OUR ECOLOGICAL CRISIS

OUR ECOLOGICAL CRISIS

Its Biological, Economic, & Political Dimensions

GRAHAME J. C. SMITH
Boston University

HENRY J. STECK
State University of New York at Cortland

GERALD SURETTE
State University of New York at Cortland

MACMILLAN PUBLISHING CO., INC.
New York

COLLIER MACMILLAN PUBLISHERS
London

Copyright © 1974, Grahame J. C. Smith

PRINTED IN THE UNITED STATES OF AMERICA

MACMILLAN PUBLISHING CO., INC.
866 Third Avenue, New York, New York 10022

COLLIER-MACMILLAN CANADA, LTD.

LIBRARY OF CONGRESS CATALOGING IN PUBLICATION DATA

Smith, Grahame J. C.
  Our ecological crisis.

  Includes bibliographies.
  1. Environmental policy—United States. 2. Pollution—Economic aspects—United States. 3. Human ecology. I. Steck, Henry J. II. Surette, Gerald. III. Title. [DNLM: 1. Ecology. 2. Environment. QH541 S6480 1974]
  HC110.E5S54   301.31'0973   72-12456
  ISBN 0-02-412710-8
  ISBN 0-02-412700-0 (pbk.)

Printing: 1 2 3 4 5 6 7 8   Year: 4 5 6 7 8 9 80

TO

Sully and Elford Smith
Trudy Perry and "Jacques"
Leon and Emily Steck
with affection and respect

PREFACE

THIS book attempts to provide the reader with a short, general, integrated, and timely examination of one of the most disturbing problems facing the American public: the crisis in our relationship with the natural environment. In this volume we have sought (1) to provide the reader with an introduction to the study of ecology and with the concepts and terminology for understanding environmental problems; (2) to acquaint the reader with the economic and cultural premises underlying the environmental crisis and with the characteristics of the marketplace economy as they relate to the crisis; (3) to give the reader a comprehension of recent developments in federal environmental policy and policy-making and an appreciation of the structure of power and political dynamics shaping the government's environmental policies. We have attempted to avoid dealing with the horror stories or journalistic descriptions that constitute so much of the writing on the environmental crisis. At the same time, we have tried to keep the book broad enough for the reader who is seeking a generalized and careful understanding of the subject but not a more highly specialized approach. Because we regard this volume as an extended essay on the subject rather than as a detailed scholarly study, we have provided lists of general and specialized readings for those who wish to go beyond our pages. We hope that this book will find an audience not only among students but also among the nonstudent populace—both of whom share a world characterized by a serious imbalance between man and his environment.

Although the book has been written by three authors, it is not a product of a "committee of three." Each author is responsible for the section of the book falling within his special area of interest: Grahame Smith wrote the section on ecology, Gerald Surette did the section on economics, and Henry Steck composed the section on environmental politics and policy. All three authors contributed to the Introduction, but Grahame Smith compiled the final version. Gerald Surette and Henry Steck wrote the Epilogue in the closing days of the 1972 national election campaign.

In addition to informing the reader about the ecological dimensions of the environmental crisis, the economics and culture underlying that crisis, and the attempts by the political system to deal with it, we have also sought to argue a case. We believe that the environmental crisis is the result of very deep forces within our society and culture and do not think that the environmental situation can be easily understood, simply defined, or readily solved. Indeed, we share a certain skepticism about those who come bearing solutions. Our understanding of the problem has just begun. The shock of discovery that characterized Earth Day in 1970 and that led President Nixon to declare that it is "now or never" has passed. It is now time for a more considered approach to the subject. At the same time, we believe deeply that the problem ultimately involves political and social arrangements and that an "ecological movement" must be guided by an ecological sensibility and an environmental ethic. Although the three authors share a broad outlook on the subject, they do differ on a number of points. We do not apologize, therefore, if our prose differs or if differing emphases do emerge. We regard this work in part as a dialogue among ourselves, and between ourselves and our readers.

We take pleasure in acknowledging the help we have received as we have worked on the volume. Appreciation goes to our editor at Macmillan, Charles Stewart, who provided us with much-needed editorial guidance.

Henry Steck wishes to express his thanks to Jean Klein and Tony Falco, two student research assistants, and to Alan Willsey for timely research funding. He and Gerald Surette also would like to express their gratitude to Ms. Angie Partigianoni and Ms. Linda Beard for their secretarial help. Henry Steck wishes to express his appreciation to various congressional committees who have generously responded to requests for help and assistance. He also thanks Daniel Beard for his generous assistance in the research on federal policy, and Leon J. Steck for his help in locating documents in Washington, D.C. Finally, Henry Steck wishes to express his gratitude to his wife, Janet, for her tolerance, patience, help, and support.

Gerald Surette wishes to express his appreciation to Robert Antin for his invaluable research contribution. He also wishes to express his indebtedness to Professor Douglas Dowd, whose teaching and friendship he has valued and continues to value highly.

Grahame Smith wishes to express his appreciation to Professor David Pimentel, who has assisted in his intellectual development. He also thanks Ms. Patricia Allen for secretarial help.

Finally, the authors wish collectively to acknowledge the suggestions for line drawings by Ms. Marcia Deihl and the excellent photographic studies by Professor Terrance D. Fitzgerald.

G. J. C. S.
H. J. S.
G. S.

CONTENTS

INTRODUCTION

SEVERAL years ago, CBS News inaugurated a special feature on their nightly program titled, "Can the World Be Saved?" Since then this question has been asked with increasing frequency and urgency as the effects of environmental deterioration become more palpable. It is not only the poets, singers, and philosophers of the young who now phrase the question: housewives and hardhats have added their voices. Ecology has become a key word in these discussions and the ecologist has been called upon to express opinions on topics that are quite often far outside the range of his professional training. What is ecology and why is the ecologist now consulted on everything from gardening problems to the economic advantage of nuclear power?

Ecology is, in the words of the President's Council on Environmental Quality, "the science of the intricate webs of relationships between living organisms and their living and nonliving surroundings." The word derives from the Greek word *oikos*, meaning "home"; it was chosen for this science to convey the idea that all components of nature are integral to its functioning just as the components of plumbing, heating, the kitchen, food, and people are integral to the functioning of the home. Ecology deals with the balance of nature. Because man is a part of nature, ecology deals not only with the relation of plants and animals to their inorganic environment but also with the relations between elements of nature, between man and nature, and, ultimately, between person and person.

It is obvious that no one discipline can possibly cover all of the implications inherent in the word *ecology*. A professional ecologist usually has a background in some aspect of botany or zoology, from which he has entered into the study of the relationship of some particular organism or group of organisms with other aspects of the living and physical environment. He differs from the botanists or zoologists in that he is trained to observe the ongoing process of these interrelationships. Although at any one time he is researching a small part of this whole, he is always cognizant of the whole. Ecology is thus a way of approaching a study, rather than a study in itself. Anyone might qualify, therefore, as an ecologist because no specific background is required; what is essential is that he have the perspective of ecology and be able to appreciate the fact that all facets of nature are interrelated and, to a considerable degree, interdependent.

[1]

The word *ecology* has come to be used and misused with increasing frequency in the last few years. Buttons, decals, and bumper stickers have recently appeared proclaiming in iridescent colors, "Ecology Now." It is important and instructive to find out what events have led to this general feeling of urgency. We appear to have crossed a threshold of some sort. The deterioration of the environment has reached a level where it has become immediately apparent to everyone. Mass media have had much to do with this change in attitude, as millions of people watching the evening news on television are confronted almost daily with the destruction caused by oil or pesticide spillage or with the controversy surrounding the placement of a nuclear power plant. However, the media have not invented this message or the ability to transmit it within the last few years. There has obviously been a change in public opinion that has made these items newsworthy.

One factor that has definitely contributed to the awareness of environmental deterioration is the space program. Photographs of the Earth taken from out in space accentuate the limited size of our planet. For the first time it is possible for us to comprehend the idea of limited land and resources. A resident of a U.S. city could easily be aware that his immediate environment has deteriorated rapidly in recent years, but a short trip out of the city through forests and farmland or to the seashore was sufficient to allay any fears he may have had that pollution was having global effects. When, however, he sees in living color on his television screen this tiny ball in the vastness of space, he cannot help but be struck by the fact that this is a rather small planet that is definitely limited in the amount of abuse it can absorb without effect. It can now be truly understood that when pollutants "go away" they are, in fact, merely being diluted throughout the planet, and with a sense of the finite nature of the globe we can now appreciate the fact that they have not, in fact, gone anywhere and will return to haunt us.

In this space age it has become increasingly common to portray the ecosystem as a closed and balanced system by using the metaphor of Earth as a spaceship. Regarding the Earth as a spaceship gives us some of the guiding principles of the economics, ecology, and social reconstruction necessary for a safe voyage. Kenneth E. Boulding has developed this idea to its greatest refinement.[1] The spaceship idea vividly conveys the concept of a closed economy in which the resources cannot be considered unlimited either for exploitation or as a carrier for wastes. In this ship, then, man must find his place in a cyclical ecological system. Although continuous inputs of energy are

[1] "The Economics of the Coming Spaceship Earth," in Garrett de Bell, ed., *The Environmental Handbook* (New York: Ballantine Books, 1970).

necessary to maintain the system, there is no overall growth; instead there is a continuous reproduction of material that will be endlessly recycled and reused. In Boulding's words, "The essential measure of the success of the economy is not production and consumption at all, but the nature, extent, quality and complexity of the total capital stock, including in this, the state of the human bodies and minds included in the system." [2] Within the spaceship, then, we are concerned with maintaining a certain stock, and technological innovations would be of advantage only if they enabled us to maintain this stock with a lessened throughput of energy.

To refer to the ecosystem in such terms is to point immediately to several crucial features of the system. First, the environment is a system: a structure of interrelated and dependent components. Obvious as this may be, its implications are not always widely understood. One significant implication is that any change, however beneficial in one element of the ecosystem, can have consequences for the entire system and that these consequences cannot be fully anticipated, known, or controlled. In this sense the ecological crisis, that is, the aggregate imbalances in the ecosphere, consists of the unanticipated environmental consequences of generations of purposive social action. We are, of course, familiar with the more lurid and widely publicized examples: the destruction of marine life by the thermal pollution caused by power plants; the destruction by Los Angeles smog of trees hundreds of miles away; the damage to human anatomy by radiation and pesticides; the destructive influence of mercury in tuna and sulfur oxides in the air. Although ecologists are accustomed to viewing the environment as a system, this model has not made itself fully felt as a guide to environmental policy; and although this model has radical implications—it forces us to regard the structure of a system as a whole—it is also quite conservative. It suggests that changes should be made with extreme care because even the most well-meaning and constructive action can have deadly consequences. To view the environment as a system, then, immediately imposes a certain constraint on the outlook of economic and political decision-makers.

A second feature of the spaceship is that its resources are finite and its systems are closed. The stock of resources—for example, energy and repair parts—is limited. These resources must not only be carefully conserved but also reused (recycled). Despite speculation about solar, wind, and tidal sources of power, the environment should not now be regarded as receiving inexhaustible inputs from some generous external source. All of our energy comes ultimately from the sun, and

2 Ibid., p. 97.

solar power may prove economically feasible, but not in the near future. In the same way, outputs—that is, wastes—can be jettisoned, but only at the risk of diminishing the finite stock. It is essential for mankind as a whole to achieve and maintain a steady balance between human societies and the limited resources available. The resources must be defined not merely in terms of energy sources but also in terms of the various subsystems that make up the spaceship: the processes by which nature maintains the balance of gases in the atmosphere and replenishes fresh water are but two examples. So far mankind has not thought in terms of a steady state but in terms of infinite quantitative growth and consumption of resources: the acceptance of the steady state by decision makers will constitute a revolutionary change in consciousness. To accept the alternative model—that is, continued growth—involves an ultimately inviable kind of politics.

The spaceship model is a powerful one, defining as it does some of the crucial environmental principles by which man must live. In some senses, however, it is a limited and somewhat misleading analogy. A real spaceship is, after all, a technological creation, designed and constructed by engineers. It is knowable, predictable, and controllable. Fail-safe devices and back-up systems can be installed; probabilities can be accurately estimated for performance capabilities; malfunctions can be corrected within the fixed parameters of the system. None of this is true in quite the same way in nature. The parameters can sometimes be estimated but with much less confidence; the performance of subsystems cannot be fully known; indeed, many critical subsystems have not yet even been identified. The properties of the environment are quite different from those found in the closed, controlled, man-made systems of the spaceship. In contrast, the systems of nature are characterized by their diversity, their spontaneity, their variety, their high degree of differentiation, and their multiple functions. The standard methods of scientific and statistical analysis cannot yet be employed in understanding these systems. An analysis of separate components cannot give the necessary insight into the importance of mixtures of effects and interactions of environmental conditions. Our concept of single cause-and-effect events cannot produce usable conclusions in the complex natural environment.

From this more realistic point of view, the ecological crisis can be seen as not merely an imbalance in the system produced by man nor simply a problem of exhausted, misused, or dirtied resources. It is a crisis resulting directly from man's own social ecology—his economics, his technology, his science, his culture. Man, as a species, is a relative newcomer to Earth and his ability to exploit and control other elements of nature is even more recent. His mastery of the controls of spaceship Earth does not stem from a knowledge of their workings but from a blundering, brute force. Unlike the spaceship, nature cannot be known to the fullest; its functioning cannot be plotted, its processes cannot be controlled. The mystery of nature is not only the province of the poet, the primitive, and the romantic; it is a hard scientific reality.

Our interest in and awareness of environmental problems may have been stimulated by the space program, but it has no doubt also been prompted by personal experience of environmental destruction on a local scale. Over a period of time the environment has been able to absorb a certain amount of interference by man, but beyond a certain point of stress the damage becomes apparent even to the casual observer. It may be that in the last few years we have passed a pollution threshold in a strictly ecological sense as well as in a sense of awareness.

All living organisms have a definite range of tolerance for various kinds of stress beyond which they are unable to live and reproduce. Australia is too hot for polar bears and the Arctic is too cold for kangaroos. These examples are, of course, rather obvious; the tolerance range of a species is seldom this apparent. For example, a species of aquatic plant may survive quite well in a stream in which two factories are depositing their wastes, but the presence of a third factory might well push the environmental conditions beyond the tolerance range for that species and it will die out. In the last decade we have produced many of these "last straws" and have caused the local extinction of a multitude of organisms that contributed to the quality of our previous environment. Examples of this can be seen in many local areas. In southern California, ponderosa pines in the San Bernardino mountains are dying from the effects of smog coming from the area of Los Angeles. The point at which the tolerance of the species is exceeded can be seen as the point between living and dead trees. The pines are replaced by other species more tolerant of air pollution, but in the future we may see these trees die also as their tolerance limit is passed by the increased concentration of air pollutants. On the eastern coast there is an area off New York harbor known locally as the Dead Sea. No higher forms of marine life can live in this region, twelve miles across. The dumping of waste materials over a period of some forty years has led to a decline in oxygen saturation from 61 per cent in 1941 to 29 per cent in 1969.[3] The tolerance range of virtually all life forms other than bacteria has been exceeded by this pollution. One of the best-known examples of pollution thresholds is Lake Erie. Here commercial fishing

3 Editorial, "To Save the Seas," *The New York Times* (October 13, 1970).

disappeared as pollution exceeded the tolerance of such species as white fish, pickerel, perch, and sturgeon.

Whatever the immediate cause, the public is concerned and interested in environmental problems as never before, and ecology, environmental deterioration, and pollution are new household words. If we develop and sharpen the ecological perspective, however, we begin to see why so much of the popular discussion of the ecological crisis falls short. The solutions of these problems require more than an operating manual from which we can determine which circuits went wrong and proceed to rewire them, because the ecosphere is not knowable or manageable in this technological sense of a spaceship. The crisis consists of aggregated imbalances produced by the straining, misuse, damaging, rearrangement, and destruction of nature by man's institutions and economic existence in the environment. Insofar as that imbalance reflects the structure of man's life, it reflects imbalances in society itself, for example, an overconcentration on technological advance. The ecological crisis, therefore, is a reflection of a crisis not yet seen in social structure, technology, and culture. (The term *man* is used with deliberate purpose because the imbalance is not confined to the United States and the other Western countries: it extends to the Communist world and increasingly to Third World nations as well.)

From this point of view, it is apparent that any thinking about the ecological crisis must be concerned equally with the structure of human society, culture, and technology. Man has become a dysfunctional element in the system, and the system is not adaptable. Whether nature has sufficient ability to purge itself of man's parasitic behavior is a question for the ecologist; whether the parasite can adapt himself to his host for his own sake is a question for the social theorist and the political actor. The ecology movement—as a political movement seeking to compel a different allocation of socioecological values—thus differs from the conservation movement as the new politics and the new economics differ from traditional models in these disciplines.

Our culture in its success has seemingly won over the natural world. Progress in the battle against nature gave the appearance of overcoming death, by inches perhaps, but a victory nonetheless. In a cultural sense progress became our most important product. We are now beginning to appreciate that the price of this progress against nature may be nature's ultimate answer: death.

It appears that the development of our culture over the last several hundred years does not serve life as much as we like to pretend it does. Our multifaceted and overwhelming interference with the natural processes of our planet has created a crisis of monstrous proportions. To begin to think of its complexity, the best that we can do is to simplify, isolate, and abstract basics. The artist and the wiseman understand intuitively that massive interference demands massive withdrawal and a righting of the balance. The scientific observer of both the physical and the social world, however, approaches the crisis with the same tools that created it. The essence of these tools, of the scientific method, is to simplify, that is, to hypothesize. He isolates from the environment that he observes, certain properties, qualities, factors, or forces and he attempts to interrelate them systematically in simulation of reality.

The ecologist tells us, on the other hand, that the quality of an ecosystem lies in its very complexity. One cannot grasp this complexity by isolation of its parts. One must strive instead for a grasp of the whole in all its manifestations and diversities. The whole is more than a sum of its parts. It is a system that one observes, a system of which the observer is a part, an integral part. A knowledge of the system is a knowledge of the self. A knowledge of the self aids in appreciation of the system. It is a circle of which the observer is a part. To set oneself apart is to break the circle and thus preclude the possibility of ever knowing what a circle is.

Beneath the façade of progress are the people who contribute to that progress. Essentially, the problem of environmental deterioration arises from the values held by the society. The complex of attitudes, beliefs, and orientations that make up the American Point of View are the institutions that largely determine our behavior. This value structure must be seen as supportive of the way we carry on our daily business. The way we carry on our daily business, in turn, reinforces this value structure, which is the character structure of the population; the multitude of attributes, mental and physical, that determine our outlook on life and the activities that arise from that outlook.

The battle against nature, the main purpose and central core of our culture of success, is directly related to the relationship of man to man. Institutions have developed that inculturate every individual with the values of the society. The nature of these institutions may vary from place to place, but they occur in any culture that is development oriented. The goal of a successful encounter with nature is not the unique property of the United States. The socialist world shares the same basic goal and is consequently creating the same ecological crisis as the capitalist world. The means of effecting rapid development are different in the two areas and these differences result in a different impact upon nature, but surely the end result will be the same.

We are faced with the seeming paradox that in the name of life and the amenities thereof we are living in a culture that creates the very possibility of ecological disaster. To increase the enjoyments of life—

that is, the standard of living of the greatest number of people—we must necessarily take an aggressive stance toward nature. That is what our logic tells us anyway. To get more abundant and variegated products then, we apparently must learn the basic principles of the natural world so as to manipulate them to our material advantage.

Our aggressive stance is linear: a forthright and straight line attack using all the knowledge of nature gained in the thousands of years of human history as a principal weapon. The weapon is in the form of technology, the concrete application of our knowledge. Technology appears in its most dramatic form as machinery. But it also appears in more subtle forms in our organization of the population engaged in the battle into efficient units.

The more successful the technological effort, the more elaborate the apparatus, the more machinelike the organization of the population will become. The goal of all technology and technological processes is to simplify, to make things easier. To make something more efficient is to get more for less. Increases in productivity per capita come about by the employment of machines and machinelike processes in such a way that fewer men can produce more. To economize is to make a given amount go further, produce more, or yield maximum returns. For a culture with an increasing population to grow or develop all of these processes must be taking place. The orientation of men in such a situation must be a rationalist orientation. The world view of such a culture must be that more and more production is good.

In a culture of success that aims to promote a more bountiful life, the increasing complexity of the technology that is developed to effect this end appears more and more unlifelike. Spontaneity and creativity, impulse and diversity, hallmarks of life give way to the mechanical and the rigid, the abstract and the linear. One is likely to find in such a culture that the degree of achievement, of pushing back nature, has brought about a corresponding increase in rigidity in those engaged in the battle, that is, the general population. One is likely to find a preoccupation with things and order. One is likely to find that superstitions and myths, mysticism and mystery, animism and intuition, and all other manifestations of the collective unconscious tend to be ironed out. Soul, or the inner man, and other unprovable concepts will have less and less place in a culture that is successful in getting more and more. The culture of success might make it possible for more and more people to live a more and more abundant life, but it is a life that would cause all our wisemen and all our artists to shudder at its emptiness. Old Testament man would not survive. Now the ecologist tells us that it is doubtful that even the new, cool, flattened man, the rationalist, technocratic, modern man himself will survive.

To our understanding, then, the present crisis of environmental deterioration is the inevitable result of our cultural heritage, value system, and political institutions. With an understanding of this sort one does not look for simple causes of the problems, or for simple cures. However, a number of such causes and cures have been widely discussed, and it is necessary at this point to consider these suggestions and to evaluate them.

LITTER

The suggestion that cleaning up litter will solve the problems of environmental deterioration is certainly one of the most cruel hoaxes ever perpetrated upon a gullible public. There is an important distinction to be made between problems of local environmental conditions such as urban decay, ugly hamburger stands, and garbage littering the streets on the one hand and the really dangerous and life-threatening problem of global pollution on the other. These are, again, not separate problems, but the litter is merely a superficial symptom of an insidious and potentially fatal disease. To scratch off the scabs and put bandaids over the sores may make the surface more immediately appealing but it does nothing to slow the progress of the disease within the body. Litter is the visible symptom and for a public sympathetic to the body but unfamiliar with medicine the most that can be done seems to be to tend these superficial wounds.

The nobler feelings of an innocent public are played upon when they are told that cleaning up litter will restore the ecology of America. This is simply a diversion from the more basic issues of where the litter comes from and what it represents. No one, of course, is advocating a removal of trash barrels, but our point is that if one is thinking ecologically one will still pick up the soda can but will think about the true meaning of that piece of trash. When one handles such a can one might think, Where did the metals come from to make it? How was the land treated when these metals were removed? Did the miners receive adequate compensation for their work in extracting the ore? Where did the energy come from to process the can? How much coal did that power plant burn? What happened to the gases and smoke from that burning coal? Where did the flavoring and the sugar come from to make the soda it contained? What did the countries get in return for growing these cash crops on land that may be badly needed to feed an undernourished population? Who owns and operates that land? What is the political arrangement between that country and this? An ecological approach would automatically bring questions like this to the mind of the Boy Scout or the Audubon Society member who picked up the can. In this sense ecology may be seen to be what Paul B. Sears [4] very aptly called a "subversive subject."

POPULATION

That the exponential growth of population has placed severe strains on the natural and social environment is widely recognized. The causes, the importance, and the long-term consequences of population growth are, however, a matter of some controversy. Paul R. and Anne H. Ehrlich, leading population experts, write in their book *Population, Resources and Environment* [5] that "the explosive growth of the human population is the most significant terrestrial event of the past million millenia. . . . No geological event in a billion years . . . has posed a threat to terrestrial life comparable to that of human overpopulation." Undoubtedly, the growth in population raises Malthusian possibilities that are reflected both in demographers' predictions and in the reality of present and predicted starvation, malnutrition, and disease. The distortions introduced into the social environment by population growth (hunger, concentrated masses of persons, the breakdown of social services and political systems, intensified pressures toward conflict) parallel the distortions introduced into the physical environment, that is, the increased demand on finite resources and the limited capability of the environment to absorb and recycle wastes. However, to focus only on a growing population as the chief villain, as many are inclined to do, is to ignore the impact of an economic system in which both consumer wants and economic incentives for the producer create a drive for production at the lowest cost.

It is not only the number of people but also their insistence on whiter-than-white clothes and worm-free apples that puts phosphates and pesticides in our ground water. It is not simply the number of people but the ever-increasing number of electrical appliances that each person thinks he needs that requires the construction of polluting power plants. To promote an expanding economy the consumer is made to feel that he wants, and indeed must have, these advantages of modern technology. The price of these appliances is kept within reach, in great part, because waterways and airspace can be used, "cost-free," as open sewers for liquid, solid, and gaseous wastes.

To focus on birthrates alone is to ignore the complex social, economic, technological, medical, and cultural variables involved. It also leads to dangerous proposals to improve the situation by lowering the human population. This implies either an increase in the death rate

[4] "Ecology—a Subversive Subject," *Bioscience*, Vol. 14, No. 7 (July 1964).
[5] (San Francisco: W. W. Freeman & Co., Publishers, 1970). p. 1.

(some form of warfare) or coercive control of fertility. The problems we face will require drastic solutions, and these solutions must certainly embrace birth control; but in addition the solutions must involve far-reaching social, economic, and political changes. The consumption of at least 35 per cent of the world's scarce or nonreplaceable resources and energy output by the 6 per cent of the world population living in the United States [6] gives one pause for thought and underlines the distinctly political dimension to the question.

TECHNOLOGICAL ACTIVITY

Advances in medical and agricultural technology have contributed to the growth in population, and we now find that the growth of population intensifies the effects of an accelerating and spreading technology. Whatever this relationship, technology and population together are propelling mankind toward the limits of the resources necessary to sustain life: space, heat, energy, nonrenewable mineral resources, water, food, and aesthetically rich environments. Even if we disregard the fact that we are approaching these limits on the argument that we have no obligation to preserve resources for future generations, the effects of technology are still of importance as they pose an immediate and severe, perhaps fatal, strain on the environment.

Insofar as technology grows at a more rapid rate than population, it would be dangerously distorting the situation to assume that zero population growth alone would arrest the stress that technology has placed on the web of ecological processes. Since World War II Americans have escalated the war against nature by the use of an increasingly sophisticated technology. Between 1946 and 1966, for example, the use of fertilizers increased by 700 per cent, of electricity by 400 per cent, and of pesticides by 500 per cent. At the same time, the population has increased by only 43 per cent. No doubt population contributes significantly to the stress placed on the environment, but it is safe to say that the use of an ecologically unsound and indifferent technology has been a critical element. Ecologist Barry Commoner has pointed out that if we still used the old Model T Ford engine—with its low compression and low temperature—we would not now face the smog we do.[7] Commoner believes that the success of modern technology is an illusion. He wrote, "For our present system of technology is a threat to the continued existence of the very machinery—the bio-

[6] C. H. Day, "The American Fertility Cult," *Columbia University Forum* (Summer 1960).

[7] *The Closing Circle* (New York: Alfred A Knopf, Inc., 1971), p. 168.

logical processes that constitute the environment—on which all productivity and the quality of human existence is based." [8]

The consequences of technology are several. Technological processes pour substantial amounts of pollutants into the environment
and these present real, known and unknown dangers to human
health. The pollutants include not only biologically degradable wastes
—which may be entering the ecosystem too rapidly to be processed—
but the by-products of fossil fuels, lead and mercury traces, detergents,
sulfuric acid, hydrofluoric acid, phenols, nitrates, nondegradable plastics, chlorinated hydrocarbons (DDT), fluorides, radioactive isotopes
and other forms of radiation, chemical mutagens, noise, heat, and concentrated toxicants—to name but a few. Such pollutants are more than
dirt- or disease-producing agents. They become, as Lewis Herber [9]
puts it, "part of the very anatomy of the individual by entering his
bone structure, tissues, and fat deposits. Their dispersion is so global
that they become part of the anatomy of the environment." Even in
trace amounts, such agents are toxic, chronically so in many cases;
the damage they do to hormones or to the structure of DNA may not
be recognized until it is too late.

Technological processes not only threaten man's health but attack
the environment as well. They do so by increasing the level of pollutants to the point where the balanced functioning of various natural
processes is impaired. The tolerance levels of some species are exceeded, the biological community becomes simplified and unstable,
and ecological cycles are disrupted. By technology, moreover, we refer
not simply to factories, automobiles, jet planes, and the deposit of
solid or liquid wastes. Agricultural processes are also a major threat
to the environment. Insecticides, herbicides, irrigation runoffs, and
chemical fertilizers assault the environment in an exceedingly ruthless
if invisible manner. The water pump and the crop-dusting airplane
no less than the factory and the auto are symbols of man's arrogant
war on his environment.

An even more subtle threat to the environment comes from the
complacent attitude that modern technology has engendered. This
attitude holds that because necessity is the mother of invention it is
obvious that, should the threat from pollution become sufficient,
science and technology will come up with a way to solve it. After all,

<hr/>

[8] Testimony before the Subcommittee on Intergovernmental Relations of the
Senate Committee on Government Operations, *Hearings. Establish a Select Senate
Committee on Technology and the Human Environment,* 91st Cong. 1st Sess. 1969,
p. 233. Commoner's views on the decisive role of technology have been elaborated
at length in *The Closing Circle.* For an exchange on the relative explanatory value
of *population* and *technology,* see the Commoner-Ehrlich exchange on *The Closing Circle* in *Environment,* Vol. 14, No. 3 (April 1972), pp. 23–52.

[9] "Toward an Ecological Solution," *Ramparts* (May 1970), p. 8.

we have been able to produce the technological means to realize man's wildest dream—to stand on the moon; surely no problem on Earth could be beyond our capabilities. This is an extremely dangerous assumption, producing the attitude that "scientists will come up with a solution when things are bad enough." This again implies the knowable, manageable spaceship Earth. Man has frequently comforted himself with the notion that a panacea can be found to cure all ills. Even if there is no hint of what form the panacea will take, he is confident that he will be rescued from imminent disaster. The ancient Greeks dedicated a temple to a nameless god whom they may have overlooked. Presumably, when needed he would make himself known and solve any problem. Because we have been so successful in solving problems up to now, however, the concept of a panacea seems even more deeply entrenched in us. Science is the god of our society and can be depended upon to provide a solution in times of stress. It seems unlikely, however, that any technological advance will solve these problems under present conditions; a change in human ecology and economic patterns will also be necessary.

HUMAN ECOLOGY

Man despoils his environment not merely by multiplying his number and employing a destructive technology. The physical distribution of his social, industrial, and agricultural activities impinges no less severely on the environment. The location of millions of people in urban areas, the dense concentration of industrial activity, and the development of large factory farms produce significant dislocations in the environment. Over millions of years ecosystems have evolved intricate balances and feedback mechanisms that promote stability. Man is, however, threatening these balances by his efforts to master nature for his own benefit through his policies on land planning, industrial location, and agricultural technique. More to the point, man is imposing on the environment the characteristics of mass society, advanced industry, and technological farming. In so doing he is making the environment over in his own image rather than adjusting to his global habitat.

Not only are the careless and exploitative attitudes of the landowners important in creating these problems, but the very size of the firms involved is also integral. Modern society has become divided into enormous urban areas and a highly industrialized agriculture, both managed by an anonymous, bureaucratized state. The huge physical presence of one of these firms affects local communities and resources such as waterways and airspace, demands raw materials and water, and creates tremendous logistical problems in the transportation of people, raw materials, manufactured goods, and foodstuffs. The presence of one of these firms also controls local economic and political organization.

The same tendencies toward simplification, uniformity, technological manipulation, and an advanced division of labor that occur in man's social ecology are carried over into man's approach to his natural ecology. The developed societies do, of course, bear a heavier responsibility for the despoliation of the environment. Insofar as they remain the model for the elites and populations of the Third World peoples, they are but the vanguard of the future. The environmental crisis is, therefore, directly tied to tendencies in the physical structure of society and the values guiding it.

CULTURE

Finally, the environmental crisis is seen to be the direct product of a deeply rooted set of cultural values that have defined the Western approach to the environment no less than Western technology. The most persistent of these values reflect the displacement of pagan animism by a godly theology that gave man, in the somber words of Genesis, "dominion over the fish of the sea and over the birds of the air and over every living thing that moves upon the earth." Having made man in His image, God promptly invited man to make nature over in his image. In contrast to the tendency of the less anthropocentric religions of Asia or of the pagans to invest natural objects with sacred spirits, the Judeo-Christian tradition establishes a dualism that separates man from nature. The destruction of the idols by Abraham and the victory of Western Christianity over pagan animism was, writes historian Lynn White,[10] "the greatest psychic revolution in the history of our culture." Whatever the theological place of nature in the scheme of things, the Latin West came to approach nature in an active, scientific manner.

Progress came then to mean industrial growth. This utilitarian outlook had medieval origins, but it was strengthened by the nineteenth-century fusion between science and technology, which produced the theoretical and empirical approaches of our natural environment. As it was formulated by the empirical philosophers, the Western practice of science was disposed to ignore the aesthetic and emotional side of man and so to develop a strict rationalist and utilitarian economics. Scientific knowledge came to mean technological power over nature.

The Industrial Revolution was closely tied to the emerging democratic revolution. This change lowered social and cultural barriers and

[10] "The Historic Roots of Our Ecological Crisis," *Science*, Vol. 155 (1967), pp. 1203–1207.

reinforced the fusion between aristocratic, intellectual "science" and the lower-class, empirical, action-oriented "mechanical arts." This change also mobilized the hitherto uninvolved masses into active participation in the economic, political, and cultural spheres. By the mid twentieth century, the democratic culture had linked mass egalitarianism to an ethos of affluence and individual consumption.

These cultural attitudes—the dualism of man and nature, the commitment to technological definitions of progress, the advent of consumer democracy, the growth of a value-free rationalistic science—are not confined, of course, to those societies that are democratic, capitalist, and Christian. Non-Christian though it may be, Marxism has reflected numerous deep-seated Western ideological tendencies. For Lenin, Communism was Soviet Power plus electrification; for Krushchev it was goulash Communism. For Russians today the heritage of Bolshevism is seen in the death of the Ural River because of industrial pollution. Similarly, the commitment to industrial progress colors the political and social goals of most Third World leaders. All in all, the result has been a political, cultural, and economic blindness to the environment in men of all races, creeds, and ideologies.

In summary, the ecological crisis is of such magnitude that it cannot be turned back by the inventions of science. Ever since man domesticated plants and animals some ten thousand years ago, his disruptions of natural ecosystems have been becoming more and more extensive. With the emergence of highly industrialized nations the disequilibrium has become ever greater, so that ecological instability is increasing at an accelerating rate. Disasters will follow if these trends continue. Every thoughtful analysis of these problems concludes that we must aim for a closed system in which materials are recycled instead of being discarded. Man must strive to live in a relationship of harmony with nature rather than one of exploitation. Any "solution" to the present crisis must take into account all aspects of population growth, technological advance, and human ecology and can come about only through radically new political and economic arrangements. The question is whether the necessary change can take place without the sacrifice of important values of Western democratic politics. The change must be substantial because, as we have seen, to think of solutions in terms of cleaning up the environment or recognizing the spaceship is inadequate. The solution lies in thinking of the problem as not merely social and political but in casting the politics and economics of the crisis in ecological terms. To do this requires a definition of man as part of and not apart from the environment. Whether this is possible is considered in the chapter on environmental policy.

Environmental deterioration is the ultimate injustice. It affects everyone, rich and poor, black and white. The poor are more immediately affected, and in proportion to their percentage of the population more blacks than whites are poor, but everyone suffers from this deterioration. These problems are all systemic: they arise from the internal functioning of our economic and political systems, which, in turn, reflect our cultural heritage. None of these are casual or incidental problems, they are definite reflections of the society that we have evolved. It is not within the scope of this book to discuss the problems of racism or poverty further, but in presenting the systemic nature of environmental deterioration we felt it necessary to illustrate that, to us, these problems are not unrelated. This was clearly recognized by C. S. Lewis more than twenty-five years ago when he wrote, "Man's power over Nature is really the power of some men over other men, with Nature as their instrument."

Recognizing that the environmental problem reveals the intimate link between the social sciences and ecology, we have attempted in this volume to bridge some of the gaps that have separated these disciplines. We do not attempt a comprehensive treatment of the subject but describe the problem from the viewpoint of an ecologist, an economist, and a political scientist. This is not intended as an exhaustive study of environmental deterioration. We do not present a list of solutions that can immediately be put into effect to solve the crisis. Such solutions cannot be proposed without a thorough knowledge of the causes of the problem and, as we have pointed out, action can then be effective only through political and social change. Some discussion of alternative political systems will be presented for consideration with these facts in mind.

This treatment should stimulate many more questions than it has answered. We posed the following questions: What is the extent of environmental deterioration? How did it arise and will it continue to worsen? Is life on Earth really threatened? What is the nature of economic and political systems that contribute to this decay? What are the attitudes and beliefs that support the economic system and how does it reinforce these beliefs? Is the structure of our political system flexible enough to adapt to a situation of this sort? A brief description of the functioning of the biological, economic, and political systems is presented. It becomes increasingly obvious that no one of us can discuss the problem without some consideration of the other disciplines. The biologist may reveal a case of environmental decay, but whether or not this will be remedied will depend on the action of the economic and political forces. The environmental problems that we face arise from the ongoing practices of our society. If the reader of this book can view his further life experiences in the perspective of ecology, its purpose will have been served.

ONE

✧

ECOLOGY

It is *becoming increasingly obvious that we have reached a turning point in history. The environment is a complex, delicately balanced system that has evolved over, literally, billions of years. This environmental system is now being subjected to a vast number of pollutants in such variety and concentrations as have never been known before. It is our firm belief that the cumulative effect of these pollutants threatens the subtle system of checks and balances on which the continued existence of the living world depends. The thin shell of life that surrounds the earth is already showing cracks. It is essential that we all become aware of the potential danger, not in a casual and superficial way but with a real understanding of why the crisis is upon us.*

Public opinion polls show that the vast majority of Americans are deeply concerned over environmental issues. It is difficult, however, for people to believe the real extent of the problems. Without an understanding of the complexity of natural systems one cannot appreciate the potential threat to all life forms that our interference poses. We are saddened when we hear that a species of wild cat is becoming extinct and upset by television documentaries that show birds sitting for weeks on infertile eggs. It is difficult to make the connection that these are portents for our own species. H. E. Daly expressed this idea eloquently when he wrote "the canary is silent." Miners used to lower a canary into a mine to test the quality of the air; it was an indication of the conditions before man would venture into the shaft. In the same way, these horror stories that we see applied to other species are portents for mankind. To see the connection one needs an understanding of ecological principles.

An understanding, even if precise and broadly distributed throughout the population, will not bring about changes in the situation. Any change must come through social action. We are the ones who make the social action, however, and this will not happen unless we are sufficiently informed and alarmed at what is now happening. In order to understand the depth and breadth of environmental problems we need an understanding of the ecosystem concept and of the way in which ecosystems are structured and function. Only with this kind of knowledge can we anticipate the ramifications of present and future technological innovations.

[17]

This section explains the study of ecology and provides the concepts and terminology needed for an understanding of environmental problems. It is essential that we all have this understanding in order to cultivate an ecological perspective and to translate it into social action.

SOME FUNDAMENTALS OF ECOLOGY

AN EXPLANATION of the field of ecology is made much easier by the fact that many people now have a full appreciation of the limitations of Earth. As long as we thought in terms of any resource being limitless in supply it was difficult to appreciate its value and its vulnerability to exploitation and to change. With a space age background, however, it is relatively easy to explain some of the more basic ideas of ecology. A general understanding of these concepts is necessary to an appreciation of the immediacy and reality of this environmental crisis.

The basic unit of ecology is the ecosystem. This is defined as a community of organisms, both plants and animals, together with their inorganic environment. This whole unit is, in theory, self-sustaining. All components are interdependent to some degree. Animals cannot exist without plants because plants produce atmospheric oxygen through the process of photosynthesis. Similarly, the plants could not exist indefinitely without animals to restore carbon dioxide into the atmosphere; this is a necessary raw ingredient for photosynthesis. The inorganic environment is also dependent for its stability and continued existence on interactions with other components of the ecosystem. The composition of the atmosphere we breathe could change rapidly if the ecosystem were disrupted; estimates are that plants would remove all the carbon dioxide from the air in about one year if it were not being constantly replaced by the respiration of animals and by fire. Nitrogen-fixing bacteria could remove all of the nitrogen in less than a million years if it were not being constantly returned by other organisms.

A self-sustaining community must have a number of components. Plants are the only organisms capable of capturing the energy from the sun and incorporating it into organic material through the process of photosynthesis. The plants are the primary producers of the ecosystem. They require considerable amounts of inorganic nutrients, such as carbon, hydrogen, oxygen, phosphorus, potassium, calcium, iron, and magnesium and a number of other elements in very small amounts. These inorganic materials are converted, through the action of the sun's energy, into organic molecules containing high-energy carbon-carbon bonds. The energy stored in these bonds is extracted by herbivores, which feed upon the plant and in their digestive systems break down the organic compounds of the plant and reform them into animal tissue. A certain amount of the energy is stored in the plant in the room of woody tissue and so on, and much of this is unavailable to the herbivore as food. Of that energy assimilated by the herbivore, not all is incorporated into body tissues. Much of the energy is used to maintain body heat, produce movements, and so on. Thus the total number of calories stored in the body of a herbivore is only about 10 per cent of the number of calories in its plant food. These herbivores may, in turn, be eaten by higher-level consumers (predators or scavengers) so that this energy is transformed once again. The efficiency of the transfer is again only about 10 per cent; that is, only 10 per cent of the calories from the herbivore is assimilated by the carnivore. There is therefore a one-way flow of energy through an ecosystem, from the sun to the higher-level consumers, with a loss of energy at each transfer and a gradual dissipation in body heat and the energy used for movement. The energy contained in woody tissue and in the excrement and decaying bodies of animals passes through a detritus food chain of worms, fungi, and bacteria, each of which extracts some of the energy and uses it in body maintenance and reproduction. Estimates show that in some ecosystems as much as 90 per cent of the energy flow may be through this detritus food chain.

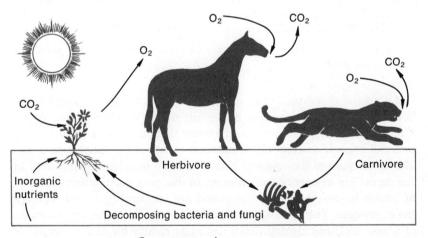

Components of an ecosystem.

Because of this loss of energy at each transfer, a smaller mass of organisms is supported at each step. These stages are defined as trophic levels. Herbivores, carnivores, and secondary carnivores would represent three distinct trophic levels. A large amount of plant material is required to feed one rabbit and a number of rabbits needed to feed one dog and a number of dogs needed to feed one lion. If we represent the number of organisms found in each trophic level as a block, we have a pyramid of numbers or biomass. In most instances such a pyramid is also produced if we represent the total biomass found in each trophic level as a block. Certain ecosystems, however, have a smaller biomass of producer organisms at any instant of time than of herbivores because the herbivores continually feed on the plants that have a rapid rate of reproduction. At any particular time the biomass of plants is not larger, but the rapid turnover allows them to support a larger biomass of herbivores. The ecosystem of the open ocean is an example of this inverted pyramid of biomass.

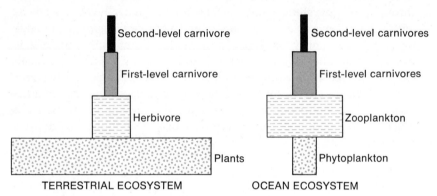

Pyramids of biomass. Blocks represent the biomass found at each trophic level.

An essential component of any ecosystem is the bacteria and fungi that decompose dead animal and plant material. Their activities are vital because they release the elements that have been incorporated into the organic matter. These nutrient elements are thus made available once more to the roots of plants and can be taken up and used in the formation of new organic matter. In this way the nutrient elements of which organic matter is composed are continually cycled through the ecosystem. The cycling process involves the inorganic environment of water, soil, and air and illustrates most clearly the interdependence of the various components of an ecosystem. The rate of release of nutrients into the ecosystem depends upon the combined activities of the inorganic elements and the decomposer organisms, and this rate of release may regulate the rate at which the total ecosystem can function.

Each organism within an ecosystem has a certain definable set of requirements for surviving and multiplying. A plant requires a number of inorganic nutrients including water and carbon dioxide and needs the energy of sunlight in order to carry on its life process, photosynthesis. Supplied with these basic requirements, however, not all plants will grow. Some species need a high temperature in order to function, whereas others can carry on photosynthesis at very low temperatures. Some species require bright sunlight and lots of water and a high level of nitrogen in the soil, and others function best in a shady, acid soil with a different balance of nutrients. For each of these environmental factors each species has a certain maximum and minimum limit beyond which it cannot survive and reproduce. This is known as the range of tolerance of a species for that factor in the environment. A particular species may have a wide range of tolerance for several environmental variables (say, water, nitrogen content of the soil, light intensity, and temperature) but may have a narrow range for one important feature, such as the acidity of the soil. A species that has a wide tolerance for all aspects of the environment will be very widely distributed. Dandelions would fit into this category. Some species are particularly sensitive in that they have a very narrow tolerance for some facet of the environment. They can survive within only a narrow range of conditions; if we know the requirements of these species we can use them as indicators of that aspect of the environment. Many species of lichen have a narrow range of tolerance to certain air pollutants and are used by scientists as a convenient index of changing conditions. If a particular species of lichen dies out in an area, we know that its tolerance to a particular pollutant has been exceeded and we therefore have an idea of the concentration of that pollutant in the air.

Cycles and Pollution

Some knowledge of the structure and functioning of ecosystems is essential to an understanding of pollution problems. For example, we know that decomposing bacteria are important in the ecosystem because of their role in releasing inorganic nutrients from organic matter. These nutrients are thus made available again to plants for photosynthesis. It should come as no surprise, then, that bacterial action in a sewerage treatment plant is able to break down the organic material and render it inoffensive to us. We should also realize, however, that the runoff water from this plant contains all of the nutrient elements that were originally present in the sewerage. In the water, plants will take up these nutrients in a rapid spurt of growth and so complete the nutrient cycle. The prolific growth of algae in the streams and ponds into which the effluent is dumped is a natural and logical function of the ecosystem. Because this heavy growth of algae replaces the species normally found in the stream, it represents a pollution problem. We could not expect this natural cycle to stop in midstream, as it were.

This everyday source of pollution has very important consequences for us. As explained, the bacteria that break down the organic sewerage release the inorganic elements into solution. The effluent from the sewerage plant is then released into some convenient river or ocean bay. Another ecological concept now assumes importance: the fact that different species of organisms have different tolerance ranges for the various important aspects of their environments. Inorganic nutrients are a crucial factor in the environment of plants, as these constitute the raw materials for the process of photosynthesis. In most situations some of these elements are in relatively short supply and are restricting the growth of plants. This can readily be demonstrated by the addition of fertilizer containing inorganic elements; a rapid response in plant growth indicates that growth had been retarded by a lack of one or more of these nutrients. Within any particular ecosystem, then, with a characteristic balance of inorganic nutrients available, the plant community will consist of species that are adapted to that particular balance of nutrients. If the balance is altered, other species that are better able to grow under this new set of conditions will replace the native species.

When the runoff from sewerage plants enters a stream, it contains not only the inorganic elements released from human wastes but also the elements contained in everyday household effluents. For example, as much as 70 per cent of the phosphate may come from detergent wastes rather than from human excreta. This is the reason for recent concern over the composition of laundry detergents. If the plant growth in a stream or the ocean is, in fact, being restricted by a relative shortage of phosphate, then the addition of detergents in effluents will alter the composition of the plant species in the stream or bay.

Why are phosphates singled out rather than any other element? Plants require a mixture of inorganic elements in certain proportions, the requirements varying from species to species. The major needs of all species, however, are for carbon, hydrogen, oxygen, phosphorus, and nitrogen. These five elements comprise more than 95 per cent of the requirements for any species and so are obviously the elements to be considered. Carbon, hydrogen, and oxygen are readily available in the form of water and the carbon dioxide of the atmosphere, so phosphorus and nitrogen are the critical elements. Nitrogen is present in vast amounts in the atmosphere but in a form that is unavailable to plants (see the discussion of the nitrogen cycle later in this chapter). Some of this inert nitrogen can be "fixed" by blue-green algae into a form that is usable by other plants, so that waters in which blue-green algae are growing are generally not depauperate in nitrates. Phosphates, then, appear to be the factor limiting the growth of plants in most bodies of water.

Effluent from sewerage treatment plants, rich in phosphates from detergents, enters a body of water and provides nutrients that had previously been lacking for plant growth. The native species are adapted to exist at normal, low nutrient levels. With the environment now rich in inorganic elements, new, fast-growing species quickly absorb the nutrients and create a population explosion of their kind. Certain species of algae are particularly fast-growing under these conditions and the water becomes green with a luxurious growth of these plants. The algae in the water are often so numerous that they prevent light from passing through the water, and the bottom-living plants in the stream die out because they are unable to photosynthesize.

The inorganic elements are rapidly incorporated into the tissues of algae, but the algae are short-lived and soon die and settle to the bottom. On the bed of the lake or stream, the natural cycle is again being completed. Bacteria feed on the bodies of the plants, to release the nutrients once again. However, in order to carry out this process the bacteria need oxygen, so that the oxygen in the water is quickly depleted. As the oxygen level falls, the bacteria are unable to decompose the bodies of the plants efficiently, so there is a buildup of ooze on the bottom, smothering any remaining native plants. As the oxygen is removed from the water by the action of the bacteria and by the nighttime respiration of the algae, other species of organisms that cannot tolerate low levels of oxygen in the environment will die out. The addition of effluent has thus created a Biological Oxygen Demand (BOD), which has resulted in a lowering of the oxygen content of the water. As less and less oxygen is available the tolerance of species after species is exceeded and fish and many species of invertebrates die out. This process is often described by the word *eutrophication*, which means, literally, "good food." The addition of inorganic nutrients that were previously lacking was good food for certain species of plants but resulted in the death of most of the species of plants and animals that made up the natural community.

Because of the repetition of this sequence of events in many bodies of water to which sewerage effluent was added, there was a move to ban phosphates from household detergents. To maintain the cleaning effectiveness of the detergents another substance, nitrilo-triacetic acid (NTA) was substituted. When broken down this substance released nitrogen, rather than phosphorus, into the water. Recent evidence [1]

[1] J. H. Ryther and W. M. Dunstan, "Nitrogen, Phosphorus and Eutrophication in the Marine Environment," *Science*, Vol. 171 (1971), pp. 1008–1013.

has suggested that in ocean environments nitrogen, rather than phosphorus, is the limiting element. When a mixture of nitrates and phosphates is added to samples of water from test sites in the ocean, the nitrogen is quickly taken up by plants, whereas the phosphorus is not necessary to spur extra growth because nitrates are released more slowly than phosphates from decaying matter in this environment. The addition of NTA to detergents, then, although alleviating to a great extent the problems of eutrophication in bodies of fresh water, may in fact exacerbate the problem in ocean areas.

This example illustrates the fact that each ecosystem operates differently from all others. What may appear to be a solution to a problem in one region may, in fact, cause even greater problems elsewhere. The only foolproof solution to a situation of this sort is to remove the nutrient elements before the effluent leaves the sewerage plant. These nutrients could, of course, be used as a crop fertilizer under controlled conditions.

ECOSYSTEM DEVELOPMENT

An ecosystem is a community of plants and animals together with the inorganic environment. The component parts of an ecosystem evolve together into an interdependent, complex entity. The system has built into it a number of homeostatic mechanisms that operate to maintain the stability of the system. A balancing device of this sort is perfected only after a long period of evolutionary adjustment.

Thus, if a herbivorous insect were to increase in numbers to the point that it defoliated trees, there would be a strong selective pressure on the trees to evolve thicker leaves or a chemical to keep the insects off. A bird might switch its attention from other prey to this more numerous species and so help reduce the number of insects. Because of the ample supply of this food the birds might produce more young and so the outbreak would be further suppressed by their feeding. Many more subtle feedback mechanisms are operating constantly in an ecosystem.

New systems tend to oscillate more violently and to be less able to adjust to change than are mature systems. In an area with a reasonably predictable climate an ecosystem will develop that has the maximum possible protection against disturbance because of the increased homeostasis of the community. This is known as the climax community for a particular area.

A climax community is a stable, self-reproducing community of organisms in which reliable and intimate relationships have evolved between species. It is regarded as the mature community in a particular area. Nutrients are tightly controlled and circulated to avoid possible loss to the system through leaching out of the soil. Much of the energy captured by the plants in the system is used in the maintenance of such a climax community. The development of this climax community results from the process of succession. Succession is a predictable, orderly change from one community to another, culminating in the steady-state climax community. Starting from water or bare rock, pioneer species of plants will grow under these harsh conditions and modify the environment to make it more suitable for other species. For example, in a pond, floating aquatic weeds die and build up the bottom of the pond until it becomes shallow enough to allow the growth of emergent weeds such as cattails. These plants, in turn, will produce much organic matter and build up the edge of the pond until the surface is clear of the water and will support the growth of some grasses. The grasses add more organic material and soil and are, in turn, replaced by species such as alders, willows, and button bushes. As these trees and shrubs grow and die the area becomes higher and higher with the accumulation of organic matter and becomes drier through the transpiration of large amounts of water by the plants. Drier conditions favor the growth of aspens, elms, and white pine, which flourish for a while, but their seedlings are unable to grow in the shade, so when these trees die the young seedlings already present are of sugar maple, beech, and hemlock. This is the climax community. The community is determined by the climate of the region and is the same whether succession started in water or on bare rock. It reseeds itself and remains constant, in theory, indefinitely.

As succession proceeds through a series of communities to the mature, climax community, we see an increasing dominance of the plants over their environment. Pioneer species are faced with a harsh environment, exposed to all the vagaries of nature. These species have a wide range of tolerance to environmental conditions. They have a short life span and during this time they alter the environment so as to make it less suitable for their progeny. Such communities are inherently unstable. These early stages in succession produce more energy than they use in respiration, so there is an overall buildup of organic matter. As we proceed through the succession toward the climax community, the biomass of the community increases and more and more of the energy produced is used in the maintenance of this biomass. Productivity in terms of energy captured from sunlight per unit of area increases as we approach the climax, but more and more energy is needed for respiration to maintain the biomass. In these more stable environments the species that exist are more specialized than the pioneer species, with much narrower tolerance to environmental changes.

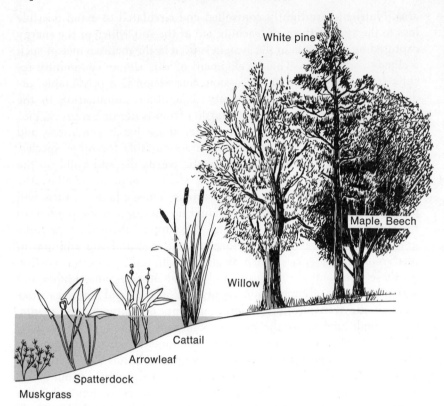

White pine

Maple, Beech

Willow

Cattail

Arrowleaf

Spatterdock

Muskgrass

Succession from open water to a climax community forest.

There is a much greater diversity of species in later successional stages than in the early stages.

The concept of succession has importance in the consideration of modern man's use of land areas. Our agriculture focuses on early successional stages. These stages have a high productivity relative to the maintenance energy of the plants. We seek to harvest this productivity. A climax community would have a high biomass in terms of plant tissue (trees, shrubs) but little that could be harvested for food because much of the energy produced is used in the maintenance of the biomass of the trees. We therefore focus on the early successional stages, which are inherently unstable. We are simplifying communities for our own use. These communities have evolved little in the way of internal homeostasis so they are prey to pests and diseases and we must constantly fight and expend energy to maintain the plants long enough to harvest the crop.

An ecosystem is generally described as self-sustaining; but there is usually some degree of interaction between ecosystems. For example, water running from a forest ecosystem down into a swamp ecosystem carries with it minerals that are used by plants in the swamp and so enter the cycle of this ecosystem. In the same fashion, a bird that feeds in the swamp may roost and defecate in the forest, thus returning minerals to the forest though in a different mixture. Because we can now conceive of the finite nature of the Earth and we recognize the interchange that takes places between ecosystems, we now use the term *ecosphere* to encompass the total of all life that blankets this planet together with the global inorganic environment. The ecosphere is the sum of all ecosystems.

The Vulnerable Ecosystem

An ecosystem is self-sustaining and, for the most part, balanced. An increase in one component is usually compensated for by another component to restore the balance. If plants increase, the herbivores increase and eat these plants, causing a decline in the plants and, eventually, a decline in the number of herbivores. This is the balance of nature. Although balanced, the ecosystem is vulnerable to outside influences, and a change in the operation of one component may produce changes in many other parts of the ecosystem. Any major change in the environment, whether man-made or natural, may have devastating effects.

A natural disruption of this type occurred along the coast of Peru and was described by Robert Cushman Murphy.[2] During December of each year warm currents of air move to the south, bringing the annual rains to the arid northern coast of Peru. In 1925 this current moved further south than usual, killing the marine life along the normally cold coastline as it went. Fish were killed in vast numbers and the seabirds that depended on them for food also died. The dead animals were decomposed by bacteria, causing obnoxious smells in the harbors blocked with their bodies. Organic materials released into the water by this decomposition nourished the growth of certain marine plankton, turning the water deep red. The plankton bloom, in turn, affected shellfish and other organisms accustomed to filtering plankton of different types from the water. On the land the unusually heavy rains left pools in which malaria-carrying mosquitoes bred and harassed the human inhabitants. Seepage into wells was increased, carrying with it human fecal matter and causing an outbreak of typhoid fever.

[2] This situation is described by M. A. Bernarde in *Our Precarious Habitat* (New York: W. W. Norton & Company, Inc., 1970), pp. 27–28.

Natural events such as the one just described may temporarily upset the balance of an ecosystem, but usually the system adjusts and returns to the normal state quite rapidly. Permanent alterations in ecosystems do, of course, occur. Volcanoes, the folding of the Earth's crust, and changes in the courses of rivers may lead to permanent changes in local environments.

These catastrophic natural events are relatively rare; most of the events that permanently affect the environment are caused by the interference of man. When the environment can be said to have deteriorated, it has often become less stable. When man disturbs the natural balance of an ecosystem in a way that makes the ecosystem less stable, he is causing the deterioration of that ecosystem. In many cases this deterioration is in essence permanent.

Comparisons of natural ecosystems have led to the general ecological principle that more complex ecosystems are more stable. In a hypothetical simple ecosystem we could have just one producing species, one herbivore, and one carnivore. Energy from the sun is thus fixed by the plant and passed to the herbivore and eventually to the carnivore. This is a food chain. Some species of decomposer bacteria would be needed to keep the nutrients cycling through the ecosystem. Suppose that this ecosystem has only crabgrass, rabbits, foxes, and decomposing bacteria. If, for some reason, all the rabbits were to die then the foxes would die of starvation. Eventually all the decomposers for flesh would die. In a more complex ecosystem, however, we might have hundreds of plant species and hundreds of consumers and predators. Thus, if all the rabbits were to die the foxes could exist on mice or birds or other small animals and the ecosystem would adjust to a new balance.

No natural ecosystem is as simple as the first example given. Instead of straight food chains of this sort, we find that there are numerous crosslinks, forming a food web. The rabbits feed not only on crabgrass but on many other plants, and the foxes feed on many different herbivores. A food web is thus a series of interconnected chains that provide a relatively flexible system. A break in one link of the web is compensated for by increased usage of other links.

Very simple ecosystems have only a few species, often with large numbers of individuals of each species. The number of individuals may vary greatly from year to year. The Arctic ecosystem is an extremely simple one. In a good year the number of snowshoe hares may increase and there will be a corresponding increase in the foxes and wolves, which constitute the next link in this very simple food web. The following year, however, the numbers of hares may decrease and the carnivorous species will also decrease. Great fluctuation in the numbers of individuals is a characteristic of a very simple ecosystem. A complex ecosystem such as a tropical rain forest has few individuals in each of many species and, because of the compensatory effect of the many links in the food web, does not show large fluctuations in numbers from year to year.

The situations cited are obviously a great oversimplification. A cause-and-effect relationship between species diversity and the stability of an ecosystem has not definitely been established, and there are many conflicting hypotheses on this relationship. Even the concept of stability is difficult to define and measure in an ecosystem. Generally, a more stable ecosystem is thought of as one that returns quickly to equilibrium after being disturbed in some way. In the simple example given, the complex ecosystem returned to a balance more quickly than the simple system when both were perturbed by the death of rabbits.

If the relationship between species diversity and community stability proves to be as consistent as it now appears, the fact that man's activities lead to increasing simplification of communities has profound importance. Our agricultural practices result in large areas of land being planted with one species of crop, and our pollution of waterways allows the survival of only those few species that can exist under these harsh conditions. The natural ecosystems are being simplified and we are required to expend more and more energy in attempts to maintain some stability.

Environmental Deterioration in History

Man has contributed to the deterioration of the environment largely by his simplification of natural communities. He actively exterminated some species as he hunted them for food or sport or because they were competing with him for some food that he used. He changed the environment so rapidly that many species could not adjust quickly enough and so died out. The alteration of the environment on this scale is unique to man because of his widespread use of tools. The deterioration of the environment is not a new process; it has been going on ever since man has existed as a distinguishable species on Earth.

Man himself is, of course, an extremely new organism in terms of the existence of life on Earth. The best evidence now available suggests that algae and bacteria had evolved 3 billion years ago, and general estimates place the origin of life on Earth at about 3.5 billion years ago. Really abundant fossils have not been found from before about 600 million years ago and the first reptiles and amphibians appeared about 300 million years ago. Dinosaurs flourished but disappeared some 135 million years ago and only since that time have mammals been important. Man as a distinguishable species has existed for only about a million years. The domestication of animals and plants dates back only a little over ten thousand years, so that from that period on man has been altering the environment on an ever-increasing scale. The process of change by man can be seen to be ever accelerating, with a notable quickening of pace at the onset of the Industrial Revolution. In terms of the life span of the Earth, then, man's existence is only a wafer-thin frosting on the cake and the period of serious change to the environment is but a dust layer on this frosting. In this very short span of time, however, he has come to dominate all of the complex ecosystems that have evolved over much longer periods of time.

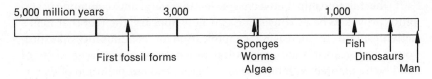

Relative time scale of the earth's history.

Man's influence on his environment has been much more widespread than most people realize. His first tool to have a significant effect on the environment was fire. Early man evidently hunted in packs and used fire to drive game into areas where it could be easily captured. The habitat had been exposed to sporadic lightning fires for millions of years, but man used fire constantly in the same area and so brought about dramatic changes in the environment. A forested area that was repeatedly burned was unable to reseed itself and so many of the world's great grasslands were formed. Many ecologists believe that the American prairies were much enlarged in this way by the addition of previously forested areas. In pockets that were protected from continuous burning the forest ecosystems have persisted.[3]

There is good evidence that heavy hunting by primitive man was responsible for the extinction of many species of animals. It is generally agreed that man first arrived on the North American continent between eleven thousand and thirteen thousand years ago. This time corresponded with the most recent of four distinct ice ages. Geological history shows that many species of large mammals became extinct in Europe and the Americas at the end of this ice age. A widely held

[3] See P. V. Wells, "Postglacial Vegetational History of the Great Plains," *Science*, Vol. 167 (March 1970), pp. 1574–1576.

theory, the Pleistocene Overkill Theory,[4] contends that man's invention of more efficient hunting tools was responsible for these extinctions. Species such as the giant mastodons and mammoths, giant beaver, ground sloth, saber-toothed cats, woolly rhinoceros, and cave bear became extinct altogether and others, such as horses, camels, and tapirs, were extincted from parts of their range. At the end of previous ice ages environmental changes had caused some species to die out but the number was insignificant relative to the dramatic change at this period. The only difference in the environment at this time was the presence of man and his hunting tools. Man was able to hunt these huge animals to extinction with only these very primitive tools. In more recent centuries there has been ample documentation of the extinction of species under man's hunting pressure.

The dodo and the passenger pigeon have gone forever; whales and the whooping crane are teetering on the brink of extinction. In the last four hundred years, about 1 per cent of the four thousand species of mammals on earth have become extinct. Another 3 per cent are considered endangered species. Over three hundred species of birds are now officially listed as endangered species.

With the development of agriculture, man's influence on the environment began on a truly large scale. The first settlements were along the fertile flood plains of the Tigris, the Euphrates, and the Nile. As early as 4000 B.C., irrigation dams and canals were built and farmers along the Nile were establishing the area that was a granary of imperial Rome.

Of particular consequence in this process of environmental deterioration was the domestication of animals, especially grazing animals. Flocks of animals grazed the hills surrounding the fertile plains on which crops were being grown. The heavy concentration of sustained grazing subjected the native vegetation to unprecedented pressures. The most succulent grasses were eaten as soon as they sprouted and could not survive. Those species of grasses that were able to survive the grazing pressure did not provide adequate cover for the soil and erosion began on a large scale.

Erosion was increased further because the trees had been cut from these hills for the building of houses and ships and for fuel. The famous cedars of Lebanon provided timber for the Phoenician ships and for the temple of the Queen of Sheba. Without trees or a ground cover of grass to hold it, rainwater ran off more quickly and floods became frequent. G. L. Stebbins [5] has suggested that Noah's flood was, in

[4] P. S. Martin and H. E. Wright, eds., *Pleistocene Extinctions: The Search for a Cause* (New Haven: Yale University Press, 1967).

[5] "Prospects for Spaceship Man," *Saturday Review of Literature* (March 7, 1970).

fact, a form of punishment for man's sins against the environment. The rushing water carried soil from the hills down into the plains and filled the irrigation dams and canals with silt. Ruins of towns can be found buried under thirty-five feet of silt, and the ancient seaport of Ur now lies 150 miles from the sea, owing to silt deposits.

THE GROWTH OF POPULATION AND THE ORIGIN OF POLLUTION

The shift from a hunting-gathering life to agriculture meant a greater and more reliable source of food. Only about 10 per cent of the food energy of a plant is incorporated into the body of a herbivore. A hunter feeding on a herbivore is not much more efficient in this transfer of energy, so that a hunter is extracting only a fraction of the energy that the plants of an area have stored. By changing to a largely vegetarian diet, man was eliminating this inefficient "middle man" in the food chain so that a given area could support more people. The greater supply of food coupled with the fact that these grains could be stored for use in unfavorable seasons meant that man was able to settle in one place and was less susceptible to the hazards of weather and the vagaries of nature.

With the population more settled and the food supply greatly increased, an increase in numbers could be supported. A tribe that existed by hunting and gathering had to keep moving to take advantage of seasonal foods; also, the food in a particular area soon became depleted and the game became wary. These people had no permanent houses and very few personal goods in the form of pots and pans and so on because they had to carry everything with them when they moved on. Because children would have to be carried from place to place a woman could not manage a second child until the first was old enough to keep up with the movements of the tribe. This was no doubt the basis for tribal taboos against intercourse while a child was still nursing and for the infanticide practiced against the extra babies produced at multiple births. Cruel as these practices may seem, they did ensure that the population was maintained at a level that the environment could support.

In areas of good agricultural potential one man was now able to produce enough food for several families. Not all individuals were required to produce food and the larger communities could now afford to maintain people in roles other than as producers of food. Artisans flourished and religious and administrative men could be supported by the rest of the community. A market system developed and towns grew up as marketing and governing centers for a region.

When man settled into villages and townships he was no longer dependent on the natural vegetation for shelter. He had removed himself from this intimate contact with nature and from the necessity for remaining in harmony with her. His agricultural practices modified the local ecosystem. Some species of animals and plants were domesticated and others were killed off for food or furs or because they posed a threat to man's growing crops. He had entered an entirely new phase of his history on Earth, one in which he could consciously manipulate the ecosystem. His was now the dominant species and those other species that continued to exist did so only under his sufferance.

At this point in man's history environmental degradation began to assume serious proportions. Perhaps we might even place the origin of pollution at this point. Pollution is a difficult term to deal with because it is a social term that can be truly defined only in terms of social values and expectations. In many instances a pollutant is a substance that is a useful resource in another context. A pollutant then could be described as a resource that is out of place in a particular environment in that it destroys some aspect of an otherwise stable ecosystem. For example, human biological wastes have always existed and have served as a fertilizer, a useful resource, in many ecosystems. The accumulation of large amounts of sewerage in a lake or stream is, however, a form of pollution. If the original ecosystem is no longer able to survive we could classify this ecosystem as polluted.

In most cases a pollutant does not kill all life, but some of the more susceptible species cannot survive. Species that have a low range of tolerance for the particular pollutant are the first to disappear. As a result of the local extinction of these species, the whole food web of the ecosystem is changed, possibly resulting in the death of other species. The growth of some species, particularly some species of algae, fungi, and bacteria, is often facilitated by heavy concentrations of certain pollutants. A substance that has caused the death of one species may be just what is needed for the growth of another species. The old adage "One man's meat is another man's poison" might be reworded in a modern context as "one species' pollutant is another species' dinner."

We have known for hundreds of years that species differ in their requirements of the environment and recent pollution events have dramatized this fact. A case in point is Great South Bay off Long Island, New York. When Long Island duckling became a menu favorite and many duck farms were established in the area, the waters entering the bay carried high concentrations of minerals from the duck farms. The change in the nutrient balance of the water in the bay caused the

death of some species of the tiny floating organisms in the bay. Unfortunately, these organisms constituted the bulk of the diet for oysters
in this area and the oyster industry was virtually wiped out. It was
found that the bellies of the oysters were full (they had filtered small
organisms out of the water), but these species could not be digested
by the oysters. These new organisms had previously been found in
only very small numbers, but they throve in water with the new mineral balance and became the dominant life forms of the bay. The
oysters could not survive. Duckling replaced oysters on menus in
that area.

Man's early alterations of his environment produced conditions that
eliminated many species but also favored the growth of a few species.
His permanent dwellings became the home of rats, lice, and fleas.
Stagnant water in his dams and irrigation ditches provided an ideal
habitat for mosquitoes. His sedentary life produced high concentrations of sewage that allowed the growth of dense populations of bacteria. The environment that man had created was one that provided
ideal conditions for the growth and transmission of many disease
organisms.

Travel between market centers in different cities and countries pro-
moted the spread of infectious diseases. Typhoid, cholera, yellow
fever, smallpox, and malaria claimed the lives of large portions of the
population. The Black Death of the fourteenth century killed about
one third of the population of Europe in a single epidemic. Wave after
wave of these epidemics swept the dense populated areas of the
world. These diseases were particularly harsh on children, so that only
about half of those born lived to reproduce. Population growth was
kept in check by disease.

THE SCIENTIFIC-INDUSTRIAL REVOLUTION

One of the products of the scientific-industrial revolution was the
rapid population increase we are now experiencing. Many people
blame environmental deterioration on population growth alone, but,
as emphasized earlier, this view is much too simple. The scientific-
industrial revolution meant not only a great increase in the production
of goods but also a further freeing of many individuals from the process
of food production. Medicine and science could now be supported by
the population, and the knowledge gained was properly recorded so
that information accumulated. The year that Jenner announced his
discovery of inoculation against smallpox was the same year (1789)
that Malthus wrote his now-famous treatise discussing the rapid
growth of the human population. He thought that this growth must

end in famine and misery. As basic knowledge about public health, sanitation, and the causes of disease were discovered, the death rate of the population fell correspondingly.

The growth rate of a population is the result of the difference between the number of births and the number of deaths. A change in either the birth rate or the death rate can result in an increase in the rate of growth of a population. There is no evidence that the reproductive ability of man has increased over the period of his existence as a species although, of course, improved diets and medical care have heightened the chances of producing a healthy child. Our present rate of population growth is much greater than in the past because of changes that have taken place in the death rate, especially in infant mortality.

Estimations of the size of the human population in the past are necessarily inexact, but they do give some idea of how drastic the change in the growth rate has been. E. S. Deevey [6] has estimated the total world population at the time of Christ to be about 200 or 300 million. In the year 1650 there were about 500 million people, a doubling of the population. Only two hundred years were needed for the next doubling of world population to about 1 billion in the year 1850. In the next one hundred years the population trebled to a total of almost 3 billion! It is obvious that not only the size of the base population is increasing but the rate of growth is itself increasing as the difference between birth rate and death rate becomes greater. At present rates the population of the Earth is expected to double in about thirty-five years.

It is tempting to attribute the environmental crisis in which we find ourselves to this growth of population alone. Population increase is a most important, but by no means the only, cause of the problem. Nevertheless, as long as population growth continues there will be a need for more and more interference with the environment. Therefore the problems that beset us cannot be solved unless population growth is slowed or stopped.

Population growth has resulted from a decrease in death rate. Improved diets and sanitation and the enormous advances made in the understanding and control of communicable diseases have been responsible for this decrease. To a large extent, then, the population explosion may be said to result from the control of pollution.

Population expansion began with the advances made in sanitation during the Industrial Revolution at the same time as new forms of industrial pollution began to affect our environment. As the popula-

6 "The Human Population," *Scientific American*, Vol. 203, No. 3 (September 1960).

tion of industrialized countries increases, the amount of industrial pollutants also increases.

There is no doubt that the rapidly increasing population can in itself lead to serious and permanent deterioration of the environment. Population biologists have for many years used the term *carrying capacity* to describe the population size of a particular species that can be permanently maintained in an area. A population of this size would not deplete the resources available to the next generation. Although all animals are able to breed quickly enough to use up all these resources, populations seldom reach the carrying capacity and very rarely exceed it under natural conditions. Populations are regulated at a level below the carrying capacity by weather, diseases, predators, or behavioral limitations. On the rare occasions when overpopulation does occur, mass starvation results and often the habitat is permanently damaged. A consequence of exceeding the carrying capacity in one year may be the lowering of the capacity to support future populations.

A classic example of the depletion of the environment due to overpopulation was provided on the Kaibab Plateau in Arizona. In 1907 the population of mule deer in this area was estimated at 4,000. The carrying capacity at that time was thought to be about 30,000 deer. The area had been set aside as a game preserve, and for their protection the deer's natural predators—mountain lions, wolves, and coyotes —were exterminated. By 1924 the deer population, freed from natural enemies, had reached 100,000. This population was far above the carrying capacity of the area, and in the years from 1924 to 1930 an estimated 80,000 deer died of starvation. The population continued to decline because the forage plants had been damaged and could not regenerate quickly enough to support the remaining animals. With fewer plants to hold the soil, erosion took place, permanently damaging the productivity of the area. Eventually the herd leveled off at about 10,000 animals, apparently near the present carrying capacity of the region.

Continuously, throughout history, man's advances have served to raise the carrying capacity of the Earth for his species. The domestication of animals and plants raised the carrying capacity enormously: a given area could now support many more people than before. Agriculture became more productive as man learned something about plant nutrition and began to apply fertilizers and to practice crop rotation to replenish the nutrients in the soil. However, these practices have not been without long-term effects in the environment. Heavy grazing led to erosion in many areas, and continuous irrigation has, in places, raised the water table to such an extent that salts rise to the surface and make the soil unusable.

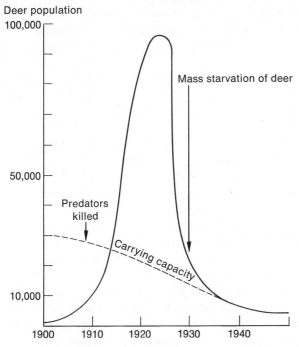

The population of deer on the Kaibab plateau. The decline in carrying capacity following overpopulation is apparently permanent.

Efforts to raise the productivity of an area for the immediate future may thus lead to a decrease in the carrying capacity of that environment for future generations. As the human population grows these pressures on the environment will increase. An attempt to provide food for all these people could lead to an eventual lowering of the carrying capacity of the Earth as a whole.

It is often difficult to predict the many and varied environmental effects that may arise from man's "improvement" of nature. A case in point is Egypt's High Aswan Dam. When construction began it was calculated that this dam would allow irrigation that would increase the food production of that country by one third. By the time the dam is completed the population will also have increased by one third. It is now apparent, however, that although population growth has erased any advances provided by the dam, other effects have altered the carrying capacity of the region. When the Nile flooded periodically it carried with it huge quantities of silt and nutrient chemicals that fertilized the fields along its banks. These floods no longer occur, and the silt is dropped into the lake behind the dam instead of downstream. The nutrients in the water entering the Mediterranean Sea nourished the growth of plankton, which, in turn, supported a large sardine industry. Hauls of sardines by several nearby countries have fallen by 50 per cent or more in the last few years and are still declining. The permanent irrigation canals provide a suitable habitat for snails carrying the parasite causing schistosomiasis, a disease of the liver and intestine in man. In some areas almost every person in the population is infected. The still waters of the lake above the dam have favored the growth of dense mats of water weeds, impeding fishing and navigation and speeding evaporation through transpiration to an alarming , degree. One ecologist has suggested that this High Aswan Dam may represent the "ultimate disaster for Egypt."

There is no doubt that the rapid growth of the human population endangers the environment for man. Population growth may soon outstrip the carrying capacity in terms of food production for mankind, causing dreadful consequences in some of the more crowded countries. Many ecologists fear that the pressure to feed this population may so overtax the resources of Earth that the carrying capacity will be permanently lowered and the human population, like the deer of the Kaibab Plateau, will continue declining with the decreasing productivity of a ravaged environment. The effects will be felt most acutely in the unindustrialized (so-called underdeveloped) nations, where the population growth rate is highest. With the historical evidence of the decrease in the carrying capacity of the areas that are now Iraq and Lebanon and with the indications that man's engineering is leading to similar deterioration of the environment (as in the High Aswan Dam), fears for the quality of the environment are well founded.

The current interest in ecology has been partly stimulated by the many eminent scientists who feel that environmental deterioration may soon reach the point at which man (and many other species) can no longer exist. Population growth, although it does contribute to the deterioration of the environment, cannot be held solely responsible for the threat that these experts sense. The effects of population growth will be most marked in the underdeveloped countries, and in these areas the environment for agriculture may be drastically altered. Although this outcome would be a catastrophe for these countries in particular and might affect surrounding countries to some degree, it is highly unlikely that the effects of population growth in these countries could threaten the existence of mankind on Earth. Scientists who are. concerned with the ecological crisis are more concerned with the worldwide effects of modern technology than with the effects of agricultural pressure in the underdeveloped countries. Although it is true that the more people there are the more these technological effects are being pressed on the environment and in greater concentrations, nevertheless the growth of population itself cannot be blamed for the sort of environmental deterioration that could threaten our species as a whole.

The dilemma in which we now find ourselves has been produced not so much by population growth as by the disproportionate growth and misuse of technology. As mentioned in the "Introduction" of this book, in the twenty years from 1946 to 1966 the use of fertilizer on a world scale increased by 700 per cent. Electrical power consumption has gone up by 400 per cent in the same period and is now doubling every ten years. Pesticide usage has increased by more than 500 per cent. In the same period the world population has increased by only 43 per cent. It is the great industrial countries of the world that are the cause of concern for the continuation of life. Even those modern products that relate most directly to agriculture are used mainly by the industrialized countries. Countries with 90 per cent of the world's population account for only 10 per cent of the fertilizer used.

Enormous quantities of mineral resources, from all corners of the world, are processed each year in the United States. As we said earlier in this book, this country, with only 6 per cent of the world's population, now consumes an estimated 35 per cent of all the minerals produced on Earth. At the current rate of growth the United States could use all of the mineral production of the non-Communist world by the year 2000. The use of these resources is reflected in our garbage cans. Today we each produce 5.3 pounds of solid garbage per day, and if current trends continue this will be 7.5 pounds per head in 1980 and in the year 2000 we will each be responsible for 10 pounds of solid wastes daily! We can all relate to something as personal as our own garbage, and when we are told continuously by people in the "ecology movement" that "we have met the enemy and he is us," our guilt is confirmed by these garbage cans. Boy Scouts and various citizens' organizations hurriedly organize trash collections and haul garbage from along one section of roadway or river bank and dump it somewhere else. Can we really believe that this is what the ecological crisis is all about? Supposing that we collected all the litter, vowed always to return our bottles to the store, and turned off air conditioners at peak periods of power usage—would the crisis disappear? It is very hard to imagine that the sins of a litterbug could threaten man's existence on Earth.

Most people find it very difficult to believe that life is really being threatened. But the environmental crisis is real. It cannot be attributed to any one cause or process; it is the result of population growth, industrialization, the American Way of Life, and the attitude of the consumer. To appreciate the basis for the predictions of doom, it is neces-

sary to understand something about the global effects of the products
of man's newest technology.

The Global Threat: The Atmosphere

The balance between the living organisms of the ecosphere and the
physical environment is delicate but apparently stable. Over millions
of years this balance has evolved; even the atmosphere as we know
it has evolved because of the action of living organisms.

It is generally agreed that the primitive atmosphere of the Earth contained very little oxygen. Early plants released oxygen as a by-product
of photosynthesis. Under present circumstances the oxygen produced
by a plant is fully used by organisms that feed on that plant, the
herbivores, and the decay bacteria. In the past, however, much organic
matter was not completely oxidized but was formed into the coal, peat,
and oil deposits that we are now using. Thus the oxygen content of the
atmosphere increased up to the present level. Theoretically, at least,
the oxygen required to oxidize these fossil deposits fully would deplete
our atmosphere of all its oxygen. However, now that new balances
have been established, the carbon dioxide produced from the burning
of fossil fuels is absorbed by the oceans and also stimulates the plants
to photosynthesize more rapidly and to produce more oxygen. Alarm
that the burning of fossil fuel would deplete our atmosphere of oxygen
appears to have been unfounded; the oxygen content has not been
altered by this industrial use of fuel.

In spite of absorption by sea water and increased photosynthesis by
land plants, the carbon dioxide content of the atmosphere has been
altered by industrialization. The percentage of carbon dioxide has
increased somewhat and many scientists have expressed concern that
this may increase the Earth's temperature by a "greenhouse effect."
Like glass, carbon dioxide allows visible light rays to pass freely but
absorbs infrared rays. An increase in carbon dioxide in the atmosphere
could cover the Earth as glass covers a greenhouse, trapping the infrared rays and increasing the surface temperature. Scientists have speculated that this warming of the Earth could cause the melting of the
polar ice caps, resulting in a raising of the sea level by as much as four
hundred feet.

To date there has been only weak evidence that a warming effect is
operating. In fact, the average global temperature has fallen slightly in
the last few decades, perhaps because man's industry and agricultural
practices have increased the smoke and dust in the atmosphere. These
could act as a screen, blocking out the sun's rays and resulting in a
decline of temperature. Speculation of the amount of particulate matter

in the atmosphere has suggested to some that a new ice age may form.

Depending upon the studies one reads, he may fear either the destruction or the increase of the ice caps because of pollution! Both suggestions are rather extreme, and optimists hope that perhaps the two effects will cancel each other out. We simply do not have the data or knowledge to make accurate predictions of these effects but the enormity of their consequences underscores the need for such information.

THE NITROGEN CYCLE

An example of the complexities of the ecosphere that maintain the atmospheric balance is provided by the nitrogen cycle. Nitrogen is an essential component of proteins. All living things have proteins, so nitrogen is essential to all life. The atmosphere is composed of about 80 per cent nitrogen, but in an inert form. Plants are unable to synthesize protein from atmospheric nitrogen and must obtain the nitrogen either as ammonia or in nitrate form. Certain bacteria and blue-green algae are able to convert atmospheric nitrogen directly into compounds used for their tissue proteins. These species are therefore very important in the ecosphere, as they provide nitrogen in a form that is available to higher plants. Blue-green algae live in water or on the soil surface, and fixation of nitrogen by these organisms is one of the reasons for the high productivity of rice paddies. Nitrogen-fixing bacteria grow mostly in association with the roots of plants belonging to one family, the legumes, which include peas, beans, and clover. Crop rotation that includes legumes at some point thus serves to incorporate nitrogen into the soil in a form usable by other plants. Some atmospheric nitrogen becomes available to plants through the action of lightning, but in amounts much less than those from nitrogen-fixing bacteria. The intense heat of lightning combines the nitrogen with oxygen to form nitrates, which dissolve in rain and enter the soil.

Plants are able to absorb nitrates (NO_3) and nitrites (NO_2) as a mineral raw material and convert these into amino groups (NH_2) in plant protein. Animals obtain their nitrogen supply from this plant protein. When animals and plants die, decay bacteria free the nitrogen in the form of ammonia (NH_3). Ammonia itself is a nutrient for a group of nitrifying bacteria that act on the ammonia and convert it to the nitrate form, which is again suitable for plant use. The soil also contains denitrifying bacteria that convert nitrates into inert molecular nitrogen, which is added to the nitrogen content of the air. Without these denitrifying bacteria all the nitrogen would eventually be removed from the atmosphere.

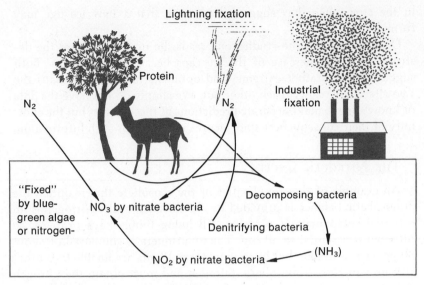

The nitrogen cycle.

This complex cycle depends on at least four different sorts of bacteria: the nitrogen fixers, the decomposers, the nitrifiers, and the denitrifiers. Together these organisms maintain a steady state in the atmosphere. The removal of any one element could lead to drastic changes in our global environment. Because plants are able to use only nitrates, some scientists have suggested recently that we attempt to block the action of the denitrifying bacteria, thus increasing the amount of nitrate in the soil and so, they say, increase agricultural productivity. This is a terrifying suggestion to any person with an ecological view of the world because such action would disrupt the entire cycle and would eventually result in the fixation of all of the nitrogen from the atmosphere. The possible consequences are unknown but would certainly alter the constancy of the atmosphere and jeopardize all living things in the ecosphere.

Barry Commoner [7] has discussed the ways in which man is already interfering with the nitrogen cycle and endangering its balance. When crops are grown continuously in an area the nitrate content of the soil is depleted by the plants. Crop rotation and manuring replace this organic nitrate in the soil. Modern agriculture supplies the plants with chemical fertilizers in the form of nitrates. This produces good yields but cannot maintain the organic nitrate content of the soil. Continuous usage of fertilizers leads to a decline in the organic matter content of

7 *The Closing Circle* (New York: Alfred A. Knopf, Inc., 1971), pp. 24–25.

the soil and the physical condition of the soil is also changed. Lacking the organic humus, the soil becomes less porous and cannot hold water or air. The roots of plants need oxygen in order to function in absorbing nutrients from the soil, and as the soil becomes compacted there is poor aeration and the extra fertilizer is not taken up by the plants. Because the soil retains less water, most of the chemical fertilizer is washed off the fields and pollutes our streams and lakes. The bacteria necessary for the continuation of the nitrogen cycle cannot exist in the soil under these conditions and the whole delicately balanced cycle is disturbed.

The Global Threat: Radiation

Radiation was chosen from among many pollutants that threaten our global environment because it is, in the words of G. M. Woodwell,[8] the "model pollutant." Although it is an extremely recent pollutant in the history of man, the hazards of ionizing radiation are potentially the most destructive addition he has made to his environment. Radioactive material was the first pollutant to be properly monitored and the first to show clearly the worldwide distribution and effects of a pollutant released at one point. It was this pollutant that alerted us to the dangers inherent in our treatment of the Earth.

Biologists had known for centuries that substances could be transported in the natural environment by the air and by water and in the bodies of animals, but this knowledge had little apparent meaning to the welfare of man until 1954. That was the year in which Project Bravo, a test of the nuclear bomb, was carried out at Bikini in the Pacific Ocean. Everybody knew of the immediate effects of such bombs on the local environment from the ghastly experiences of Hiroshima and Nagasaki, but the test at Bikini showed much broader, delayed effects.

High-energy radiation is released into the atmosphere by a nuclear explosion and gradually falls to Earth as fallout. The distance traveled by the fallout depends on the height of the explosion and the weather conditions. Fallout particles lose their radioactivity rapidly at first, but then more gradually. Some of the smaller particles may be picked up by winds and carried large distances, falling to Earth weeks or months later and still carrying some radioactivity. High-altitude winds carried the particles from Project Bravo much further than had been anticipated. Several thousand square miles of the Pacific Ocean received a dosage of radioactivity that would be lethal to man. Tests of fish

[8] "Radioactivity and Fallout: the Model Pollutant," *Bioscience*, Vol. 19, (1969), pp. 884–887.

throughout the vast Pacific showed that measurable amounts of radio-activity, thought to be at a harmless level, had been spread extremely widely.

Residues from Project Bravo were expected to be spread by wind and water over the Pacific and diluted to undetectable levels. However, fish available in Japanese markets showed much higher dosages than would be expected with this sort of dilution. Studies have shown that these high concentrations are due to the biological food chain. Radioactive particles in the water are taken up by tiny plants that are eaten by small animals that, in turn, are eaten by larger animals. There is a concentration of radioactivity in the bodies of organisms as we move up the food chain. Man, as a general predator on the large fish, stands at the very end of this food chain.

One of the dangerous radioactive particles is radioactive iodine, I^{131}, which emits gamma rays. The half-life of this substance is short (only about eight days) so that it was considered to be of little danger to man. It has been shown, however, that in the few weeks that it does exist in hazardous form it may reach high levels of contamination in man even though contamination in the environment is low. This substance reaches man through a very simple food chain; the particles fall in rain or snow and are on the grass which is eaten by cows and their radioactive milk then contaminates man. The danger to man lies in the fact that iodine is highly concentrated in the thyroid gland. This gland controls the rate of metabolism in the body. It has been shown that relatively low levels of irradiation will cause tumors in the thyroid glands of children. The toxic effects of a contaminant such as this may not be manifest for as long as ten years. Children who were exposed to this fallout at Rangelap Atoll in 1954 showed evidence of thyroid abnormality ten years later.

The food chain path that I^{131} is known to follow is an extremely simple one. When we consider the sorts of interactions that occur in nature and the intricate food webs that exist, it can be appreciated that this is one of the simplest of routes. How much more complex this process might be with other contaminants and other communities of organisms! Even for this extremely simple situation, however, it is virtually impossible to predict the rate of movement of a pollutant through a natural community or the concentration that will show up in man or, indeed, what the long-term effects of a given concentration might be for man.

The rate of movement of I^{131} from a bomb site to a man in another area will first of all depend upon the weather conditions. Winds may move the particles great distances, and deposition takes place most heavily in rain or snow. When the fallout particles have settled on the grass the amount taken up by the cow will depend on the density of the forage; if she eats from a wide area she will pick up more iodine. She may also, of course, be receiving a supplementary diet of grain or stored hay that would decrease the iodine intake. Individual cows will vary in the efficiency with which the iodine is secreted into the milk. The amount of contaminated milk that a person consumes will determine the dosage he receives. Even with this most simple of food chains, many factors determine the flow to man and it is virtually impossible to make accurate predictions.

An unpleasant surprise concentration of radioactive elements occurred in the bodies of Eskimos in Alaska. The radioactive isotope cesium[137] has a long half-life (about thirty years), emitting gamma rays. Chemically cesium[137] behaves like potassium, a constituent of all cells, and so becomes widely distributed in the biological realm. This element also passes through a food chain. The first link in this tundra region was lichens. In an environment poor in nutrients, the lichens readily extract the cesium[137] from rain or snow and concentrate it in their tissues. During the harsh winter months the lichens are the main food source for caribou, which, in turn, are the main food source for the Eskimo in many areas. In the bodies of the Eskimo the element is concentrated to twice the concentration in caribou, so that these people were receiving substantial doses of radioactive material.

The next question is obvious: What levels of radiation can be considered safe? Ample evidence is available to show that there is no really safe level of exposure. With most environmental factors that affect man there is a threshold below which the effects are not noticeable. However, there is evidence that genetic mutations may be caused by very low dosages of radiation although the frequency is increased only slightly over the natural rate. We have already faced this problem in medicine. The value of X rays has been considered to outweigh the small chance that these dosages could produce mutations and modern man has agreed on a compromise. In the natural situation it is impossible to make this sort of compromise agreement. We cannot anticipate with any degree of accuracy the degree of exposure in a particular area. Also, the radioactive material is spread throughout the world so we are no longer faced with the prospect of making choices on an individual or even a local basis. Natural concentration processes through the biological food chains compound the problem and may result in particular individuals' receiving much higher doses because of their location or diet.

Recently controversy has arisen over the concentration of the isotope strontium[90] that may be considered safe. This element is concentrated in cow's milk, where it substitutes for calcium. It is passed along the food chain to a human and there is deposited in the bones and the teeth. Although this isotope has a long half-life its effects were thought to be minimal. Experience had shown that young women employed to paint luminous watch dials did show an increase in leukemia and bone cancer, but they had been exposed to large doses over long periods of time. Victims who survived Hiroshima and Nagasaki had been carefully observed and only a small number of leukemia cases were reported. There seemed little cause for alarm over the very small amounts of this isotope released from nuclear bomb tests and diluted over the surface of the globe.

It has been discovered, however, that radiation effects are much more marked in the highly sensitive reproductive cells and in an embryo in the first few weeks of its life. Experiments with X rays on animals and observations of pregnant women who were exposed to these rays showed that the embryo may be twenty to fifty times more sensitive to the effects of radiation than an adult. These embryos had a much greater probability of developing leukemia and other cancers than did an adult exposed to an equivalent dosage. Other experiments indicate that very small dosages of radioactivity affect the reproductive cells of the parents, resulting in genetic damage.

There are sources of radioactive contamination of our environment other than nuclear weapons. Chief among these, of course, are nuclear reactors used to produce electricity. The fuel for these reactors has to be reprocessed periodically, producing the isotopes of cesium and strontium that are known to be biologically hazardous. These wastes should be stored where they cannot escape to contaminate the environment for at least one thousand years. Some of the storage tanks that have been used to date are known to be leaking after only about twenty years! It has been suggested that these reactors may be replaced by thermonuclear power plants that operate by fusion instead of fission and so will not produce these particular isotopes. They will produce new contaminants, however. Important among these pollutants is tritium (H^3) which can become a constituent of long-lived radioactive water and would contaminate all the waters on earth. Many workers consider tritium to be harmless, whereas others have stated that this pollution would reach unacceptable levels by the year 2000. An alternative method of producing electrical power is with the "fast-breeder" reactor, which is generally considered to be clean of radioactive fallout but requires the use of considerable quantities of plutonium. Plutonium has been called the most dangerous element known to man. It is radioactive, with a half-life of twenty-four thousand years. A few pounds of this substance is used in the production of an atomic bomb; a suggested program for the development of fast-breeder reactors would require the handling of thirty tons of this material over the next ten years!

THE GLOBAL THREAT: PESTICIDES

Unlike radioactive isotopes, persistent pesticides are difficult to detect in the environment. For this reason their use went unchecked and unquestioned for several decades. Recent evidence has shown that these chemicals are spread throughout the Earth and that they threaten the web of interacting life forms even more than do radioactive particles. The threat to the global environment from persistent pesticides is real and complex; it arises from their effects on all living organisms. The question of their use is complicated by industrialization, by population growth, by the attitude of the consumer, and by international politics and health care.

The scientific-industrial revolution precipitated our present dilemma in ways other than the development of medicine with its consequent lowering of the death rate. One of the earliest and most successful applications of this new technology was to agriculture. The development of farm machinery allowed one man to do the work of many and freed others for work in the industrial centers. Large-scale farming became an economic necessity to make the investment in machinery pay off. Instead of small fields managed by many farmers and interspersed with hedgerows, wood lots, and fallow fields, mechanization made necessary the monoagriculture that we know today. Huge fields were cleared and planted in one crop. Trees and hedgerows were eliminated as the machines efficiently and systematically ploughed and planted mile after mile of corn and wheat.

In one quantum jump our ecosystem had been simplified once more, this time to an alarming degree. Where trees and shrubs had provided nesting places for birds and shelter for hundreds of types of insects, spiders, and small mammals, none now existed. A variety of crops had provided food for many types of animals, which, in turn, provided food for many predatory and scavenging species. Suddenly this complex food web had been drastically simplified, with the basis of the whole ecosystem now represented by only one or two species of plant. A simple ecosystem is a more unstable ecosystem than a complex one. Those few species of insects that were able to feed on this crop now found themselves with miles and miles of food while their predators (other insects, spiders, and birds) had largely disappeared. Under these conditions these insects underwent a population explosion of their own and so posed new problems for the scientific technicians of the day.

Train track running through a natural meadow that forms an integral part of a complex mountain ecosystem. [Photo by T. D. Fitzgerald.]

A new industry was born to produce pesticides that would kill any insect on contact. Outstanding among these, of course, was DDT. This chemical, incidentally, is one of the important ingredients of the human population bomb that now threatens to explode. It has been used on a grand scale in the control of insect-borne diseases, particularly malaria, which was previously responsible for an estimated 750,000 deaths a year in India alone. Treatment of large areas with DDT resulted in dramatic declines in the death rate in some underdeveloped countries. Characteristic of these is Ceylon, where the annual death rate was halved in a ten-year period following the introduction of DDT.

In the agricultural areas of the industrialized countries insecticides such as DDT resulted in a further simplification of the ecosystem. In a field there may be hundreds of species of insects, but only a few of these are actually causing damage to the crop. A broad-spectrum insecticide such as DDT kills all insects on contact, so that not only the harmful insects but also their natural predators were killed. The predatory insects, which moved about in search of their prey, were especially susceptible to poisoning while some of the harmful insects underneath leaves or inside the body of the plant escaped unharmed. In the absence of their natural predators, the few remaining pest species could readily increase to even higher numbers. This situation also demonstrated perfectly the principle of natural selection. The population of the pest species was high and the selective force (DDT) was very strong. Individuals that had some genetic resistance to the effects of DDT were at a tremendous advantage, and thus the next generation was composed of resistant individuals bred from those that had escaped the spraying. Well over one hundred insect pest species are now known to be resistant to the effects of DDT. Many of the predatory insects have been killed directly or have been poisoned by eating other insects that contain the poison. Without these general predators feeding on all insects, new pests are created; mites were not considered a pest of crops until DDT removed their natural enemies. The side effects of DDT on crop pests were thus threefold: it produced insects that were resistant to it, it removed insect predators, and it created new species of pest insects.

Another side effect of the early effectiveness of DDT was the fact that consumers became accustomed to pest-free produce. A worm in an apple is no longer tolerated by a choosy housewife. As DDT resistance became apparent and as new pest species became established, the farmer became desperate to keep them in check. The requirements for a marketable crop had changed; it now had to be completely insect-free. The farmer had to spray more and more often with heavier and heavier dosages to produce this sort of crop. Many farmers now spray twelve times per season, whereas once was sufficient in the early days of DDT.

It is extremely difficult for the ecologist to convey to others an appreciation of the manifold changes that occur when one portion of the environment is disturbed. Many people are familiar with Rachel L. Carson's now-classic book *Silent Spring*,[9] which describes the food-chain effects of DDT. The chemical in fallen leaves and in the soil is eaten by earthworms and robins are then affected by feeding on the poisoned worms. More and more of these food-chain effects are being documented as DDT monitoring becomes more routine and observers are more aware of the consequences of what they see.

In remote villages of Borneo the World Health Organization came into the thatch huts and sprayed the houseflies, which, they feared, might carry disease. The dying flies were especially easy prey to the gekkos, small lizards that live in the thatch and regularly feed on what flies they can catch. Having eaten many flies and concentrated the poison from each one in their bodies, the gekkos in turn became ill and fell prey to the cats. As the cats began to die, the village was invaded by rats, which may have been carrying plague. Because of the fear of plague live cats were parachuted into these villages in the jungles of Borneo to restore the balance of nature that man had unwittingly disturbed.

Looking along a food chain it is easy to see that birds that feed on insects and predators that feed on these birds will be accumulating DDT from every meal. Because DDT is not metabolized or excreted, at each trophic level concentrations become higher. There are a few well-documented examples of this accumulation of pesticides along a food chain. Measures of bottom mud in Lake Michigan showed a concentration of DDT and its breakdown products of 0.014 parts per million. In a shrimp within the lake, concentration was more than ten times as high, at 0.44ppm. Fish such as the alewife, the chub, and the whitefish showed another tenfold increase. Concentration in the herring gull, the omnivore at the top of this food chain showed a further twentyfold increase, at 98.8ppm. The body of the gull had concentrated the DDT to seven thousand times the concentration in the mud![10]

General predators at the end of food chains can be expected to receive heavy and frequently fatal doses of DDT. The death of general predators such as hawks, owls, and eagles allows rodent populations

9 (Boston: Houghton Mifflin Company, 1962).

10 G. M. Woodwell, "Toxic Substances in Ecological Cycles," *Scientific American* (March 1967).

to increase, effecting a whole new food chain. Although we may not see these birds falling dead in the streets there is ample evidence that they are being affected by DDT. This pesticide accumulates in fatty tissue and has been shown to upset the hormonal balance of the birds, interfering with their calcium metabolism. Birds containing high doses of DDT lay eggs with very thin shells that are easily broken in the nest. Recently a nest of a bald eagle was found to contain an egg with no shell at all, just a thin membrane. Many eggs contain so much DDT that the embryo is killed and cannot hatch even if the shell has not broken. Many species of predatory birds are now considered doomed to extinction because of the effects of DDT. Among these are the peregrine falcon, the Bermuda petrel, the osprey, the Cooper's hawk, the Californian brown pelican, and the national symbol of the United States, the bald eagle. All of these are top predators, accumulating DDT from every meal. The sterility effect has been shown to lower the production of offspring in several species by 30 per cent per year.

Man occupies the role of a top predator and has been accumulating DDT in his tissues for many years. Deposits of DDT are found in fatty tissues, which has led to some recent speculation that a crash diet, in which fatty tissues are rapidly depleted, may result in the release of large amounts of stored DDT into the bloodstream and the consequent danger of pesticide poisoning. Recent measurements have shown that citizens of the United States have large amounts of DDT stored in their bodies. The allowable content of DDT in meat for sale in the United States is 7ppm, but Americans have, on the average, 12ppm in their fat tissues. This has prompted the comment that "Americans are not for eating." Little is known of the effects of DDT on human health, but a recent study of persons who had died of liver cancer, leukemia, or high blood pressure showed that their body tissues at the time of death contained two to three times the residues of DDT and related pesticides that were contained in the body tissues of persons who died accidental deaths. Alarm has also been expressed about the DDT content of human milk. Levels of 0.15ppm to 0.25ppm have been found in the milk of American mothers. This is the sole diet of infants and it means that they are consuming four times the maximum daily intake of DDT recommended by the United Nations and five times the content allowable for the interstate shipment of cow's milk!

The alarm about the effects of DDT seems justified in light of the evidence already in hand. It is surprising to note that this pesticide was used for twenty-five years in vast quantities before the alarm was sounded. The reason for this indifference to its effects is that it was very difficult to monitor, so concentrations went unnoticed. Only with the development of gas chromatography techniques, in about 1960, did rapid monitoring become possible. At first the small concentrations in water and soil appeared harmless, but as knowledge of food-chain effects increased so did public awareness, and DDT use was curtailed in many areas.

Chlorinated hydrocarbon pesticides such as DDT, aldrin, dieldrin, and endrin are alarming chiefly because they are long-lived. DDT is not readily broken down in the environment but is active for ten years or more and is stored in living tissue. In areas where DDT applications have been curtailed, observers have been amazed to see the concentration in water and muds continue to rise for several years. This may be due to worldwide circulation of DDT and the fact that plants and animals die and release stored DDT into the environment. Large quantities of DDT are washed from fields and forests into the streams and eventually to the sea, being distributed over the entire surface of the Earth. Penguins in the Antarctic, probably never closer than 1000 miles to the nearest area of spraying, have been found to contain significant amounts of DDT in their body tissues, illustrating graphically the widespread nature of the chemical and the universal rule of food-chain concentration. There is probably no living organism on Earth that does not contain measurable amounts of DDT in its fatty tissue!

A new note of urgency was added to this alarm when, in 1968, C. F. Wurster [11] reported the startling discovery that DDT has a deleterious effect on the photosynthesis and rate of cell duplication of marine phytoplankton. These tiny organisms are the "grass of the sea" and all food chains in the oceans ultimately depend upon them. Unlike the grass on land, these organisms are eaten whole, so a continuous supply of food for all organisms in the sea depends upon the rapid division of these tiny plants. A decrease in the rate of production of these organisms could have disastrous effects on the whole ocean ecosystem. The ocean ecosystem was cited earlier in this chapter as an example of an inverse pyramid of biomass. With a change in the rate of turnover of phytoplankton the whole pyramid could collapse. We know that DDT is present in all oceans and will continue to build up for many years as the residues from decaying organisms on land are added to the supply. The potential danger to the productivity of the oceans at a time when man is turning increasingly to them as a source of food is enormous and frightening.

If the use of DDT is necessary for a farmer to produce a marketable crop and if it will save the lives of several million potential malaria victims each year, what choice do we have but to keep on using

11 "DDT Reduces Photosynthesis in Marine Phytoplankton," *Science*, Vol. 159 (1968), pp. 1474–1475.

it and so endanger our environment? An alternative is available in the form of numerous organophosphate pesticides. The main advantage of these chemicals is that they reportedly lose their effect in a few days. Thus the problems of accumulation through food chains and distribution throughout the globe do not arise. A major disadvantage of these products, however, is the extreme toxicity at the time of application. One of the most commonly used chemicals, parathion, is estimated to be three hundred times more toxic to humans than DDT. It is a poison that acts on the nervous system and can be absorbed through the skin. A few drops of the undiluted chemical is enough to kill a man, and in the last few years USDA statistics show that 132 people have been killed by parathion poisoning. These organophosphates are considerably more expensive than DDT. Some countries and some states within the United States have banned the use of DDT completely because of its long-term effects on the environment. However, organizations such as the World Health Organization strongly oppose a complete ban on the grounds that they cannot afford the new chemicals and they do not have personnel trained to handle these extremely toxic substances.

There are ways of controlling pests that are more ecologically sound than the application of sprays that kill any insect on contact. An insect becomes a pest when its growth is unchecked, often because, as explained earlier, its natural enemies (predators and parasites) have been killed off. Many pest species have been introduced from other countries where they were not pests and have increased in numbers to attain pest status here. The increase in numbers here is presumably due to the absence of natural enemies in this country. An ecologically reasonable procedure, then, is to attempt to restore the balance of nature by introducing the predatory species that do not occur in this country and to foster the growth of natural predators whose numbers have been decimated by earlier sprayings. This form of "biological control" has had a few remarkable successes in the past.

Biological control of insect pests was the first form of defense used on American farms. In the late 1800s the cottony cushion scale was accidentally introduced from Australia and infested the orange groves of California. The industry was severely threatened. To counter the pest the United States introduced vedalia beetles, the natural predator of the scale insect in Australia. The success of this introduction is now cited as the classic example of this type of control. An industry worth millions of dollars was saved at little cost and the insect populations are permanent; no further expenditure is required to keep the groves free of the scale pest.

Since that time more than 650 species of predatory insects have

A simple man-made ecosystem. A wheat farm in Saskatchewan, Canada. [Photo by T. D. Fitzgerald.]

been imported into the United States for this purpose of natural control. Not all of these experiments have been successful, but those that did succeed were impressive. Other biological enemies of pest species, such as diseases and viruses that attack only these species, are under development. Field tests have been encouraging. These diseases are selected for just that pest species so that other insects and the plant crop are not affected by these applications.

To establish a workable control system only the pest species must be affected. Recently scientists have developed some attractants, including sex attractants, that lure a pest to traps where they may be killed or sterilized. Other pest species are actually being reared by scientists, sterilized by irradiation, and released into the natural population. The idea behind this is that males are sterile but compete with wild males for the attention of the females. Those females who mate with sterile males lay eggs but the eggs are sterile. If a sufficient number of sterile males is released, a large proportion of the female population are sexually satisfied by these males but do not produce any offspring. This means that the next generation will be considerably smaller, so that a release of the same number of sterile males at this time will result in an even greater proportion of the females' producing no offspring. Over a period of several generations a local, isolated population of a pest species may be completely exterminated by this method.

A return to a more complex community adds stability to the ecosystem. Farmers are beginning to discover that this can be profitable, too. One way of keeping pests such as lygus bugs out of crops like cotton is to offer them an alternative food supply that they prefer. In California, cotton farmers now cultivate strips of alfalfa beside the cotton fields to act as decoys, attracting the lygus bugs to feed on the alfalfa instead of the cotton. This saves the farmer insecticide costs, and the absence of general pesticides, coupled with the more complex environment, preserves many of the general predatory insects. Not only lygus bugs are lessened as a pest, then, but all other species of insect that feed on cotton are kept down in numbers by these general predators.

The Global Threat: Toxic Metals

Only very recently, interest has been prompted in the amounts and types of metal wastes being introduced into our ecosystem. Most of these findings have come as a complete surprise to scientists and, apparently, to federal authorities. Contamination of the environment by these metals is considered by some to be the most insidious pollution of all. Unlike radioactivity and pesticides, these metals do not degrade at all in the biological environment. The amounts already present (and they are considerable) will simply be cycled and recycled throughout the ecosystem.

Perhaps the most generally recognized of these metal pollutants is lead. The main source of contamination by lead is the automobile, spewing out an estimated 300,000 tons of the metal each year. This is distributed by air and water movements throughout the Earth's surface. Concentrations of lead in the Pacific Ocean have increased tenfold, and the snow layers of the Arctic provide a record of the yearly increase in lead content.

At recent hearings the Assistant Secretary of the Interior stated that chronic lead poisoning is now fairly common. Women who work in areas with heavy concentrations of lead show high incidences of stillborn births and miscarriages. It is suggested that along a moderately traveled highway the lead content is high enough to abort a cow grazing on the contaminated vegetation nearby. A recent U.S. Public Health Service report on water quality showed that more than half the residents of Vermont are drinking water that is rated only "fair" or worse because of contamination by lead and other metals. Even as these reports come to light it has been revealed that industrial plants are dumping forty-eight hundred pounds of lead into the lower Mississippi River every day!

Everyone is familiar with the Mad Hatter in Alice in Wonderland—he was probably mad because he used compounds of mercury to treat the felt of hats. At least that is the modern interpretation. Mercury is known to act on the red blood cells and nervous tissue and many accidents from mercury poisoning have been reported in recent years. In the years between 1953 and 1960, 111 people in Japan died from mercury poisoning. The mercury came from a plastics factory and was concentrated in the bodies of shellfish that the victims ate. Nineteen congenitally deformed babies were produced by mothers who had eaten the shellfish.

An estimated 5 million pounds of mercury is used by industry each year in the manufacture of fungicides, disinfectants, pigments, and plastics. Only in the last year or so have concentrations of mercury been detected that are harmful to the U.S. citizen. Recently the province of Ontario stopped all fishing in five large lakes along the U.S. borders because of mercury contamination. In Montana hunters have been warned not to eat the pheasants and partridges they kill because these birds have been found to contain concentrations of mercury from seeds treated with a fungicide.

There are many other lesser-known metals circulating in our environment. Considerable dosages of arsenic are being discovered in some water sources. The Kansas River has been found to have concentrations of arsenic between 2 and 8 parts per billion; the USPHS recommends 10ppb as a maximum safe dosage in drinking water. The arsenic comes from detergents, pesticides, and mine wastes. Because it is a cumulative poison, its full effects are not known as it may take years for symptoms to become apparent.

Dr. Henry Alfred Schroeder of the Dartmouth Medical School feels that cadmium is the single most important pollutant in our environment today.[12] Cadmium replaces zinc in the body. The zinc is vital for the breakdown of fats; a body poisoned with cadmium cannot break down fats and the fats build up in the circulatory system. Twenty three million Americans suffer from hypertension (high blood pressure) and there is evidence that cadmium is a major factor in this disease. The cadmium in our diet comes from refined rice, white flour, and white sugar. In the processing of these foods zinc is removed and replaced by cadmium.

The metals may follow the biological food chains, becoming concentrated in man, the top predator. The most alarming fact in this poisoning, however, is that these metals will never be degraded and as long as man keeps dumping these great amounts of metals into his environment the problem can only get worse. Even when dumping is stopped we have no way of removing the metals already present in the water and the soil.

INTERACTION OF POLLUTANTS

The fact that all biological populations are dependent upon the other organisms in the environment and upon aspects of the physical environment has been stressed. Substances such as radioactive isotopes and pesticides enter this biological realm in ways that are complicated and unpredictable. How much more complex this becomes when we consider that there are an estimated 500,000 man-made substances now present in the environment! These substances do not enter the environment as separate pollutants; industrial and municipal wastes contain mixtures of compounds and are often heated as well. We must also realize that there are interactions between these pollutants that alter (usually increase) their potential damage.

Generally speaking, the danger of a pollutant to the environment is calculated from its immediate effects on certain target species that are chosen for toxicity tests. It is understood that such factors as the

[12] Testimony to Senate subcommittee, reported in *The New York Times*, September 1, 1970.

age, the sex, and the nutritional condition of the test plant or animal may drastically alter its response to a particular concentration of a substance; nevertheless some idea of toxicity can be obtained. Tests take into account only short-term effects; the consequences of small dosages over long periods of time are generally ignored.

The interaction of chemicals was first given broad attention in the use of pesticides. Because of the pressure to decrease the amounts of pesticide being used in the environment discoveries were made that led to the development of synergists. The presence of a synergist greatly increases the toxicity of the pesticide, so that dosages could be reduced to one tenth of the former level without loss of effectiveness. Often a synergist has no biological effect when administered alone. Some synergists are themselves pesticides, but the effect of two chemicals combined is much greater than a higher dosage of either one alone. A reaction is termed synergistic when the effect of several substances together is different from the simple sum of all the substances when applied singly. In the case of pesticides this synergism may arise from some direct chemical combination of the substances, or the synergist may act on the target insect in some way so that more of the pesticide is absorbed.

The concept of a greater than additive effect has been acknowledged in medicine for some time. Pharmacologists prefer the term *potentiation* for this effect, but the term *synergism* is more commonly used to cover these situations as well as those in which the effects are purely additive. It is commonly recognized in medicine that the effectiveness of one drug may be greatly enhanced (or reduced) by the presence of a second drug. Reduction of effect is termed *antagonism*. An unexpected synergistic reaction recently dashed the hopes for an experimental birth-control pill for men. The pill had been tested on men in prisons and had proved to be an effective spermicide. However, when tested on men leading normal, civilian lives it was found to intensify the effects of alcohol so greatly that one moderate drink was enough to incapacitate the average man!

Only very recently has information on the synergistic effects of environmental pollutants been obtained. Some of these results are startling and frightening. For example, a mixture of 0.025ppm of copper and 1.0ppm of zinc is more toxic to fish than 0.2ppm of copper or 8.0ppm of zinc alone. Plants react to sulfur dioxide in the air in a predictable fashion dependent on the concentration of the gas. In the presence of ozone the effects of sulfur dioxide are greatly intensified, acting on plants as if much greater concentrations were present. A change in the physical environment may also produce synergistic effects. Thus, a rise of 10°C. in the temperature of a stream generally doubles the effectiveness of a poison. The toxicity of hydrocyanic acid to fish has been shown to increase more than one thousandfold because of a change in the acidity of the water! A change of this magnitude in the acidity of the water could easily be produced by industrial or mine wastes.

Several pollutants acting together may also pose a greater hazard to health than either could alone. For example, sulfur dioxide fumes, a major industrial pollutant, are usually absorbed by the linings of the upper respiratory tract. However, in badly polluted areas it may be carried into the sensitive tissue of the lungs on large particles of soot or dust, thus increasing the harmful effect manyfold.

Estimates of the degree of toxicity of complex mixtures of pollutants can be greatly in error if based on the toxicity of each component in the absence of synergistic or antagonistic substances that may be present in the environment. Effluents rarely contain just one pollutant, and the interactions between these substances are just beginning to be investigated. In addition, some form of pollution may increase the temperature or the acidity or alter the oxygen content of an environment, completely altering the toxic effects on biological organisms. One can never be sure of the effects a pollutant will have on an ecosystem because synergistic and antagonistic effects are so little known.

With an estimated 500,000 man-made chemicals now present in our environment and about 500 new chemicals being produced each year, the possible number of combinations (synergistic or antagonistic) of these chemicals and the natural chemical present in the environment is astronomical. This situation complicates the prediction of the effects of a particular pollutant immensely. One can never be sure what effect a pollutant will ultimately have or what concentration can be considered acceptable because there is this potential for synergistic interaction with other chemicals in the environment.

THE LAST HORIZON: THE OCEANS

As world population growth presses on food supplies more and more people are thinking that the world's oceans will provide the food to close the gap. In the battle against hunger and malnutrition the oceans are already extremely important. An estimated 20 per cent of the world's supply of protein now comes from the sea. The vastness of the oceans holds promise because, it is felt, its very size will deny the effects of pollution. Here, if nowhere else on Earth, dilution should reduce the harmful effects of man's contaminants.

Alas, instead of increasing, the yield of food from the seas of the world may soon begin to decline because of pollution and overfishing. Despite appearances to the contrary, the oceans are not uniform bodies of water. Ryther has classified 90 per cent of the ocean as a biological desert. The open ocean has only a small productive area in the top few feet where light penetrates; in the vast bulk of the water productivity is almost zero. In shallow areas close to shore and in the few areas of the world where upwelling currents bring nutrients to the surface, productivity is very great. These are the only areas that produce our marine protein. It is also in these shallow inshore areas that pollutants are most concentrated and the effects of man are most drastic.

Estuaries and coastal wetlands are particularly important in marine productivity. John H. Ryther [13] estimates that up to one half of fisheries production is dependent, directly or indirectly, on estuaries. Many estuaries are being disturbed by man's operations, and the water draining from industry and farmland is extremely concentrated in pollutants at this point. Coastal wetlands are fast disappearing along the northeast coast of the United States as land fill for housing and highways progresses. The state of Connecticut alone fills about one acre every working day of the year. This "useless" land is, in fact, one of the most biologically productive habitats known. In addition to the shellfish and the birds that live in these areas there are many fish that use coastal marshlands and estuaries as spawning grounds or nurseries. Seven of the ten most commercially valuable Atlantic fish depend in some way upon these tidal lands for their continued existence. Perhaps nowhere else is the interdependence of ecosystems in our total biosphere more apparent than at the interface of sea and land.

All of the aspects of pollution discussed so far are exemplified in the oceans. Their seeming vastness leads most people to conclude that a few pollutants when added will become so diluted as to be harmless. However, mixing of sea waters is not complete so that some areas, particularly the productive areas close to shore, are heavily polluted. The biological food chain concentrates pollutants to levels that may be harmful to the biological community and to man. Fish and shellfish are contaminated by fecal bacteria and by heavy metals such as copper and mercury. These may then spread diseases such as typhoid and hepatitis to man or may poison him with high concentrations of metals. Some of the species are more susceptible to environmental change than others and this susceptibility may lead to a complete change of the community, as in the Great South Bay of Long Island.

The oceans are vulnerable to the effects of pollution, and contami-

[13] "Photosynthesis and Fish Production in the Sea," *Science*, Vol. 166 (1969), pp. 72–76.

nation of the seas is already more widespread than most people recognize. Travelers report garbage and lumps of oil floating in parts of the sea most distant from land. G. R. Taylor [14] has estimated that 13 million tons of oil and oil products end up in the sea annually. A sample of sea water from any part of the Earth contains measurable radioactivity. G. G. Polykarpov,[15] a Russian scientist, has shown that the development of some fish eggs is seriously affected by quite low doses of radioactivity (0.2 microcuries). He concludes that "further contamination of sea water is inadmissable."

Dramatic evidence that the ocean can, in fact, be overwhelmed by pollution can be provided by a twenty-square-mile area just off New York harbor. The dumping of wastes in this area has produced a region where marine life cannot survive. Even those marine worms that are very tolerant to pollution cannot live here. Fish that pass through are attacked by bacterial and fungal diseases. The saturation of oxygen in the zone dropped from 61 per cent in 1949 to 29 per cent in 1969. In the center of the area the level of oxygen is only 10 per cent. This drop in oxygen content, which is the scientist's way of measuring the pollution of this "Dead Sea" region, has long been evident to marine life and even to the casual observer in his fishing boat.

It is obvious that we can no longer think of the oceans as a limitless dump. Forty-eight million tons of wastes were dumped into the seas off the coasts of the United States in 1968. These wastes included the radioactive wastes from nuclear reactors. Recent concern over the dumping of excess nerve gas by the U.S. Army caused a good deal of comment in the mass media, but the disposal eventually took place anyway. In addition to these solid wastes the oceans are the eventual depository of all the industrial, mining, and municipal wastes spewed into waterways and of the fertilizers and pesticides washed from the farmlands. We can already see the effects of these contaminants on marine life, and we have not really looked very hard.

Life arose in the sea. The marine environment has remained relatively constant over the ages. The organisms of the sea are probably even less able to cope with rapid alterations of the environment than are terrestrial organisms. At current rates of dumping the ocean's ecosystems may well be destroyed before we even begin to understand their workings. It will then be too late to talk of farming the sea to feed the hungry populations of the world.

[14] "The Threat to Life in the Sea," *Saturday Review of Literature* (August 1, 1970).
[15] Ibid.

COMMENTS

This chapter has been an attempt to deal with what appear to be the main misconceptions that most people have concerning the deterioration of the environment and pollution generally. It has dealt briefly with the mistaken notions that the ecological crisis is due to population growth, that these are only recent changes and are easily reversible, and that serious problems occur only on a local level. It concerns not the regional annoyances of oil-fouled beaches, smog, and rivers that are used as sewers but rather the global implications of environmental change and the suggestion that this could result in the alteration of the planet to such a degree that man, among other species, could not survive.

One of the major objectives has been to show that the "environment" is not static. The word has been used so frequently and loosely in popular literature that one gets the impression of the environment as equivalent to an art object that must be protected from heat, dust, and so forth in order to maintain its static beauty. The environment, on the contrary, differs from place to place and most certainly changes over time.

No biological organism is without effect on the total environment. Even the composition of the Earth's atmosphere is a result of the activity of the earliest, most primitive plants pumping out oxygen as a by-product of their daily metabolism. The mixture of gases in our atmosphere has now apparently reached a steady-state composition that is maintained by the activities of many organisms. Plants remove carbon dioxide from the air and replace it with oxygen; animals do the reverse; and a balance is maintained. Even the billions of bacteria on Earth are involved in the maintenance of this steady state, as was illustrated with the example of the nitrogen cycle. There is continual interchange between biological organisms and the inorganic environment in these cycles of nutrients. These cycles illustrate the ways in which the growth of living organisms is linked to the chemical composition of the air, the water, and the soil, and they are responsible for the maintenance of a balance of atmospheric gases.

The environment of which we so blithely speak is the totality of these interactions, which are taking place continuously and have been for millions of years. An ecologist studies these interactions of the biological and the physical world and tries to instill in others an appreciation of the interrelatedness of all facets of the environment. Ecology is the understanding and appreciation of this complexity. Unfortunately, most people have the impression that ecology is concerned only with litter and with the maintenance of an attractive neighborhood.

To the ecologist as a citizen these are legitimate concerns but to the professional ecologist the problem is much broader. He is concerned with the potential that these interruptions have to interfere with global cycles or with the functioning of a local ecosystem so that it can no longer maintain an equilibrium and exist.

Environmental deterioration may cause this balance to be disturbed, and irreversible changes will then take place on our Earth. A natural environment is not static but is in balance; if one portion of a cycle is affected, other sectors compensate to return to the equilibrium. In some instances man upsets this balance in such a way that this compensation is not possible. An example given was the effects of artificial fertilizers on the nitrogen cycle. These sorts of interference could lead to permanent alteration of the global environment.

The geological record of life on Earth shows that drastic changes have occurred in the past and life has survived, although in forms quite different from those that existed previously. The alteration in atmosphere due to the actions of primitive plants is the most dramatic example of this change. Prior to the existence of these plants all life had existed in the absence of oxygen; this was a drastic change in the environment and many organisms no doubt died out as a result. Ninety-nine per cent of all species that have ever lived on Earth have become extinct because of environmental changes. The species that survived each change expanded their populations and gave rise to new species that were adapted to this new environment.

The difference between these environmental changes, wich have occurred throughout the history of life on this planet, and the changes that man is now imposing on the global environment lies in the rate of change. Natural alterations, such as the addition of oxygen to the atmosphere, took place over millions and millions of years. Existing species had time to incorporate genetic changes over many generations, that is, to adapt to these different conditions by the process of natural selection. Man's alterations, however, take place on such a massive scale and so rapidly that most species are unable to adapt. In a period of twenty-five years man imposed millions of pounds of DDT on his environment. Some species of insect were able to adapt but many longer-lived species, such as fish and birds, have been unable to change quickly enough and are threatened with extinction.

Since man first became recognizable as a species he has contributed significantly to the deterioration of his environment. His disregard for natural mineral cycles and his abuse of the soil has decreased the productivity of large areas of the world, probably forever. Early hunters apparently caused the extinction of many of the large mammals and from that time man has continued to simplify the world community of biological organisms. The simplification of a community leads to instability and man's attempts to remedy this instability seem, instead, to make matters worse. A case in point is the use of pesticides in an attempt to control the insect species that thrive in the newly simplified environment. These pesticides have the effect of removing the top predator species and so make the community even less stable than before. Continuing blind attempts at a restoration of this natural balance may well alter the ecosphere to the point where man can no longer survive.

Without an ecological appreciation of the interrelations of organisms it is difficult to appreciate the loss that is involved when a species becomes extinct. The loss of a species means that the result of millions of years of evolutionary adaption to a particular environment is lost forever. It can never be reconstructed and we can never study the mechanisms that enabled that species to cope with that environment. More important in an ecological sense is the fact that each organism is interrelated to many others in the ecosystem. The removal of one species places others in jeopardy and alters the entire balance of that system. The role that one particular species plays in the economy of a community is not often clearly understood.

Recent concern for the continued existence of the alligators in the Everglades of Florida resulted in a study that showed that these animals are essential to the fabric of the Everglades. During the dry season the alligators scrape out refuge pits in which deeper pools of water form. These pools enable fish to survive drought periods. As the number of alligators was reduced it was found that there was an increase in the number of garfish, the alligators' major food source. The garfish then replaces the smaller species of fish on which the birds feed. If the alligators were to die out the whole system would be altered, with many species of fish and birds becoming extinct, and the entire ecosystem would be irreversibly altered. Public realization of this fact has led to a ban on the sale of alligator hides, probably ensuring that the Everglades will survive as a complete system for some years to come.

In most instances we have very little knowledge of the importance of a particular species to its ecosystem or to man. How, then, can we think of any species as expendable? Organisms that may appear quite inconsequential to our well-being are often vitally important. Charles Darwin lauded the lowly earthworm as the most important organism in the shaping of the Earth through its role in the maintenance of soil structure. Most Americans would define ants as "organisms that bother us on picnics." In fact, in some areas of the world the major parts of the soil profile are the work of ants. Termites are an important part of the ecosystem of tropical forests in Africa because they cycle nutrients from decaying wood and leaves back into the soil and so, eventually, back to the living trees. Russian scientists [16] have found that a nest of red ants can destroy 3 to 5 billion insects in a single summer. An Italian reports a study in which he found that ants on 2.5 million acres of forest each year consumed twenty-four thousand tons of food including perhaps as much as fourteen thousand tons of pests! These efficient animals can be used to help control insect pests. If ant nests are placed strategically in forests they can successfully check outbreaks of sawflies, webworms, and silkworms. The use of this form of biological control would reduce the need for heavy dosages of pesticides and the problems that these have been shown to cause on a worldwide scale. In destroying the complexity of the environment we have often threatened or made extinct species that help to maintain a natural balance.

Even if the importance of a particular species cannot be established as clearly as for these ants, we can never say that a species is completely without value. We should proceed on the assumption that all species have evolved a role in the ecosystem and that the removal of even one species may result in the alteration of that system. For example, it has been found that certain soil fungi are essential for the uptake of nutrients by some tree species. If the soil is fumigated and these fungi killed the trees are unable to exist.

In a more self-centered way some of these species may have immediate importance for man. Who of the millions who owe their lives to penicillin would have objected to the extinction of the lowly bread mold prior to the discovery of the wonder drug? A recent Russian discovery of plant "phytocides" show that some plants excrete volatile substances that are capable of killing pathogenic fungi and bacteria at a considerable distance. It has been found that in parks of conifers the bacterial content of the air is two hundred times less than that of the city air.[17] Another recent discovery shows that sodium alginate, a derivative of some seaweeds, is able to purge $strontium^{90}$ from human and animal bones without displacing the calcium. These marine plants, whose existence is now threatened by pollution, may assume great importance in the future if radioactive strontium in the biosphere is increased by accident or war. We cannot, therefore, be casual about the extinction of any species of organism no matter how inconsequential it may appear at present.

Imagine that some polluting chemical were to kill one of the bac-

[16] D. McKinley, "Who Needs a Rhinoceros? We Do!," *State University of New York Forum* (Summer 1970).
[17] Ibid.

terial types important in the nitrogen cycle. The atmosphere and the entire global ecosystem would be altered. All life would have to adapt very rapidly to a change in the nitrogen cycle and those species that could not evolve rapidly enough would die out. A similar situation would arise if something were to interfere with the process of photosynthesis. Although the possibility of such an occurrence may seem remote, recall that DDT has been shown to interfere with photosynthesis in marine phytoplankton. We are assured that the concentration at which this effect was noted was higher than is generally found in the oceans, but we are also aware that biological organisms are capable of concentrating these substances far beyond the concentration found in the water. In addition a synergistic or potentiation effect with one of the half million man-made chemicals or the multitude of natural substances present in the sea could conceivably bring about such a crisis.

Another fact that the biologist appreciates is that all living organisms on Earth have many basic similarities. Although introductory biology courses and television programs dealing with wildlife often stress the variety of life that exists on Earth, there is a remarkable degree of similarity in the biochemical organization of all life. Every species of organism contains the same macromolecules, including the nucleic acids DNA and RNA, which contain the genetic information necessary to transfer hereditary information. All cells also contain proteins, lipids, and organic cofactors. Of even greater import is the fact that many sequences and patterns of biochemical reactions necessary for the functioning of life are virtually identical, even in their most subtle details, in nearly all the forms of terrestrial life that have been studied. In the chemistry of life, cabbages and kings differ very little. This evidence has been used to support the idea that all living organisms are derived from one ancestral type, as the similarity of life processes is too striking to be coincidental. In the context of our present discussion this fact has enormous importance. Because all living thing contain the same molecules and carry out the same chemical reactions, any interference with one of these basic processes could perhaps pose a threat to all life forms.

A pollutant is often defined in terms of its concentration beyond the level at which some of the members of the biological community can exist. This has led to the platitude, "The solution to pollution is dilution." This discussion has attempted to show that this simplistic phrase does not contain the clue that will provide the solution we seek. Even the vastness of the oceans has been shown to be insufficient to dilute the pollutants we are producing. We recognize that Earth is a finite and limited body that can dilute only to a limited extent.

The growth of population alone is not sufficient to explain the amounts of pollutants currently being produced. We must take into account the disproportionate growth of technology. Because industry has had access to a limitless supply of air and water on which no one ever set a price, production systems have been devised by which these resources are used to remove waste products. The removing of waste products has been accomplished outside the factory so that the population in general suffers (and eventually pays for) the inefficiency of the production line. If the production system were truly efficient there would be no waste. Products now wasted should be recycled or used in some other process.

The growth of population and technology means that there are greater quantities and varieties of pollutants being produced each year. These substances are spread throughout the whole planet by the actions of wind and water, which aid in the dilution of the pollutants below a level that is immediately toxic. However, on a few occasions when this dilution did not occur we have seen the results that can occur. The terrible smog conditions that killed hundreds of people in London in 1956 and in Donora, Pennsylvania, in 1948 were examples of a lack of dilution. As quantities of pollutants increase we may expect these sorts of conditions to occur more frequently and on a larger scale.

Natural processes frequently reverse the trend toward dilution. The best-documented instances of concentration by biological organisms are the food-chain effects of DDT and of radioactive isotopes. This concentration effect has been documented in nature for a number of food chains, and the concentration may be several thousand times the dosage found in the surrounding environment. Recent studies have also shown that some heavy metals are also concentrated by these food chains. Mercury has been concentrated from water to pike on the order of three thousand times and more. The biological cycles of nature, ignored by biologists for many years, are now shown to be reversing the dilution process. The greatest dosages of the pollutants are received by the top predators of the food chain, a position held notably by man himself.

The effects of synergistic reactions and of the potentiation of one chemical by another are only now being discovered. They do, however, give ample cause for concern. Dilution of a particular chemical does not prevent its harmful effects if some other aspect of the environment increases its action. It is conceivable that we might reduce the concentration of a particular substance very substantially only to find that, in the presence of small quantities of a new pollutant, its effects are more noticeable than before.

A consideration of the biology of pollution shows that we can no longer tolerate an attitude that accepts any resource as being limitless and the dilution of wastes to be a reliable solution. With this in mind we must seriously question the assumption that resources such as air and water are freely available to industry to be used recklessly to dilute the wastes of their production.

Garrett Hardin in an essay, "The Tragedy of the Commons," [18] has likened free access to these resources to the free usage of a pasture that is open to all for grazing their stock. Each grazier finds advantage in using the commons to the maximum extent and eventually the pasture is overgrazed and becomes worthless to everyone. The endless addition of pollutants to our air and water may also render these resources useless and even fatal to life.

To a biologist this appears to be the crux of the matter. If the use of these resources by a few individuals is going to threaten the lives of all other individuals and, indeed, all other species, then surely the pollution must be curtailed or stopped altogether. By definition do we not all have a right to use the commons even if we do not own any sheep? We should, then, be able to walk and picnic in the commons without dirtying our feet and clothes in endless manure and without having our lives endangered by the bull belonging to one of the few graziers. It is surely a right and not a privilege to breathe clean air and to drink clean water. Evidence is being compiled at an alarming rate that shows that air and water pollution is endangering our health. To a biologist there seems no question that drastic action is needed to curtail this pollution.

Any person with an ecological perspective can see that action is needed but is frustrated when he investigates possible courses of action. He is dismayed by the inertia of the government and of the public in general. The reason for this inertia is largely the attitude that pollution is an unavoidable by-product of the "good life." Our economic system, and the political institutions that protect it, appear not to be able to provide us with both the high standard of living we now enjoy and a healthful and pleasant environment. Need this be so? In order to make any critical and reasonable statements concerning the abatement of pollution it is essential that we have an understanding of the economic and political systems in which we operate.

SUGGESTED READINGS

Brookhaven National Laboratory Symposium in Biology, No. 22, *Diversity and Stability in Ecological Systems,* 1969.

[18] *Science,* Vol. 162 (1968), pp. 1243–1248.

Discussion of theories concerning the relation between biological diversity and community stability.

COMMONER, BARRY. *Science and Survival.* New York: The Viking Press, Inc., 1963.
The subject of pollution by radioactivity and the hazards of nuclear warfare are very well treated in this book.

CROWE, B. L. "The Tragedy of the Commons Revisited." *Science,* **166** (1969), 1103–1107.

DETWYLER, T. R. *Man's Impact on the Environment.* New York: McGraw-Hill Book Company, 1971.
This collection of papers includes an excerpt on the Pleistocene Overkill Theory and other papers of interest relating to man's effect on all types of ecosystems.

DISCH, ROBERT, ed. *The Ecological Conscience,* Englewood Cliffs, N.J.: Prentice-Hall, 1970.
Collection of readings, including some on values and ethics in relation to ecology.

HAMMARD, A. L. "Phosphate Replacements: Problems with the Washday Miracle." *Science,* **172** (1971), 361–363.

MARX, WESLEY. *The Frail Ocean.* New York: Ballantine Books, Inc., 1967.

ODUM, E. P. "The Strategy of Ecosystem Development." *Science,* **164** (1969), 262–270, reprinted in R. L. Smith, *The Ecology of Man: An Ecosystem Approach.*
A very thorough discussion of the process of succession.

RUSSEL-HUNTER, W. D. *Aquatic Productivity.* New York: The Macmillan Company, 1970.
An excellent general discussion of the ocean ecosystem and nutrient balance.

SHEPARD, P., and D. McKINLEY, eds., *The Subversive Science.* Boston: Houghton Mifflin Company, 1969.
Collection of readings on ecology and man's place in the ecosystem.

SMITH, R. L. *The Ecology of Man: An Ecosystem Approach.* New York: Harper and Row, Publishers, 1972.
An excellent collection of readings on the ecosystem concept.

WHITTAKER, R. H. *Communities and Ecosystems.* New York: The Macmillan Company, 1970.

TWO
❖
ECONOMICS

ECOLOGY *and* economics *derive from the same Greek word, the word for "home." Economics means, literally, "home management." The way in which each society has undertaken the management of its environment is its economic system. Our system is oriented to growth and continual expansion and we must examine what this implies in terms of our local ecosystem and of the ecosphere as a whole.*

In an examination of economics as it relates to environmental problems, it is customary to accept the system as it exists and to attempt to devise remedial measures that will lessen its impact on natural ecosystems. Growth and progress are usually assumed; exceptions are considered radical proposals. Most economists, confronted with environmental issues, draw up a ledger of cost-benefit analyses. This approach attempts to show the cost of installing pollution control devices on factories on the one hand and the benefits of a cleaner environment on the other. The environment usually comes out in the red, largely because the benefits to the environment as a whole are so difficult to quantify. The cost of installing devices on factories to cut down on soot and smoke must be balanced against the hidden costs to the consumer for the cleaning of clothing and drapes, the more frequent repainting of homes, and so on, as well as the cost of absence from work due to illness from respiratory diseases and other related health problems. There are, of course, many effects of pollution that cannot (economists say) be included in cost-benefit analyses. These would include such intangibles as the value of beautiful vistas for future generations and even the irritation of the eyes produced by air pollution. It is as difficult to estimate the cost of damage to man-made art objects as it is to assess the value of natural beauty. It has been reported that Cleopatra's Needle has deteriorated more since its arrival in New York in 1881 than it had in the three thousand years in Egypt prior to that time. It is, of course, impossible to express this deterioration in terms of dollars.

This chapter does not attempt to construct a cost-benefit ledger. Instead, it examines the basic structure of our economic system. An economic system can work only as well as those individuals who make up the system. The system is based on a set of assumptions about the "economic man" of which it is composed; his system of values and

[71]

needs; real or perceived, is what allows our economy to operate. To the people of Dogpatch in the musical version of Li'l Abner, "progress is the root of all evil." Obviously, our values differ greatly from theirs. The progress that Western people have enjoyed over the last few centuries could not have taken place unless the general populace held to a belief in that progress.

This chapter examines the economic premises on which we operate. Our economic man has certain attitudes. In order to appreciate these attitudes we need a historical perspective of the development of our economic system and some examination of the way in which society shapes this man in his beliefs and values.

Ecology and the Developmental Bias

ECOLOGISTS detail the thousand ways in which our present culture interferes with nature's balance. They impress upon us that the increasing magnitude of our incursions into the various ecosystems surely spell our doom if they continue unchecked. We may wish to quibble with their time tables and critically examine their evidence but we are left with the suspicion that they are probably right. We may fortify our optimism with a recital of other doomsayers at other times and the failure of their predictions to hold; we may satisfy ourselves temporarily with the 20/20 hindsight of historical perspective that man has prevailed against great odds at critical moments in his time on Earth. Nevertheless, our intuition nags us; there is something out of kilter. What if they're right? When forced to reflect, we recognize that each of us is a part of life, a particular manifestation of some larger scheme of things. We do after all share with pigs and peonies the capacity to respire, reproduce, and expire. We may have the gift of being self-conscious of our existence as we suppose other forms do not, but we still are of nature, in nature, from nature. Our particular cultural programming may blind us to this realization, but when we stand back and look at ourselves from a point out of this space and time we cannot deny its validity.

At the very least, we must take the question of environmental decay seriously; that is, we must entertain the notion that man's activity at the present time has affected the functioning of the Earth's ecosphere in disastrous proportions. Further, we must admit the possibility that numerous biological and geophysical thresholds are being approached that, once reached, may at the least not allow life to go on as we now know it and at the extreme may spell the doom of the human species.

If we take these assertions as a starting point and accept the main facts and ideas presented in the first chapter, the main question becomes, What is there about contemporary society that has brought about this possibly fatal degree of interference? It is true that whenever and wherever and however men have existed there has been some degree of interference with the ecosphere, probably because of man's ability to reason, to foresee, and to be self-conscious of his actions. These traits, supported by his ability to construct and transform (and destroy) grounded in his apposable thumb and his sophisticated larynx, allowed of a flexibility, spontaneity, and unpredictableness (free will?) that affected the operations of the surrounding ecosystem. But through most of human history the effect of man's activity has not been global; it has been confined to certain areas, and although there were temporary backlashes from nature from these disturbances, the diversity and spread of man throughout the Earth allowed for his survival as a species.

Today this appears no longer to be the case. Certainly the sheer number of people now living and making use of the Earth's resources is part of the problem. We now have a 3.7 billion population and in the next several decades it promises to double. But population pressure is just part of the problem; even more important is the manner in which this expanding population is using the Earth's resources. That is, sheer population increase certainly taxes the ecosphere, but increasing consumption per capita threatens to alter it in such ways that even lowered consumption couldn't be supported. Complicating this picture of total population and its increase and the effects of rising per-capita consumption upon the natural system is the fact that resources and consumption are distributed in such an unequal fashion that policies aimed at averting disaster become highly politicized.

It has been estimated that between 40 per cent and 50 per cent of the world's production of minerals is consumed by the productive processes of the United States. With 6 per cent of the world's population we generate 40 per cent of the world's income. As Paul Ehrlich has observed, the birth of an American baby has several hundred times the ecological consequence than the birth of an Indonesian baby. These are formidable statistics. Their importance lies in the inescapable conclusion that although sheer population pressure on the world's resources is a threat to the ecosphere, the production-consumption patterns of the advanced nations, particularly the United States, are the primary source of disruption of this ecosphere. Most nations of the world have economic development as one of their main goals. To the degree that they are successful in this pursuit, then to that degree the threat to the environment is exacerbated. As of today, the highly developed economies of the Western world and those of the socialist world constitute the main threat to the environment. Any inquiry into the ecological implications of the activity of contemporary man must initially examine the developmental bias of the cultures of the materially advanced societies of the modern world.

The essence of development is the growth over time in per-capita production and consumption. When a given population produces and consumes more and more goods and services in the second year than in the first, that society is said to be growing, advancing, or developing. There are a variety of reasons that may bring about such growth or development: increase in knowledge, increased skill levels of the working population, increase in the capital stock of the society, technological innovation, reorganization of the population into more efficient working relationships, and so on. In one or another of these terms most societies have effected some amount of growth and development. The developmental bias of the materially advanced cultures of the present day calls for changes in all of these ingredients in a systematic fashion. That is to say, the modern economy is based on the self-conscious increase in material abundance, and therefore on the tendency to produce and consume more.

In traditionalist cultures change is and was viewed as disruptive of more important human values. For instance, certain Southeast Asian peasants today think that each grain of rice should be individually picked. The introduction of machinery to do the task more efficiently would be viewed as leading to the deterioration of the environment and the animism with which it is imbued. Similarly, the introduction of the railroad into China in the late nineteenth and early twentieth centuries was seen as destructive of *feng shwei,* the natural balance of the environment with man's activity. Change introduced insecurity; insecurity was a threat to life. Most traditionalist cultures have evolved institutional arrangements that have minimized change, at least discernible change. To the Chinese the role of man was to be in harmony with nature. This was symbolized in the classical Chinese painting style, in which man was a very small and insignificant part of a natural scene dominated by the surrounding mountains and sky. A better mousetrap to the Chinese of the nineteenth century represented a change that could threaten their whole way of life.

In contrast, the modern materially advanced and advancing societies are the product of a culture of development and progress. The origins of the host of institutions and attitudes that today comprise the central features of our dynamic and ever-changing way of life reach far back in time and often are obscure. Commonly, we date the beginnings of the modern world with the Industrial Revolution of the nineteenth century. It becomes more and more apparent, however, that the Industrial Revolution itself was the result of many advances or changes in science, values, and institutions such as banking that occurred in hundreds of years before it.

The rise and spread of Protestantism is only one example of the attitude change that preceded the scientific-industrial revolution. In the Protestant movement man developed the attitude that he was on his own in his dealings with the nontemporal world. The role the Catholic Church had played in dictating the relationship of man to man and of man to God and the implications of this role for economic activity were eliminated wherever the Reformation took effect. The release of men from the assigned role and behavior prescribed by the Church had its effect not only on the relationship of man to God but on his attitude toward the proper scope of economic activity as well. To prove oneself worthy of salvation one had to be productive and show evidence that he had worked industriously during his tenure on Earth.

At this period in history, everyone had to be productive because there was real scarcity, and each man had to work in order to survive. But there was a difference in the attitude of this new Protestant. He was motivated to work not merely to survive in this world but to ensure his entrance into the next. The accumulation of worldly goods was proof of success in this world and a qualification for salvation. An individual accumulated wealth not for his own pleasure but to prove his devotion to God. This attitude toward work was one of the prime characteristics of the Puritans, who established this outlook on the North American continent.

As an individual's success in the world came to be measured by the extent of his wealth, so the success of a society was calculated in terms of its accumulation of material goods and the progress it made in the development of its resources. Progress was now viewed as a logical development that took place over time. Progress or change had previously been so slow, because the accumulation of knowledge from generation to generation was minimal, that time was considered unimportant. At the end of a man's life it was expected that his son would follow in his footsteps, experiencing the same things and having the same beliefs, engaging in the same work and having the same level of knowledge. Life was a circle and there was little concept of change from one generation or one era to another.

The concept of time as linear and of progress as a logical development along this linear scale allowed modern man to adjust his thinking so that he need no longer live in the present concerning himself with the everyday business of survival but could contemplate the future. The Protestant was particularly concerned about the future of the individual after death. He worked to safeguard his future by pleasing

God. This work produced an increasing accumulation of wealth, which proved to him that his attitudes must be correct because, by his new definition, his society was eminently successful: it was developing, growing, and producing more and more material abundance. The application of knowledge to agriculture and industry meant that each man could produce more goods and that man had more control over his environment, bending it to serve his ends.

Control of the environment meant control of nature. Although nature was eloquently praised in poem and hymn, man's attitude toward it had changed. Recognizing that "all things bright and beautiful" were made by God did not conflict with man's feeling that success and evidence of a worthy life spent in the service of the same God meant a submission of nature to the will of man. Where nature had played an integral part in the life of former cultures, man's relation to the environment and to other living things was now repressed. Fields and towns were formalized, as epitomized by the gardens of the day, which represented man's most immediate contact with nature. This new attitude was illustrated by the denial of man's sensual or animal nature, and was expressed in manners of eating, rigid social rules, and the sublimation of the sex drive to a purely reproductive function. Man was attempting to separate himself from his place in nature, and he created an artificial society that exploited natural resources relentlessly. Man as the chosen creature of God was made in His image and had the dignity of God within him. His life on Earth and his activities were the workings of God, and the preservation of his individual life was paramount while he proved himself to God. All other forms of life were subsidiary to this effort.

We might sum up the attitudes and values of the Protestant movement as a fight against death that became, ultimately, a fight against life. The application of science in support of these attitudes did lead to the prolonging of life and a dramatic lowering of the death rate of man. The same values that elevated scientific rationality contained the view that the sole aim of sexual activity is reproduction, and thus a decrease in the birth rate was not to be expected. These two ingredients, the decrease in the death rate and the attitude toward reproduction laid the basis for the current population dilemma.

Although the Protestant movement accounts for some of the attitudes and values that facilitated the evolution of the development-oriented society, it should be remembered that many, many other simultaneous changes were occurring. A society does not develop economically simply because of a change in its theological orientation. Other values must change as well. Some of these values reinforce the change represented by the Protestant movement, others do not. Gen-

Recreational vehicles in a used-car lot. [Photo by T. D. Fitzgerald.]

erally speaking, a culture that promotes rapid economic development would have to place a high value on efficiency, diligence, orderliness, punctuality, frugality, rationality, enterprise, and honesty. There would have to be ready acceptance of change, an alertness to opportunity, cooperativeness, and a futuristic orientation.[1] The attitudes, values, and behavioral patterns described are necessary but not sufficient for the society to advance materially. There must also be mechanisms that make for technological advance. Increases in the productiveness of the population do not come about from ideas and motivation alone. There must be the wherewithal to increase the size of the pie faster than the ability to consume it. Increases in the size of the pie can only come about from increased use of the natural materials provided by the environment, from changes in the way these materials are combined, and from reorganizations of the population working these materials.

All of these factors have been present in the history of modern society. Tremendous increases in the productivity of man began in the sixteenth century and have continued since then, with the curve of increases rising exponentially as we move into the twentieth century. There were times in the progress of productivity during which changes in the production of goods and services increased faster than at others. One of these periods was of decisive importance: the Industrial Revolution.

During the Industrial Revolution the methods of producing goods underwent great change. The production of goods became industrialized. Industrialization is defined as the rapid, systematic introduction of machine and machinelike processes into the production process. With the introduction of machines and machinelike processes, the wholesale threat to the world's ecosphere begins. The introduction of the mechanical processes of production not only brought about a tremendous spurt in the productivity of the society but created a wholesale redistribution of the population into urban centers, the concentration of production in factories, the close alliance between industry and science, the development of new sources of energy, a growth in new products, and the beginnings of the massive, impersonal society that we know today. The spread of industrialization changed the face of the Earth. With the ascendancy of the machine came the ascendancy of a complex of attitudes that reinforced acceptance of the industrialization process and the results of that process: increasing material abundance.

The invention of machinery and its introduction into the produc-

1 Gunnar Myrdal, *Asian Drama* (New York: Pantheon, 1969), pp. 61–62.

tion process heralded a new relationship between science and business. The materialist orientation and the marriage of science to industry necessitated a rationalist outlook. The industrialization process
grew in a cultural milieu that valued maximum output at minimum
cost.

The host of signs of environmental deterioration: pollution of air
and waters, and the spread of trace metals through the food chains;
the pesticides, fungicides, and herbicides used in modern agriculture
and drained into our streams and oceans; the leveling of our forests
and the destruction of wildlife for the purposes of mass transit and
mass communication; the depletion of fossilized fuels such as coal
and soil to provide the energy for expanding production and consumption; the effluent from a growing population, the growth of elaborately
packaged and merchandized consumption goods that clog our sewage
and waste disposal systems, indeed even the less tangible threats of a
diminished world oxygen supply; the world mean temperature changes
promised by the "greenhouse" effect and the disruption of the ocean's
ecology—all these signs are the direct result of growth, particularly
the unplanned growth of the decentralized economies such as the
United States.

All are direct results of a set of attitudes and behavior patterns—
a consciousness—that supports this economic growth. It is to this consciousness that we next turn.

Ecology and Education

The developmental bias of modern society, the basis for our initial
inquiry, comes from our history. It involved the evolution to predominance of a materialist motivation, a future orientation, a rationalistic world view, and diligent, orderly, efficient, enterprising behavior.
This mind set, combined with the development of the mechanical
methods of production, the systematic investigation of the physical
world and its properties, and the introduction of the fruits of these
investigations—technology—into the productive processes are the
hallmarks of all development-oriented cultures.

The large-scale interference with the operations of the physical
world comes directly from the very success of the economic activity
of these cultures, West and East. There is an important distinction
that should be drawn, however, between the manner in which Western
and Eastern development-oriented societies operate. The economic
development of the Western economies, particularly the United States,
has been decentralized, whereas that of the East has been effected by
deliberate central planning. Both have produced massive interference

with the Earth's ecosphere, but in the case of the centrally planned economies this was the result of a deliberate movement toward rapid industrialization. Presumably, a change in priorities would allow a consideration of the ecological consequences of growth.

In the decentralized economies, such as the United States, such a course of action would be extremely difficult. The next order of inquiry thus becomes, What is the nature of the growth process in the United States? How and why is technology innovated? What is the social framework within which economic development is furthered?

It is possible to gain insight into the American way of life, its attitudes, motivations, behavior, and institutions, by generalizing from some of the essentials of the education process. It is in our educational system that we inculturate the incoming generation.

It is in education that one can observe the introduction of the materialist motivation and the host of other attitudes that are necessary but not sufficient for economic development. It is here that one sees the emphasis on discipline, efficiency, rationality, machinelike memorization, being productive (i.e., contributing), working hard, denying present pleasure, thinking of the future, a career, smoothness of interpersonal relationships, the eradication of superstition, the metaphysical admiration of the machine, and the stressing of milestones in technological progress. It is during the school years that one is taught to control one's more animal impulses, and to acquire manners and good taste. The animal impulses are channeled into romantic notions of reality, sublimations into the abstract away from the concrete and sensual. One is taught to invest the animal with human traits, to humanize wild animals and mechanical objects. Those who advance furthest are those who manipulate the abstract the best. Those who are mentally more facile get ahead.

It is also through observation of the educational system that one can gain insight into specifically American attitudes that form the basis for some of our institutions. It is apparent that there is a high degree of emphasis on the individual. It is stressed that each individual is in competition with other individuals. A system of rewards and punishments, of carrots and sticks, is built into the educational system to elicit the desired attitudes and behavior. These rewards and punishments reside primarily in the grading system. The individual is given to understand that his best chance of advancing beyond his fellow students is by achieving the best grades. Of course, this grading procedure is designed to bring out the potential in each individual, but the grading system also sorts the students into various occupational groupings according to each individual's success in the grading system. If some advance, others are behind.

The grading system in the earlier years of education sorts groups of individuals into a tracking system. After an individual is channeled along a specific track, his career opportunities are severely limited by the particular track into which he has been channeled. Not everyone can get all A's, just as not everyone can get into the top-paying jobs or the most prestigious and powerful occupations.

The grading system prepares the incoming generation for a social structure in which a complex variety of increasingly subdivided functions are performed. These functions yield varying degrees of income and power. The American system of development is a hierarchical system of production and consumption in the shape of a pyramid with a large base of relatively low income and power moving up to a narrow apex of high income and great power. The earlier experience in the educational system defines the measures of success of many individuals in the society. True, most complex human societies have developed institutions that track the incoming generation into different functional groups—including non-development-oriented societies such as traditional China. The distinguishing feature of the American pyramid is the inculcation of values biased toward change, mobility, advancement, and enlargement rather than stability.

In addition, the individuals are pitched against rather than with other individuals.

Another major function of the American educational process is the inculcation of a sense of private property. This begins with the development in the earlier years of a sense of personal possession, of a sense of the individual's identity's being defined by his appearance and his personal accouterments. Over the years, this sense grows with the child's ability to accept refinement and sophistication. The student is imbued with a sense that his personal worth is intimately associated with his material worth. If he doesn't come into the educational process with a decent show of material worth, then his salvation is in acquiring worth by his own effort (i.e., getting good grades or developing a unique talent of, for example, athletic, artistic, or entertainment value).

The stress here is on saving (future orientation), and accumulating (denial of present pleasure), with the knowledge that such activities and their results are sanctioned by the society through a legal system that protects whatever is accumulated. Beginning with the sense that the individual is judged on material accouterments, the student progresses in later years to an appreciation of and support of the institution of private property. In the hopes of achieving a secure position (in a very insecure, rivalrous environment), the individual learns to accept not only private ownership of personal belongings but ownership and control of material possessions that may affect thousands of other lives.

Our educational system develops in the student a psychological outlook that supports the American advancement or progress ethic, which is hierarchical, nonegalitarian, and competitive. Our educational system inculcates an acceptance of the ownership and hence the control of the means of advancement—technology—by private individuals. The student is taught to accept the notion that private individuals in positions of ownership and control of technology have the right to make decisions about the use of the bulk of our natural and human resources. Further, the student accepts it as natural that such decisions should be made in the best interests of the individual making them.

The hallmark of the American way of development is that a relatively small percentage of the population plans production (and sometimes consumption) and that they make their plans for their own benefit, whether they are independent farmers or large corporate executives. In this elitist sense American society differs little from previous societies. However, unlike the small controlling groups in previous societies, the status and power of those who now control American production is directly dependent upon enlarged production, expanding markets, the increased use of raw materials, and more sophisticated technologies whose impact becomes more massive and disruptive of natural processes as time goes on.

Of course, the educational system is just one of the socializing institutions in American society. It reinforces the value structure and is in turn reinforced by it. The function of mass education in any society is to facilitate the adaptation of the new individual to that society. The main business of mass education is to ensure the survival of the individual in the society and thereby the survival of the society itself. The educational system formalizes more clearly than any other socializing institution the attitudes and behavioral characteristics necessary for the social and economic survival of the individual. Its message and the medium through which this message is transmitted are meant to train the population to perform a variety of skill functions and to develop a consciousness that is consistent with economic development. (It is ironic that the increasing sensitivity to the environment issue shown by the introduction of ecology curricula may be defeated by this central purpose of education.)

The test of the efficiency of education is how well the individual is trained to survive and advance in a competitive production system known variously as the free enterprise system, capitalism, or a market economy. It is in this production system that the growth consciousness is played out.

Man's ingenuity in nature's niche. [Photo by T. D. Fitzgerald.]

ECOLOGY AND THE MARKET SYSTEM

From the time man first evolved complex, urban civilizations based upon agriculture, there have always been markets, capitalists, and a degree of free enterprise. What distinguishes modern Western society from previous societies is that markets, capital, and "freedom" have become the predominant institutions affecting every life. Where exchange once existed to facilitate life, it now dominates life. Where buying and selling previously maintained a standard of life but were incidental to getting along, now buying and selling are overwhelmingly necessary for getting ahead. Everyone is steeped in buying and selling. Our lives are preoccupied with it.

Supply and demand, or markets, determine existence in contemporary America. Economic growth and its attendant disruption of the environment are direct consequences of a market economy. The market economy has its foundation in two primary institutions; the profit motive and private property.

The market is a battle arena into which each of our citizens enters to live his economic life. The market is decentralized in that exchange takes place everywhere, every time. It is in the market that one wins or loses or just gets by. It organizes our resources and stimulates production. It is the source of all consumption. The allocation of resources, the decisions about what part of nature will be used, and the distribution of product and income are carried out through the market system. It is sometimes called capitalism, or the free enterprise system. Both synonyms derive from qualities of the market system: *capitalism* from the central role as producer-organizer of the owner of the capital stock; *free enterprise* from the inherent right of the individual to accumulate capital stock and dispose of it wherever his best opportunity lies.

The producer-owner enters the buying/selling arena and mixes with other producer-owners, many times in an antagonistic fashion. Certain rules guide the interaction, and the government is the agency that supervises the rules of the game. Within these guidelines (and sometimes outside them), all's fair. Each entrant is out to maximize his own position.

Maximizing one's position means getting ahead. Getting ahead means a higher standard of living over time. Higher standards of living over time necessitate the involvement of everyone in increasingly mechanical processes. Everyone is involved either as a direct participant in the production process or as the owner of property used in the production process. Each member of the society who desires progress in his own life is participating directly in the technological progress of society.

The materialist ethic is reinforced by both rewards and punishments. Money income and accumulated money—wealth—are the rewards. The punishment is, of course, not having money, which is nonpower or impotence, a poverty existence that is often internalized, creating thereby a fear that one is worthless.

In the market culture, there is a great drive toward success measured in money-power terms. Success or nonsuccess is intimately related to one's connection with the exchange production process. It is in the market that one expresses money power as a consumer. It is also in the market that one derives one's money power as a producer. An individual is connected with the exchange production network as a supplier of labor, capital, or natural resources.

It is in capital, and its management and control that the central features of our industrialization process and our economic order stand out most sharply. The development of the mechanical processes manifests itself in a formidable array of capital goods (investor's goods, producer's goods), goods whose ultimate purpose is the production of a greater and more varied supply of the consumer's goods that go into making up the American standard of living. As the distance between the ultimate consumer goods and the natural resources of which they are made grows greater with progress, a larger amount of the activity of the owners of these capital goods is used to produce for other capital goods producers.

The interstices between the consumer and the natural resources (coal, oil, lumber, water, air, minerals, and so on) become denser with intermediate production. This intermediate production is where technical progress is most profound—where the advance of the sciences is most readily apparent. The progress of industrialization rests in the development of the technologies of the interstices; their automation, their cybernation. Those who control these processes and capital goods are dependent for their survival upon these technologies. They are the capitalists, the owner-producers.

Natural resources are the factor of production the use of which has created the current ecological crisis. Natural resources are "natural" and "resources" relative to the technology of the time. Materials found in their natural states, such as oil or coal, are useful only as they are required in the industrial processes at any particular level of economic development. The advances of technology have brought about dramatic changes in the uses of the natural products of the Earth. The general trend has been a dependency upon more and more synthetic material. The ownership and control of valuable sources of natural resources are connected with what is valuable at the technological moment.

The market culture affects growth through changes in the composition of the capital stock. The innovations of a more sophisticated technology, a technology that leads to greater productivity per man, reduce costs. The reduction of cost leads to a better chance of getting ahead for that percentage of the population who own and control the capital stock. Changes in the composition of the capital stock change the resources needed for production. Materials that a few years before were so abundant that they were free become relatively more scarce. Oil at one time was useless and could be had for the asking. Timber, when trees were abundant, was exchanged for the labor of converting it into lumber.

Changing patterns of resource use, combined with a dramatically increased use of the resources needed over long periods of time, are at the core of the environmental problem. In a market economy, operating through the institutions of buying and selling and getting ahead— in which everyone is trained to survive by the inculcation of the attitudes and consciousness consistent with these institutions—creates a dilemma. Everyone wants to get ahead but the resources necessary for getting ahead are scarce relative to these desires.

To state the problem somewhat differently: development-oriented societies, which operate through market mechanisms that purportedly allow maximum freedom for individual initiative, which believe that man is inherently self-seeking, which program their young through a host of overt and subtle socializing institutions with attitudes consistent with the profit motive and private property—all of these societies, create a population attuned to more and more, ad infinitum. Nature in all its diversity and seeming abundance is, after all is said and done, finite. The essential economic lesson of enviromental decay is that ultimately nature has no more to give to a culture geared to infinite taking.

This is, of course, the ultimate. We do not live in the ultimate. We are too busy surviving in the here and now. The "ultimate" solution lies in restoring attitudes consistent with nature, in deemphasizing taking, getting ahead, more and more—economic growth. To such considerations we shall return. Let us turn now to the present.

ECOLOGY AND MARKET FAILURE

Most economists take for granted the development bias, the acquisitive urge, and the maximizing behavior of modern man. The owner-producer is the embodiment of this bias, urge, and behavior.

The idea of rational maximizing behavior as the prime motivating force in man has been around a long time. Its widespread acceptance among those who speculated upon or studied human behavior, i.e., the intellectuals, can be traced back to the rise of the philosophic radicals, Locke, Hobbes, Hume, and so on. It gained increasing adherence as time went on and was one of the primary innate characteristics of man as seen by Adam Smith, the oft dubbed "father of economics." It has had many guises over the last several centuries: the utilitarianism of Bentham and James Mill, the hedonistic calculus of Stanley Jevons, and the "economic man" of Alfred Marshall and many contemporary textbooks are but a few. It is still with us as the basic psychological assumption underlying consumer behavior (demand) theory and the theory of the firm.

In some senses man is, by definition, self-interested and out to increase his own material worth, that is, he acts rationally. Like most assumptions about man's inner nature this one seemingly has some empirical verification. However, in those instances in which man does not behave this way, the assumption can be protected by an assertion that he is behaving "irrationally." However, the most that can be said is that within a particular cultural context the psychological basis of behavior appears to be material acquisition.

But most economists take it for granted that such motives are at work within our particular culture, and the analysis begins on this basis. It is logical to argue from this assumption, that man makes decisions that maximize his material happiness (utility), to the principle of nonsatiety. The argument runs this way. If man is innately a maximizer then he can never achieve maximization. Given an open-ended situation—that is, allowing no constraints on his maximizing activity —then he will always be striving for a maximum but never reaching it. What, after all, is a maximum if it can always become larger? Man then can never be satisfied in the aggregate. He may be sated with one particular material object, but he can never achieve his fill of an ever-changing bundle of goods. In short, his wants and desires are infinite.

Of course, one man, given enough income to get all he desires may become satiated (again only on the material level; after all, as it is said, money can't buy happiness). It is conceivable for one man to reach this point given all he needs to do so, but it is impossible for all men do to so unless there are infinite amounts of wherewithal.

Wherewithal comes from a connection to the production process. Income is generated by input, either through ownership of productive capacities or through the supply of a factor necessary to those capacities, perhaps both at the same time. One man may receive a sufficiently large income from his connection to productive capacity but all men cannot. This is because capacities to produce and the combinations of resources that go into productive capacity are scarce, that is, they are finite.

These productive capacities and the resources involved are fixed not only at a moment of time but over time as well. The wresting of increasing output from a fixed capacity is limited by the law of diminishing returns. When capacities increase with the introduction of technology and its associated efficiency, the proportionate increases in output over the long haul may eventually lead to diseconomies of scale.

The interaction of infinite wants and limited ability to satisfy these wants is the essence of the economic problem. Choices have to be made. Because everything can't be produced, what will be produced? Who will get what is produced? What criteria are to be used in distributing the limited output among the population? Who will decide what resources will be used and in what way? Economists maintain that all societies somehow answer these questions. How they are answered distinguishes one society from another. Most textbooks in economics first state the problem and describe the questions the problem raises; then they move on to describe the operation of the U.S. economy in these terms and the smaller problems that arise from the overall dilemma. The concern of economics is thus a logical deduction from given assumptions that are seemingly grounded in the empirical workings of the culture. No serious question is raised about the assumptions, nor are the cultural bases for such assumptions ever examined.

Given this context, the environmental decay problem is a problem of market failure, not the problem of the entire culture and its interaction within and through the environment. The disruption of the world's ecosphere as the direct consequence of the production/consumption activity of modern advanced societies becomes an engineering problem.

Let us trace how the destruction of the environment would be seen as an engineering problem given the traditional assumptions already described. How does the problem look from the inside of the culture rather than from the outside? We confine the analysis to the market system or "free enterprise" system characteristic of the United States. To put the present in perspective, a model will be built that typifies conditions prevalent a hundred years ago but that today are only seen in a very small part of the total U.S. productive activity. Many of the characteristics of the market system previously discussed will be reintroduced.

First it is assumed that there are thousands of demanders and suppliers of a particular commodity. The two interact and their relationship results in a market. Both groups are rational maximizers. Whereas all suppliers are demanders, all demanders are not suppliers. In the aggregate then, the productive activity is directed by a small part of the

population. Everyone presumably contributes to production in one
way or another, but only a few control and make output decisions.
In the exchange of any one commodity, the roles of supplier and demander are antagonistic at any one moment of time. The demander is
attempting to maximize his satisfaction in the consumption of this
particular commodity when he consumes it in combination with all
other goods produced; he is attempting to maximize his total satisfaction from the consumption of all goods given a limited or finite claim,
income. In other words, he is buying a consumption mix. The price
(share of income) that a particular commodity claims is of great importance to the demander. The lower the price the less income he has
to use to buy it, then the more of it and other goods he can consume,
hence more satisfaction. The supplier, on the other hand, is attempting
to maximize his source of income (and the source of income from the
rest of this productive activity). The higher his income, then the higher
would be his consumption satisfaction in the present and the higher
his possibilities of future income would become through investment
in expansion of capacity—in general, the higher the price, the more
suppliers. If the price increases then those who had already produced
at the lower price would receive a surplus.

At this point further assumptions are necessary. It is assumed that
the individual supplier cannot differentiate his particular production
from that which is being produced by other suppliers. It is further
assumed that the conditions of production are such that any supplier involved in this product line may leave or enter at his rational
discretion.

The price will emerge from the interaction of suppliers and demanders of this particular good. There will be *a price* out of all possible
prices that will clear the market, i.e., quantities supplied will equal
quantities demanded. Any price higher or lower than this price would
be unstable. For instance, if the price were higher suppliers would
respond with more quantity than demanders were willing to take and
as a consequence some supplier stuck with an excess of the good would
lower the price, thereby setting off a general reduction in price. Similarly, if the price were lower consumers would set off a price increase
in seeking the relatively scarce supply at that price. The price that
clears the market is known as the *equilibrium price*. With the assumptions given, after all is said and done, every good produced would
settle at an equilibrium price. Once established, this price would be the
price that everyone concerned with the good would have to accept.
No supplier or demander produces or consumes a significant enough
share of the good to affect the overall supply and demand.

The equilibrium price could be upset only if the conditions affecting demand and supply were to change. At any one moment of time it is assumed that there is a structure of prices of all goods that is fixed. It is also assumed that: 1) at a moment of time there is a fixed amount of income with which to consume all that is being produced; 2) the size of the population is constant; and 3) this population with a fixed income has a set of tastes and preferences that do not change. These are the conditions of demand. On the supply side, it is assumed that there is a given state of technology and that the prices of the factors of production (raw materials, labor, machinery, and so on) are constant. In these fixed circumstances, then a particular price is generated when exchange takes place.

If these fixities become unfixed, movement of overall supply and demand will take place in the direction of and to the magnitude of the change. For example, if the tastes and preferences for this particular good increase with everything else remaining fixed, then there would be an increase in demand and a new equilibrium price (higher) would be generated in the marketplace. Because of the new, higher price the suppliers would bring more quantity to market by increasing the use of their capacities, and also new firms would appear. On the other hand, if tastes and preferences are held constant and technology changes (i.e., progress), then supply would increase, price would drop, and consumers would be in a better position. When all these fixities change at once—the real world—there is seeming chaos. Underneath this chaos, however, the market forces of supply and demand are working within a particular social milieu that has a predetermined end, the equilibrium price.

The model of supply-and-demand interaction presented is commonly called the perfect competition market model. In equilibrium, the price that consumers pay is equal to the cost on the average of producing the item: no producer can get excess profit, that is, a return over and above the average return for supplying the service of enterprise (the activity of deciding what will be produced and how it will be produced). The capacity of a particular firm would be used at its most efficient level: the most output for the least input. If all goods were produced under these conditions then it would follow that 1) society's resources, being scarce, would be husbanded; 2) consumers would dictate the goods that would be produced and suppliers would simply be the intermediaries between the demanders and the host of resources available at a particular time (consumer sovereignty); 3) everyone would be allowed to maximize his own self-interest but at the expense of no one else: in fact, each individual seeking his own maximization would enchance the self-interest of all; 4) the price would direct resources to their best use, and distribute the total output

in a fair if not equal way; and 5) the overall unemployment of resources would be impossible: there might be temporary difficulties in
adjusting to technological change but they would be only transitory.

Progress would be the inevitable result of such a system because
the main innovators of technology (the suppliers) would see their own
best interests being enhanced by the lowering of the costs of production. They would undertake to reduce costs to benefit themselves.
Although others would follow in their footsteps, the innovators would
get the competitive edge of being the first. All of this activity takes
place within an institutional setting in which the rights of ownership
and control over productive capacities are protected by the laws of
private property. Private, maximizing decision-making is seen as consistent with the best interests of all.

However, even in this the fairest, most progressive model of economic activity, the origin of a problem can be seen. Each producer is
out for himself even though he supposedly acts at the behest of the
dollar votes of the consumer. He sees the world through the narrow
perspective of his own survival and profit, and he has the right to do
with his capacity as he sees fit in the pursuit of his own gain. The
question arises: In the search of his own advantage isn't it possible
that he may generate costs that he does not have to bear directly? In
other words, isn't it possible that private decision-making for personal
advancement could lead to social effects that are more harmful than
the benefits that come from allowing such private decision-making?
In the use of his capacity, in its enlargement, the supplier may very
well take a share of a common free good such as water or air and so
use it in his productive process that he despoils it and renders it of no
use to others who have need of the same free good. An example should
suffice.

A clear stream flows by a lumber mill. Lumber technology requires
the use of clear water. In the process the clear water is taken in, used,
and then discharged back into the stream but not as clear water. It
carries acids and pulp that foul the once-clear stream. The aquatic
life system is disturbed, and fish may die. It is noxious to the sight and
taste of humans. The water is polluted. An industrial process that
transforms one set of resources into another has produced by-products
that disrupt the ability of the surrounding ecosystem to maintain an
equilibrium.

The lumber mill operator in seeking his lowest cost has created diseconomies to other users of the water. A town downstream may have
to install filtering devices to make the water potable, a cost borne by
local taxpayers. Fishermen lose a source of livelihood. Those seeking
the aesthetic enjoyments of a stream and a wood in their natural

state avoid the area. These are the direct costs, some measurable in money terms, others not, of the private decision-making of the lumber mill operator. Seen from the viewpoint of the ecologist there may be other less directly attributable consequences of disturbing an eco-system.

Further complications could arise. Presumably the lumber mill is located where it is because of its proximity to the resources of trees and water. It is reasonable to suppose that other producers would be located nearby. Some of these mills would have to be downstream of others. The farther downstream the more foul the water—so foul that it may become necessary for a producer to install filtering devices to make the water useful to him, thus increasing his costs. The price of the product would have at least to cover these costs or he would not produce. The producers upstream, with cheaper costs, get more return as a consequence. The society pays a price for lumber that is just sufficient to keep the marginal producer in business, which price gives a higher return to the upstream producers. This higher return comes simply from engaging in an activity that increases the costs of others who produce the same product.

To avoid the social costs incurred by private decision-making it would be necessary to disallow any producer from discharging his waters into the common good, water. This would raise the costs of the production of lumber and thus raise the price of lumber to the con-sumer. The problem then could become a technical one. Suppose it were possible to compute the social costs of polluting the common stream (how are aesthetic values measured in money terms?). Then these costs would be added to the cost differential between the high-cost producer's product and the low-cost producer's product. This total would then be compared to the increase in price necessitated by the installation of technology to clear the water of wastes. If the former were greater than the latter, then it presumably would be best for society. If the reverse held, then the use of the resources is inefficient.

But of course the problem is not merely a technical one—because the issue of the power relationships arises. Production is taking place within a private property system in which rights of control over re-sources are guaranteed by law. This body of law is not static, nor is it without its exceptions. The heightened sensibilities of the community may lead to a restriction on unfettered activity. But there is always a gap between this sensibility and its expression. There has been and promises to continue to be difficulty in the restriction of private prop-erty rights. Such restrictions are slow of enactment but not impossible.

There is clearly a limit to the freedom of action of our lumber pro-ducer. His freedom doesn't end at the end of his fist and the beginning of the community's nose, but if he presents a clear and present danger

—for instance, pouring poison into the community's water supply and thereby killing nearby residents—he may be legally culpable. The result of most producer activity is not as clear-cut as in this example. It is likely to be less tangible than an immediate, fatal poisoning. The problem is considerably further complicated by the fact that our lumber producer is not only a source of community cost, he is also a prime source of community benefit. He provides jobs, thereby income, thereby life. It is the continual saga of measuring these costs against these benefits that so muddles the environmental water, as we shall see.

To those communities dependent upon highly competitive industries, such as lumber in the Pacific Northwest, coal in Appalachia, textiles in the Northeast and now the South, restrictions upon the producer's rights can have severe results. It is no surprise then to see the plight of many small, single-industry towns in the United States that accept polluted air and water as the price of remaining economically alive. If one were to ask Jack Benny's famous question of these communities—"Your money or your life?"—there would be and has been and is likely to be hesitation before the reply.

The relatively unrestricted maximizing activity of the producer is at the heart of the matter of environmental decay. When the by-products of this activity create social costs in terms of air or water pollution, the question of legal responsibility is always raised, and the resultant legislation is less than clear in terms of both its stipulations and its enforceability (see Chapter 3). What should be understood is that the producer in a competitive market structure is in a trap not of his own making. To survive as a producer he is forced to seek his lowest costs of production and many times he can do this only by making use of the common "free" goods of nature—air and water. What is rational (i.e., leading to maximization) for the individual producer often produces irrationality in the aggregate. When an individual seeks to promote his own advantage by standing up to see a football game better he is temporarily better off, but he inevitably sets off a chain reaction: others behind him stand up, and eventually everyone is standing up, so that everyone is worse off than before. This phenomenon is also seen in the Tragedy of the Commons.

Although air and water pollution are irksome and to some degree dangerous, the competitive market arrangement can have far more insidious and intangible consequences. Agriculture, a market closely approaching our model of perfect competition, produces little in the way of air pollution and smaller amounts of water pollution than lumber, but its development over time has created a far more serious threat to the environment. Wheat farming offers a good example.

The individual farmer produces a small part of the total wheat crop, and he finds it impossible to differentiate his particular wheat in the eyes of the consumer. He has no edge over other wheat producers. He is not conscious of other farmers as rivals but rather tends to think of them as being in the same boat. How does the farmer in this situation advance his position? How does he get his "something for nothing"?

The farmer can advance his revenue returns from the sale of wheat by selling more wheat. To sell more wheat he has to produce more wheat, for the result of such a market structure is that he can sell all he wants to sell without affecting the price. There are two principal ways of producing more wheat: he can extend the acreage under cultivation or he can try to produce more wheat per acre. An increased crop, and thus increased revenue, requires further investment. Such investment funds can come from his savings—or more likely from borrowing from a bank.

As a maximizer, the wheat farmer must reduce his costs in order to get a higher return. Improvements in production techniques, such as the application of chemical fertilizers, the use of labor-saving machinery, and a more rational use of labor both in terms of the lowest return possible and in terms of its organization, are the prime ways in which costs can be reduced.

The innovation of labor-saving devices and the use of chemical fertilizers are capital investments. The farmer, because of his market position and his maximizing drive, demands the investments that affect cost reduction.

The chemical industry and the makers of such items as trucks and tractors, reapers, and balers become the suppliers; thus the farmer is participating in several different markets. On the one hand he is the supplier of wheat; on the other hand he is the demander of those items that will make his productivity per acre higher, or at least will ensure its stability. Once the farmer becomes dependent upon chemical fertilizers and labor-saving devices then he enters into a technological development that is beyond his power to control. In order to survive, and especially in order to maximize, he must innovate. If he chooses not to, then someone else will and eventually he will find himself in a losing position.

The effect of innovation is to increase the supply of wheat, which will bring about a decrease in the price if the demand for wheat has not increased by the same amount. Historically, the demand for agricultural products has not increased as fast as the supply of agricultural products. The result has been a decrease in the price of agricultural products relative to the prices of other goods and thus a decrease in income for the farmer.

The competition in agriculture today, as in the past, has spurred the increased use of machines and machinelike processes. Machines have a logic of their own. The more complex they are, the more costly they are, and the more it pays to use them extensively. The introduction of complex technology in agriculture tends to simplify the production process. It becomes more massive and linear. The costliness of the complex technology makes it necessary to spread this costliness over higher and higher amounts of production. This is called spreading the overhead. Today, the most successful farmers engage in extensive or high-acreage farming. It pays to raise thousands of acres of a single crop—to become monoagriculturists.

One consequence of the extensive monoagriculture in America to-day is the increasing need to use chemical agents to control insects. Extensive monoagriculture simplifies ecosystems. As noted in Chapter 1, simplified ecosystems are unstable ecosystems. One source of the instability is the vulnerability of whole areas of monoagriculture to insect or fungus attack; thus, the development and large-scale use of insecticides, fungicides, herbicides, and pesticides. The chemical industry, as the supplier of these toxic agents, has, consequently, a vested interest in monoagriculture.

Another consequence of the development of extensive monoagriculture is the increased need for replacing the soil nutrients used up. The primary soil nutrients consumed by extensive monoagriculture are nitrates. Thus again, the chemical industry, as the primary supplier of nitrates, has a vested interest in extensive monoagriculture.

The American public has become conditioned to receiving insect-free, wholesome-appearing produce. The quality of the farmer's product must satisfy this conditioning. The "high"-quality agricultural product originates in the nature of the competitive market structure. The farmer in seeking to maximize his position must sell a good that is of the same quality as that of other farmers. If one farmer, seeking to maximize this position, is able to differentiate his particular product from that of other farmers producing a like good, then he will gain an advantage. One way of gaining this advantage is to give the appearance that his particular good is of better quality—more wholesome, more nutritious—than that of another farmer. To the extent that he is able to convince the buying public that this is so, then to that extent he will be able to charge a higher price, thus increasing his returns from his efforts. The excessive use of pesticides to produce 100 per cent worm-free apples and the use of chemical dyes to produce oranges that are oranger are results of farmers' seeking this competitive edge. The public becomes accustomed to this appearance of quality and rejects those products that do not seem to be of "high" quality. A vicious circle results in which the buyers seek the appearance of quality and the farmers have to respond if they wish to survive.

The sophisticated technology applied to agricultural production has had the overwhelming consequence of allowing fewer and fewer of our population to produce the food necessary for the rest of the population. Less than 5 per cent of the population in the United States produces most of the variety of foods consumed by the other 95 per cent of the population. The production and processing of foods has become more concentrated because of technology. It has been estimated that the successful farmer constitutes only 25 per cent of those engaged in farming. The other 75 per cent are marginal producers. So successful has agricultural productivity become in the United States that the major problem in the agricultural sector of the economy is seeking ways to curb excess supply. One of the solutions has been the wholesale destruction of farm products and the taking of land out of production.

What is rational, maximizing activity for the individual farmer (or any other producer in a highly competitive market structure) is by no means rational for all farmers or the general society. Acting in his own best interests, the farmer undertakes a certain activity, such as innovating technology, which may give him a temporary advantage. However, if he has no way of preventing other producers from following his lead, then the net effect will be the wholesale introduction of technology by his competitors. This leads to progress in the dual sense of further mechanization and increased productivity per man or unit of land, both of which translate into increases in supply. An uncontrolled and (in any competitive market structure) uncontrollable increase in supply defeats the original intent of the individual maximizing farmer—that is, it brings about a drop in his price per unit. Faced with a declining price, the farmer as a maximizer is forced to seek even more cost-reducing technology.

The total society reaps the benefits of such a situation in cheaper, more abundant, and more varied food products. But of late, many in our society are beginning to appreciate the social costs of such benefits. Our foods may seem to be more wholesome and cheaper in terms of our expanding incomes, but we are now informed to the increasing residues of toxic agents in our vegetables, the non-water-soluble DDT on our fruits, and the mercury treatment of our "miracle" grain seeds. We are all confronted by eutrophication of our water sources due in part to the runoff in excessive nitrates. The old-fashioned farming methods that emphasized diversified crops, organic fertilizers, and intensive use of land look more appealing as the social costs of progress in agriculture become more apparent.

There are no prospects that in the near future science will replace the chicken as the only producer of eggs, or cows of milk, or soil of wheat. Up to now, progress in agriculture has primarily been the introduction of machines and machinelike processes to increase the efficiency of the chicken, the cow, and the soil. Because these basic elements cannot as yet be replaced, there is a limit to the mechanization possible in agriculture. There is every prospect that there will be further developments in making these basic elements more productive through elaborate mechanical devices and chemical ingenuity. The economic imperatives of the producer for this innovation are just as strong, if not stronger today than in the past. The dangers are, of course, just as formidable and many times unforeseeable. The circumstances that most farmers find themselves in allow them little choice as to whether they will use the latest technology that is made available. They still operate in their own best, short-term interests. As they see it they must survive.

Traditionally the environmental deterioration problem within the market structure just outlined has been analyzed as an example of market failure: the operation of the market mechanism has produced social costs that private enterprise left to itself cannot reduce. If these costs are unacceptably high, as most sensitive observers contend, then interference by government is warranted. The government has a variety of means at its disposal: so the question becomes one of which means are the most efficient, that is, which means reduce to a minimum the amount if interference with private enterprise.

The government has no constitutional power, except in states of emergency, to interfere directly in pricing and output decisions. It does have the power to influence decisions made in the private sector. Aside from moral exhortation, the government's primary influence is in regulation and taxation and spending policy. It can ban certain productive processes, chemicals, unsafe techniques, and equipment if they are deemed detrimental to the public good. It did ban the use of DDT and its power to do so was upheld by the judiciary. It has formulated guidelines for safe automobiles. It has established emission standards for automobiles. It can and does establish heights of chimneys for more efficient diffusion of industrial effluents. It formulates sewage disposal standards for municipalities. As described in Chapter 3 of this book, there is an increasingly complex network of regulation that may or may not meet the degree of environmental danger.

Economists, although not ignoring regulation, would look to the fiscal powers of government to overcome market failure. The government, through its formidable spending power, can direct demand to antipollution technology. It can subsidize technology to control the unwanted environmental effects of privately developed technology. Through its taxing powers it can provide discouragement of the use of certain processes and incentives for the use of others. The one thing the government as now constituted cannot do is do away with economic development or outlaw the profit motive.

Indeed, there is even a great question as to whether the federal government does not contribute directly to the environmental problem. One of the primary aims of the Department of Agriculture is the development of a more efficient agriculture through the introduction of more chemical agents. The Department supports research at land-grant colleges across the country to promote increases in productivity in farming. The government spends billions of dollars a year on the interstate highway system, whose ecological consequence is merely not seen in the cementing over of the land and the consequent destruction of natural ecosystems, but also in the direct stimulation of the automobile industry by making automobile travel more attractive to the population. The government supports a great deal of various kinds of research and development, but its primary thrust is improved military technology.

When dealing with highly competitive industries, such as agriculture, textiles, lumber, and mining, the government could negate or reduce the environmental impact of private decision-making by blanket industry regulation and taxation. As long as all firms are subject to the same taxation and regulation, then no one firm is unduly hurt and the social costs of market failure can be reduced and the market mechanism of resource allocation still left intact. After all, firms in competitive market structures are all in the same boat; they do not see each other as rivals. If the shape and direction of the boat is regulated, no one in the boat is more adversely affected than anyone else. The best of all worlds.

Unfortunately, only a small part of production in contemporary America fits this idealized market structure. Most production for the market is the effort of firms who feel very much threatened by rival firms, and who are constantly seeking a competitive edge in one way or another. If the environmental crisis arises from the workings of the perfectly competitive market structure, the economist can give fairly clear-cut policy recommendations. However, if the same crisis arises from the workings of a highly concentrated, rivalrous, powerful set of vested interests, the picture is much more confused. Thus we are led to consider the more murky world of corporate America and its relation to the environmental problem.

ECOLOGY AND THE CORPORATION

In the manufacturing sector of the American economy the profit motive and private property remain central institutions, but the production processes allow of more complete mechanization and therefore a higher concentration of ownership and control. In the production of automobiles, or steel, or computers, there is no natural limit imposed as in agriculture. Although agriculture has been possibly the preeminent example of the industrialization process, we see our standard of life and our future in manufacturing.

The possibilities for the application of scientific knowledge are seemingly unending in the manufacturing spheres of economic activity. The market for any one product line is likely to be in the hands of a few firms. The business form of these firms is invariably the corporation—a legal device that limits the liability of owner-producers and a convenient mechanism for amassing the costly technology from a number of saving sources. There are few generalizations that can be made about the activity of the few controlling firms of an industry. In many instances it "just depends." It depends on the history of the firms in a particular industry, on their interdependence, on the particular personalities involved, on the government's role, and many times, most importantly, on luck.

Concentration in American industry has increased over the decades of the twentieth century. This concentration is primarily the result of what is known as horizontal integration, i.e., the merger of firms producing the same product line. A more recent rash of mergers, known as conglomerate mergers, has led to a different type of concentration: concentration of an increased percentage of the national output into fewer and fewer corporate empires. A conglomerate merger is the combination of two firms producing noncompetitive products or services. The CBS acquisition of the New York Yankees was a conglomerate merger.

There have been two primary forces behind the increasing concentration of production in the American economy: finance and technology. Both forces reflect the institutions of profit motive, private property, and rivalry. The technological imperative is obvious: simply a desire to lower costs. The financial imperative reflects a desire to eliminate competition through merger. It has led to the "rationalization" of an industry by reducing the number of firms producing and therefore to a more effective control of price through a more effective control of supply. This financial imperative led to a degree of concentration that was not necessitated by technological considerations.

There is a logic to concentrated corporate activity, although it is

The Gross National Product keeps on rising. [Photo by T. D. Fitzgerald.]

not as compelling as the logic of highly competitive industries. The logic comes from the massive dimensions of corporate activity, the increasingly sophisticated technology, and the direction of that activity (profit motive). Massiveness with rational maximizing direction spells an intricate organizational structure, a hierarchy with many subdivisions of expertise mobilized toward one goal: growth. The subdivisions are staffed with skilled personnel whose object is personal advancement through the hierarchy. Advancement comes to those whose talents and motives match the needs and direction of the whole. Increasingly, sophisticated technology spells more subdivision, more expertise, and more planning for the future.

The ownership of these massive structures is diffuse. Thirty million Americans participate in the trading of common stock, the shares of ownership of the corporation. This does not mean, however, that they control corporate activity. In most instances, the very large-scale owners of stock are those with the controlling voice. Their voice is heard by the board of directors, which sets the overall policy of the corporation. The administration of this policy is left to the decision-making executives, who usually own significant numbers of shares themselves. The major interest of the owner-controllers is the growth of the firm. It is the growth of the firm, its future potential as shown in that growth, that affects the appreciation of the share of stock. More profit as a consequence of growth is reflected in higher returns or dividends. Administrators of corporate industry are good or bad to the degree that their strategies in the marketplace are effective in increasing returns.

The automobile industry is an eminent example of the logic of concentrated industry. It is vast, uses sophisticated technology, has been the growth industry for much of the twentieth century, and has been very profitable. It epitomizes American life. It is a sleek complex mechanical gadget; other industries (such as the oil industry) have grown around it and its ugliness; the smog of our cities, the lead poisoning of public-housing children (because many public-housing projects are located adjacent to major highway arteries), and the paving over of a large part of our country have been caused by it. Anywhere from 11 per cent to 15 per cent of the nation's output of goods and services is tied up in cars, their maintenance, and their accessories.

The modern aspects of the automobile industry first appeared with the rise of Henry Ford. Before his Model T there were many types of automobile and many producers. The designs were highly individualized, their similarity residing only in the use of one basic form of locomotive power, the internal-combustion engine. (The steam and electric engine were also popular early in the twentieth century.) Each designer made his own car, assembling it himself. Such custom design was costly and consequently these early automobiles became the play-things of the rich. Ford owed his success to the development of a "better idea." He began to produce one basic design in large quanti-ties. The large-scale production of a standard product reduced the costs substantially. These cost savings were passed on to the middle-income consumer. Ford boasted that the American public could have "any color car it wanted as long as it were black."

The automobile caught on and became a growth industry. The tremendous economies of scale came largely from mass-production techniques: the vertical integration of the production process, the as-sembly line, and the use of interchangeable parts. All meant savings, but they also meant high overhead costs. The plant and equipment necessary to the mass-production processes increased over the years as these processes became more sophisticated, and by the 1950's it was virtually impossible to accumulate enough capital to start an auto-mobile-manufacturing plant.

To realize the savings that resulted from mass production, it was necessary to produce a large number of automobiles. Again, by the 1950s it was estimated that it was necessary to have anywhere from 5 per cent to 10 per cent of the national market benefit from these savings.

The implications of this cost situation (plus the advertising consid-erations discussed later) for the structure of the industry—that is, the number of firms producing—were enormous. The cost situation was one of the major forces bringing about the current dominance of the automobile industry by the Big Three, particularly the predominance of General Motors.

In the 1920s, Ford, Chrysler, and General Motors were the largest producers of automobiles. Early in that decade their product changed little from year to year. By the middle of the decade, however, the "used-car" problem arose: the current production was competing with the production of the preceding years. The market was saturated. The solution to the used-car problem was the introduction of changes in style. Stylistic changes and the retooling costs they necessitated, com-bined with the cost structure of the industry in general, made the industry what it is today. The rivalry among the three firms was in-tensified. This rivalry began to be expressed not in price competition, as had been the case in the past, but in quality competition, or advertising.

Advertising exists to disseminate information. It also disseminates misinformation: it plays on public fears, promotes status conscious-ness, and makes use of other psychological susceptibilities. Large-scale advertising by the automobile industry makes use of all of the possibilities. Befitting its size, General Motors spends more money on advertising than does any other corporation.

The manufacture of automobiles today is highly centralized (in Detroit), but the distribution is highly decentralized (in dealerships). The exigencies within which the Big Three corporate leadership operates are those that affect most corporations. There is an imperative to expand, to seek higher profit returns. Each of the major firms seeks to expand by enlarging its share of the total market through advertisement and the introduction of new models and model changes. All seek to expand the market for the product. The expansion of the entire market is effected by built-in obsolescence and by goodwill advertising. No one firm can take a chance on a major product line's failing (such as the Chevrolet, the Mercury, or the Plymouth), so the basic structure is the same but its trimmings differ: its fins and chrome give the appearance of diversity. The product is administratively priced (as are many major consumer items); that is, the price is arrived at by the establishment of a target profit rate at medium use of capacity. Higher use of capacity yields higher returns, lower use, lower returns. It is generally acknowledged that General Motors, as the largest firm, establishes the prices. The other firms follow suit. The aim of the industry is to make a "good" automobile that will sell at this administered price rather than a purely functional product that would sell more cheaply. In this aim, at least, General Motors has been successful, generating, as it does, one of the highest profit rates of any industrial activity in the nation.

Most Americans tend to believe that they have a wide range of choice in the car that they buy. Several years ago a national magazine made the observation that the potential automobile buyer had virtually a million and one options in his choice of product: he could "custom-design" his own car as to color, optionals, and gadgets. This assertion gives the illusion of tremendous choice; but most automobiles within the same price range are more alike than different. The planning that goes into any particular year's model was conceived on some drafting board several years before. Out of necessity the large corporate empires engineer in advance; they cannot be responsive to sudden changes in consumer whim. If consumer whim threatens, then it must be controlled. Advertising is an effective tool in such control, but the stabilization of production in the hands of cooperative mass-producers is even more effective in limiting the range of choice. The complexities of the current mass-production, multinational corporations with assets in the billions of dollars and yearly production in the hundreds of millions are not susceptible to consumer control. This is most true of the high-priced durable-goods industries. It is to their interest to create wants rather than meet needs.

Charles Wilson, Secretary of Defense under Eisenhower and a former president of General Motors, once said (while in public office), "What's good for General Motors is good for the country." In a sense he was right. The automobile industry and other industries of like size and dimension are the main vehicles for our continued development. The achievement of an ever higher standard of living is in the hands of the current corporate establishment. The growth of the GNP is attendant on the growth of these corporations. Whatever affects their growth potential affects the standard of living not only of the employees of a particular corporation but of all the population. The corporate establishment, the prime undertaker of investment spending, comprises a vested interest of overwhelming importance. This investment spending has brought about our "success" but it has also brought about our "failure." The rate and direction of this investment spending is decided by the forces generated by market survival. The rate and direction of investment spending is basically the composition and magnitude of our technologies. It is these technologies that threaten the operation of the world's ecosphere.

Ecology and Contemporary Economy

The logic of corporate economy and its connection with the environmental crisis is obvious in some instances, less so in others.

First: the central thesis of this essay has been that decentralized economic development is intimately connected with threats to the world's ecosphere. The highly mechanized, massive nature of contemporary technology is the engine of this economic development. This technology, its direction of growth, its uses, and its scope are controlled by a relatively small percentage of the population. Further, this technology is used to advance private ends.

Second: although within any given corporate empire rationality is a byword, the several corporations in any one production line create an irrational whole. Because of rivalry between giants, what is rational for one creates, when effected by all, irrationality. No one automobile company could afford to reduce the efficiency of its engines by applying emission-control devices. Its sales would suffer. Consequently, they all produce unmuffled engines that exact great social costs.

Third: unlike agriculture (farmers see themselves as being in the same boat), firms in highly concentrated industry are in separate boats seeking the win. They see the other boats and are constantly aware of their positions relative to the other boats. The pressures are greater to stay ahead or keep abreast, and more massive interests are at stake. Research and development departments within each firm seek the advantage. This advantage is tested in the market. Refinements and new applications of old ideas are constantly developed: at one time packaging, at another time a new "discovery," some new additive, a new way of getting a whiter wash or a shinier floor. To get the advantage, time is of great importance. There is little time to research the environmental impact of these refinements.

Fourth: the sheer size of concentrated industry, its vast distributive network, and its command of transportation and communication facilities quickly spread a refinement. The whole economy is more tightly intermeshed. The environmental impact of the new product comes immediately, massively, and sometimes recklessly.

Fifth: the centralization of economic activity leads to careful, unilateral growth. Internal processes are made efficient. Immense quantities of selected resources are gobbled up. The petroleum industry as we see it today is very much a creature of the internal-combustion engine. Only 37 per cent of the petroleum industry's products are used for heating and for generating electricity. The petroleum industry fuels the automobile industry. There is a vested interest in the internal-combustion engine. Oil becomes the important energy source of society. Other possible energy sources, such as the winds, the tides, the sun, the waters, tend to be ignored. There are no vested interests in these resources.

Sixth, as an extension of the fifth point: much of the pattern of consumption and production in our society was decided in the past. Ford made decisions consistent with his best interests that gave us our automobile society. Other industries that we take for granted come from similar backgrounds (such as Watson's IBM). If these industries constitute a threat to the environment, we are relatively helpless. Our economic growth comes as a direct result of these past decisions. If we seek to undo them, then we create unemployment and loss of income. At best we can hope to control some of the unwanted by-products.

Seventh: although difficult to establish, the highly concentrated industry has more than only economic power. It also has political influence. The larger the corporation, the more important its continued success becomes for the society at large. Not only does it generate taxes and employment, but one of its clients is likely to be the government. (And there is some evidence to suggest an interconnection of personnel between government and business.) It has huge sums at its disposal to create goodwill through lobbying. Its point of view—its logic—is likely to have greater moment in governmental decisions than the more amorphous environmental movement. Government decision-making criteria may be less clear-cut with regard to the highly concentrated industry than with regard to industries with hundreds of producers who are all in the same boat.

The qualities and imperatives of the corporation become increasingly the qualities and imperatives of the total society. To repeat the historical cliché: "The business of America is business." When that "business" is on a small scale, diffuse, and relatively decentralized as is true of some industry today (but was more true of all industry yesterday), the danger is localized and more easily absorbed by the surrounding ecosystem. When that "business" is massive, centralized, all pervasive, and even global, then of course the danger to the stability of the ecosphere is increased in direct proportion to the growth of the source of the danger. The air and water pollution that has always been the by-product of American industry increases as that industry grows, becomes a social problem, and sets the public mind to seeking a solution.

The solutions offered vary with the degree of the perceived threat (already there is a backlash to the ecology movement) and the degree of loyalty to the ideological and institutional basis of our culture. Most solutions involve putting some restraints on the source of the pollution. Generally, these restraints involve forcing industries and municipalities to filter their effluents. The cost of such restraints is passed on to the consumer in one way or another but usually in the form of increased prices and taxes. The technology of filtration and the corporations developing it promise to be one of the fastest growing areas of the economy. There is little doubt that programs can and will be implemented that will effectively decrease concentrations of noxious effluents in our air and water and food supplies. The timing of such implementation is the unknown quantity.

However, it should be understood that air, water, and trace-metal pollution is just the tip of the icebreg. The danger to the environment is more insidious. It is in energy dislocations, land use, and ocean dumping grounds that the danger most exists and is least calculable. It is in these areas that massive, centralized corporate industry in effecting its growth poses the greatest threat.

The centralization of industry into fewer and fewer corporations (two thirds of America's manufacturing assets are under the control of two hundred corporations) spells a gloomy picture for the future of the environment. These massive business units develop technologies aimed at reducing costs and increasing efficiency. They seek, through elaborate conjunctions of physical processes and chemical systems, both products of scientific advances, to produce the most output for the least input of labor and to reach the maximum output consistent with the highest rates of return or profit. This profit aim is supported by attempts at consumer manipulation through advertising in the mass media. In the process, an overall growth of the economy is achieved, per-capita consumption increases (in quantity, not necessarily in quality), and an exponential rate of increase in the use of the world's resources of minerals and energy results, along with powerful vested interests in the use of certain resources (such as oil), certain technologies (such as the internal-combustion engine), and certain land-use patterns (such as an elaborate interstate highway system). The last thing that a successful corporation would like to do is to make its major products obsolete. Too much capital is tied up in resources, technologies, and land-use patterns to risk change. As our economy becomes more centralized we can expect an amalgam of interests to continue along paths they have already ordained.

Given that the world's resources are finite, that there is only so much oil, and that land can be used for only one major purpose at a time, and given that the desires of corporations for growth are non-finite—always expanding—then something has to give. Either the system of perpetual growth and the institutional arrangements allowing for this growth must be altered, or the sources of this growth will be exhausted. The logic of the U.S. economy as described in this chapter contributes to this dilemma. All development-oriented cultures that are built on the same logic will come to the same end.

There is evidence of much planning in our economy. The operations of General Motors are predicted upon a careful assessment of sources of supply, production control, and the marketing of the product. The Pentagon is one of the largest planning organizations in the world. Planning in our economy is fragmented, however, because it pursues a careful estimation of specialized goals. There is no overall planning of the national objectives except during periods of war. Our sociopolitical structure does not support the idea of central planning. But even if overall planning were possible, the objectives of that planning would still be in question. Would it be toward growth? If so, the threat to the environment would remain.

The dominant assumption in our culture is that growth will be the means of achieving the greatest degree of liberty for the individual. His wants are unlimited. Little discussion is made of his needs. It is presumed that there is no difference between needs and wants. Because we are unable to distinguish between wants and needs, the idea of a nongrowth culture seems alien. But even if we were to arrive at an acceptable distinction between wants and needs, it would be useless, given the current way in which production and consumption decisions are made, that is, the corporate form of doing business. Such an acceptable distinction would certainly mean a redistribution of the nation's wealth and income and thus of its power.

SUGGESTED READINGS

BARAN, PAUL, and PAUL M. SWEEZY. *Monopoly Capital.* New York: Monthly Review Press, 1966.

COMMONER, BARRY. *The Closing Circle, Nature, Man and Technology.* New York: Alfred A. Knopf, Inc., 1971.

DALES, J. H. *Pollution, Property and Prices, an Essay in Policymaking and Economics.* Toronto: University of Toronto Press, 1968.

DALY, HERMAN. "Toward a New Economics: Questioning Growth," *Selected Readings on Economic Growth,* p. 146, Committee on Interior and Insular Affairs, U.S. Senate Part II, Serial No. 92–3, September, 1971.

D'ARGE, R. C., A. V. KNEESE, and R. V. AYERS. *Economics of the Environment: a Materials Balance Approach,* Baltimore: The Johns Hopkins Press, 1970.

DORFMAN, ROBERT and NANCY S., eds. *Economics of the Environment.* New York: W. W. Norton & Company, Inc., 1972.

GALBRAITH, J. K. *The New Industrial State.* New York: New American Library, 1967.

GARVEY, GEROLD. *Energy, Ecology, Economy.* New York: W. W. Norton & Company, Inc., 1972.

GELLEN, MARTIN. "The Making of a Pollution Industrial Complex" in D. M. Gordon, ed., *Problems in Political Economy: an Urban Perspective.* Lexington, Mass.: Raytheon/Heater, 1971.

HERFENDAHL, ORRIS C., and ALLEN V. KNEESE. *Quality of the Environment: an Economic Approach to Some Problems in Using Land, Water and Air. Baltimore:* The Johns Hopkins Press, 1965.

HERTZ, DAVID. "The Cancer of Growth," *Selected Readings on Economic Growth,* p. 65, Committee on Interior and Insular Affairs, U.S. Senate Part II, Serial No. 92–3.

MISHAN, E. J. *Technology and Growth, the Price We Pay.* New York: Frederick A. Praeger, Inc., 1970.

MYRDAL, GUNNAR. *Asian Drama,* New York: Pantheon 1968.

RAMSEY, WILLIAM, and CLAUDE ANDERSON. *Managing the Environment.* New York: Basic Books, Inc., Publishers, 1972.

SOLOW, ROBERT M. "The Economist's Approach to Pollution and Its Control." *Science,* 173 (August 6, 1971), 498–503.

VEBLEN, THORSTEIN. *Absentee Ownership: The Case of America.* Boston: Beacon Press, 1967.

THREE

❖

POLITICS

THE DESTRUCTION *of the ecosphere is not merely a by-product of progress, growth, and development. It is not just a case of incidental bad management. It is a result of the nature of our patterns of production and consumption, which, in turn, reflect our cultural values. Now that our technology has reached the point at which our interference with natural processes is so great as to threaten the very structure of the ecosphere, our relation to nature is determined by political management.*

The political framework within which we operate is as much a reflection of our value structure as is our economic system. The two systems are intimately tied together. Policies of government have developed to protect and enhance the attitudes and beliefs that we have evolved.

In view of the global environmental problems that have recently become apparent, we now see that our belief in constant expansion and growth is no longer valid. It is now obvious that what is good for General Motors is not necessarily good for the country or for the world. Business interests are not unaware of this threat to their unbridled growth. The advertising and public relations efforts of many large companies have been directed to assuring a concerned public that their activities are actually improving the natural world. We are told that fish really like offshore oil rigs and that lead-free gasoline will solve all air pollution problems. But the very nature of the ecological crisis is such that it cannot be bought off; we are not concerned merely with the survival of whooping cranes or the white rhino but with the very fabric of the ecosphere.

Ecosystems are all interdependent to a degree and we cannot, with any precision, define the boundaries of an ecosystem. This fact has important implications in terms of controlling pollution, for pollution cannot be controlled at the town, state, or even, effectively, national boundaries. We are faced with conflicts between local, national, and even international interests. The Stockholm conference on the human environment held in the summer of 1972 was a first step toward establishing guidelines for management of the environment at the international level. For the time being, however, we must examine the national policies of the United States with the hope that international cooperation will develop in the future.

[109]

If we are to alter the direction in which we are headed and which, we are assured by scientists, will bring environmental disaster, we must do so through governmental action. We are at a point in time when our basic beliefs are being questioned and reevaluated, particularly by young people. What we must now ask is, How responsive is government to change in these basic beliefs? Our political structure was designed around a set of beliefs and values that are no longer tenable, but is it so controlled by vested-interest groups that it cannot be realigned to new attitudes? Is it possible to operate under the present system of American politics and at the same time maintain the integrity of the ecosphere?

This section of the book examines the response of the political system to the ecological crisis. It first focuses on the response of the federal government to environmental problems, from the conservation policies of Theodore Roosevelt to the environmental policies of the present. It seeks to examine the strengths and weaknesses of policies toward environmental questions, primarily pollution control, and to investigate the character of the political system generally as it relates to environmental problems. This section asks a number of questions. What have been the shortcomings of federal policies in recent years? Are these shortcomings the result of the stance of a political party? Or are they attributable to particular individuals in power, or to the political process as a whole? How much of this federal legislation is actually enforceable? Can the National Environmental Policy Act provide the basis for a genuine attack on the existing range of environmental problems? Can the Environmental Protection Agency break through the network of interests and values to regulate economic processes to significantly improve the environment? Finally, this section asks whether the character of the political system is such that an environmentally sensitive public can make itself felt on the structures of power.

The Environmental Movement:
From Conservation to Ecology

The widespread and somewhat fashionable concern with the environment did not begin with the demonstrations held on Earth Day, April 22, 1970. Despite the publicity given that event, ecological deterioration had been a matter of increasingly pessimistic concern to a growing public composed of environmental scientists and ecologists, some public officials, conservation groups of varying outlook and purpose, and ecologically sensitive political activists. From time to time, of course, environmental issues had created a wider stir, as when Rachel Carson published *Silent Spring* or when the mutagenic effects of nuclear fall-out became known. The question of man's relation to his environment had not, however, been a major political question when compared to other issues that have tormented American politics. With other questions demanding public attention it was hardly surprising that ecologists with their scientific knowledge and so-called nature freaks with their organic foods could not readily gain a hearing. Nonetheless, by the last days of the 1960s a body of informed opinion had developed that was sufficient to constitute a basis for the ecological movement. Between the Santa Barbara oil spill in the spring of 1969 and Earth Day in the spring of 1970, the environmental question was placed on the agenda of American politics. Ecology was promptly declared by many observers to be "the issue" for the 1970s.

It is difficult to say whether this judgment was accurate. In any case, the politicization of the environmental question hardly began with Earth Day. Indeed, what was termed the ecological movement for the 1970s was referred to in the late 1960s as the "new conservationism." The term is significant, reminding us that the ecological movement has ample precedent in American history. This is hardly surprising. More than that of most nations, perhaps, the history of the United States can be written largely in terms of the relationship between man and nature. For Americans the relationship between man and nature has been generally characterized by an unchecked exploitation of nature. At the same time, however, voices have consistently been raised throughout the course of American history against the assault of the pioneer and the industrialist on nature. As early as 1854 the best known of these voices, Henry David Thoreau, cried out in anger: *"Flint's Pond!* Such is the poverty of our nomenclature. What right had the unclean and stupid farmer, whose farm abutted on this sky water, whose shores he had ruthlessly laid bare, to give his name to it?" Three years earlier, in "Walking," he spoke on behalf of nature as follows: "I wish to speak a word for nature, for absolute freedom and wildness, as contrasted with a freedom and culture merely civil—to regard man as an inhabitant, or a part and parcel of nature, rather than a member of society." [1] This view, which we can term an ecological view, was echoed in the succeeding years by such persons as John Muir, George Perkins Marsh, and Aldo Leopold, to name only three. The writings of these men contributed to the rise of the conservation movement in the early twentieth century. But from our point of view, their distinctively "ecological" view was not, as we shall see, the dominant outlook of the conservation movement during its most influential

1 In Carl Bode, ed., *The Portable Thoreau* (New York: The Viking Press, Inc., 1947), pp. 444 and 592.

period. Nonetheless, the conservation movement gave rise to a tradition and a movement that sought to create and maintain a respectful and wise approach to man's relationship with his natural environment.

The conservation movement has been characterized by important limitations and by striking ambiguities. Nonetheless, it was successful in becoming, in the judgment of Grant McConnell, "apparently the strongest political force in the country" during its brief existence.[2] Its strength derived from several characteristics. It was led by an effective and strong-willed political figure, Gifford Pinchot, who had as ally an unusually strong President, Theodore Roosevelt. Furthermore, the conservation movement was part of the rising Progressive tide of the early twentieth century. At the same time, however, Pinchot's ideas about conservation were quite consistent with the needs of a society beginning to make the shift from the era of the robber baron and the open frontier to an age characterized by a corporate economy and an urban way of life. For Pinchot, conservationism involved the wise and efficient use of natural resources: it looked toward the rational readjustment of men's fundamental attitude toward nature. A somewhat different approach was developed by John Muir, who, in his quarrels with Pinchot, sought to preserve wilderness areas in their natural state. As historical figures, the two had more in common than either had with the rampaging activity of those who indifferently uprooted nature for profit. The accomplishments of Pinchot and Roosevelt were, however, hardly sufficient to change an entrenched set of cultural attitudes.

Because of the limited understanding during that time, it is perhaps natural that land reclamation, the creation of wildlife preserves, parks, and national forests, and the initiation of modern management of public lands were rather far-reaching measures. Although a few had more profound intuitions about man's relation to nature, the conservation movement of the Progressive era did not develop an ecological definition of what might be termed the man-nature problem. Pinchot took as his guide a distinctly materialistic and explicitly utilitarian approach to conservation. As he once said, "The object of our forest policy is not to preserve the forests because they are beautiful . . . or because they are refuges for the wild creatures of the wilderness . . . but [to make] prosperous homes. . . . Every other consideration becomes secondary." [3] For Pinchot the dollar count and the head count were the best and most efficient yardsticks of measurement. At the same

[2] "Environment and the Quality of Political Life," in Richard A. Cooley and Geoffrey Wandesforde-Smith, eds., *Congress and the Environment* (Seattle: University of Washington Press, 1970), p. 4.

[3] Quoted in Samuel P. Hays, *Conservation and the Gospel of Efficiency* (Cambridge, Mass.: Harvard University Press, 1959), pp. 41–42.

time, the ultimate choices in deciding questions of value, e.g., more logs for homes or more wilderness for people, lay with scientific experts: decisions regarding environment were to be made by scientifically sensitive experts in the most economically rational way. There is no doubt that this thinking represented an advance over the thoughtless ravaging of the robber baron. There is no doubt either that had this restricted conservationism continued strongly beyond Pinchot and Roosevelt, it might have minimized the degradation of the environment that we are experiencing today. But the disregard of nontangible questions of human value constitutes a critical defect in the Pinchot brand of conservation.

However inadequate in conception the conservation movement might have been, it succeeded brilliantly in execution during its short lifetime. These successes were largely due to the potent combination of presidential leadership and the efforts of a small group of men who made the conservation of natural resources and the preservation of natural forms their major concern. Unhappily, however, they could not unleash the political forces that would have revolutionized the prevailing approach to nature. Consequently, the conservation movement languished as a major political force after Roosevelt and Pinchot. Though government policy had changed in some respects, there was no real check on the continued exploitation of nature by an expanding industrial urban society. Despite the unflagging efforts of various individuals and groups, conservation had little more than a minor priority in the values controlling American political and economic life.

Conservation did not reemerge as a visible public issue until the advent of the New Deal during the 1930s. Lacking the dynamic leadership that had characterized the conservation movement earlier, conservation was not a major political issue during the 1920s. Nonetheless, both the idea of conservation and the federal government's role in conservation policy moved forward substantially. The conservation programs that had found expression in various federal resource agencies continued to expand and mature. Although this growth in the federal role in conservation was unobtrusive, it was undeniably significant. As Donald Swain has pointed out, the definition of conservation was broadened to encompass the protection of wildlife and the preservation of natural beauty. During the latter part of the 1920s, in fact, conservation policy began its departure from the ultilitarianism that had characterized Pinchot's definition of conservation. With the advent of the New Deal, conservation enjoyed a dramatic revival as a pressing concern of both the President and the Congress. For Franklin D. Roosevelt, conservation and resource policy were essential elements in the New Deal. As Stuart Udall points out about the period, "The economic bankruptcy that gnawed at our country's vitals after 1929

was closely related to a bankruptcy of land stewardship." [4] Conservation policy and resource planning thus paralleled New Deal attempts
at remedying a profound economic and social disaster. Given Roosevelt's commitment to conservation and given the all too visible severity
of dust storms, floods, erosion, and the resulting human dislocation,
it is not surprising that the 1930s saw a quickened recognition of the
crucial role that the federal government should play in conservation
policy and resource planning. Effective environmental management
required a degree of comprehensive planning and coordination that
only the federal government seemed able to provide. The reforestation
of land, the concentrated attention to water resource planning and
flood control, the creation of the TVA and the CCC, the development
of resources on a regional basis, the development of river basins, the
creation of national forests—all these were reflections of the President's perceptions of the distortion of man's relationship to the land.
The quickened response of the Roosevelt Administration was such that
some historians have claimed that "the record of achievement . . .
surpassed that of any previous administration." [5]

Nonetheless, it seems fair to say that despite the renewed concern
about conservation, the conservationism of the 1930s, insofar as it was
expressed in federal policy, did not fully define the man-environment
relationship in truly broad ecological terms. Like the conservation
movement that had preceded it by twenty years, this wave of conservationism was also constrained by its time. It was, on the one hand,
simply one aspect of New Deal policy. On the other hand, it was dependent on the political effectiveness of a particular president and
those around him who shared his personal commitment to conservation. Despite the initiation of a wide-ranging set of policies and the
establishment of several important federal agencies, and despite Roosevelt's pride in his "national plan" of conservation, the New Deal failed
to create a genuine national plan for the environment, an institutional
structure for dealing with environmental questions, or a broad-based
conservation movement.

A more serious drawback lay in the ideological conception of conservation that Roosevelt expressed. Sensitive as he was to nature and
the ravages worked on the land by man's indifference, Roosevelt's
view was as imbued with a commitment to wise management for
economic purposes as Pinchot's had been. "Let us," Roosevelt said,
"use common sense and business sense. . . . Economic foresight and
immediate employment march hand in hand in the call for the refor-

[4] The Quiet Crisis (New York: Holt, Rinehart & Winston, Inc., 1963), p. 137.
[5] Anna Lou Riesch, "Conservation Under Franklin D. Roosevelt," in Roderick
Nash, ed., The American Environment (Reading, Mass.: Addison-Wesley Publishing Co., Inc., 1968), p. 147.

estation of these vast areas." [6] He failed to perceive that a more profound approach to the environment would involve not a rationalizing of man's economic exploitation of nature but rather a restructuring of man's way so as to reconcile him to his ecological niche. It would be altogether too much to expect such a view at that time. Those whose intuition and understanding led them to that view were few in number and, in the absence of overwhelming evidence of the impact of economic and social organization on the environment, a wider appreciation of the situation was impossible.

Thereafter environmental questions were generally ignored until the 1960s. Although Truman maintained a formal commitment to the conservation directions charted by Roosevelt, the circumstances of Truman's Administration were such that this commitment could not be converted into a major element in his domestic program. President Eisenhower showed virtually no interest in conservation policy, much less in any conception of what might be termed environmental policy. Despite the relative disinterest of both Democratic and Republican administrations after World War II, there were a number of tentative steps taken toward laying a foundation of what we now call environmental policy. Thus, in 1948 the Water Pollution Control Act was enacted. The significance of the Act was that it marked the modern entry of the federal government into water pollution control. Unfortunately, the Act was already inadequate for the job at hand. Because it was designed primarily to provide loans for sewage-plant construction, was cumbersome in its operation, and depended on states and localities for its effectiveness in pollution control, the Act made little headway. It did, of course, foreshadow the kinds of political and budgetary games that were to be repeatedly played with pollution-control legislation: though $22.5 million was authorized for low-interest loans, no funds for the loan program were appropriated. By 1955, funds for the enforcement of the Act had sunk from $3 million in 1950 to a paltry $1 million. The provisions for pollution abatement were so cumbersome that in 1956 the House Appropriations Committee cut out all funding on the grounds that the law was "almost unenforceable." When the law came up for revision eight years later, the mayor of Independence, Missouri, desperately told Congress, "We are losing the battle against water pollution. At the present rate of construction, in 1966 we will be twice as far behind as we are now." [7]

In 1956 a Democratic Congress strengthened the Act in a number

---

[6] Quoted in Udall, op. cit., pp. 139–140.

[7] Quoted in James L. Sundquist, *Politics and Policy—The Eisenhower, Kennedy, and Johnson Years* (Washington, D.C.: The Brookings Institution, 1968), p. 324. The discussion of the Eisenhower, Johnson, and Kennedy periods draws on Sundquist's excellent account of developments in these years.

of ways. The result, the Federal Water Pollution Control Act of 1956, became the legal framework for federal-state water pollution control and abatement. The model established by the Act also became the model for subsequent air pollution control legislation. Its basic elements—the primary role accorded the states, the enforcement procedures, the system of grants, the provision of research programs—remained unchanged for the next fifteen years. At the time its defects were not dramatically apparent. Perhaps it did not matter at the time, as the Eisenhower Administration showed little enthusiasm for enforcement of water pollution control. Indeed, as late as 1960 Eisenhower successfully vetoed a somewhat stronger Democratic measure. For Eisenhower, water pollution control—which he regarded as a uniquely local problem—was one of the central arenas for implementing a philosophy based on fiscal restraint and decentralized government. The only difficulty was that the assumed beneficiaries of Eisenhower's policy were already looking to the federal government for help. From the start, municipalities joined with conservation groups, Democratic Congressmen, and other interests such as the AFL-CIO in pressing for water pollution legislation. Nonetheless, there was not enough congressional support for pollution control to override Eisenhower's 1960 veto.

The situation was even more dismal in other areas. No federal policy existed with respect to air pollution despite the evidence that smog was clearly a health hazard. A meager bill providing funds for research passed in 1955, but even its sponsor argued that air pollution was a problem for states and localities. Subsequent attempts by the Secretary of Health, Education, and Welfare to secure some enforcement powers were defeated by opposition on the part of the Public Health Service and various economic interests. The Manufacturing Chemists Association expressed the prevailing view of the time when it told Congress that air pollution was "a matter which is peculiarly that of the community and States." The same outlook prevailed in other environmental areas. Although Eisenhower was willing to permit rehabilitation of the national parks, budgetary priorities as well as opposition from commercial and propertied interests blocked the acquisition of seashore and lake shore areas or the purchase of wilderness areas on anything but a piecemeal basis.[8] Although conservation groups like the Sierra Club did win a major victory in the struggle to stop the construction of the Echo Park Dam in the Dinosaur National Monument, the combined opposition of mining, lumbering, and tourist interests, on the one hand, and bureaucratic agencies on the other,

---

[8] See the account in Sundquist, op. cit., pp. 333–336.

blocked legislation limiting the discretion of federal agencies to apply a "multiple-use" policy to national forests. Western political and economic interests continued to resist the attempts to stem the economic exploitation of the wilderness. As a representative of the Washington Department of Commerce and Economic Development put it, "We live in a raw materials economy. . . . Our new jobs . . . must come from greater use of our raw materials. . . . We need greater access to these raw materials rather than less." [9]

There is little excuse for this indifference to conservation policy and presidential indifference to an already worsening environmental condition. Some legislation was passed, but at best it was inadequate and piecemeal. As far as the political system was concerned, such initiative as might be said to have existed lay with a handful of Congressmen and Senators. Faced as they were with the indifference and opposition of the Administration and the entrenched position of a wide range of private interests, they could not make headway with even modest proposals. As for the public at large, the complacency of the Eisenhower years was completely undisturbed by the very few conservationists and preservationists crying alone in the wilderness.

In a number of obscure ways, the situation began to change in the early 1960s. Prodded by municipal agencies, conservationists, and a few Congressmen, the political situation began to change ever so slightly. The return to power of the Democrats guaranteed a slightly more expansive approach to the question of the environment as well as to other public purposes. Kennedy himself, who had won a shaky mandate to "get America moving again," did offer the conservation-minded a broader commitment to environmental policies as well as a greater readiness to enlarge federal powers and loosen the purse strings Eisenhower had so tightly tied. The changed attitude was suggested in a 1962 White House Conference on Conservation when the focus turned to the deterioration in the environment rather than conservation in the older sense of wise use. In the early 1960s, then, a beginning to a start was made.

Despite Kennedy's more open attitude and despite the passage during his term of some significant legislation, conservation and antipollution interests—the environmental movement was still in the future—still had a protracted struggle ahead of them. Despite the desire of municipalities, conservation groups, and their allies in Congress to press forward, Kennedy was unwilling to go much beyond the water pollution control bill that Eisenhower had vetoed the year before. When legislation was finally passed, in the form of amendments to the

[9] Ibid., pp. 339–340.

1956 Water Pollution Control Act, it was only marginally stronger than the modest bill that Eisenhower had rejected. Although it did extend the role of the federal government, and although it did create some abatement procedures, the bill represented incrementalism as usual against a background of Kennedy rhetoric.

Even as the 1961 amendments were being passed, municipalities and conservation groups sought legislation that would provide more funds for control of pollution, for stiffer abatement enforcement, and, in the case of the conservation groups, for the transfer of responsibility from the "medicine men" in the Public Health Service to an independent authority within the Department of Health, Education, and Welfare. In 1963 conservation forces found an ally in Senator Edmund Muskie, who had become Chairman of a Special Subcommittee on Air and Water Pollution of the Public Works Committee. Early in the year he introduced legislation that sought to place water pollution control on quite a different basis than that established by earlier legislation. Although the bill was amply supported by conservation and municipal groups, it was opposed by a broad range of industries (the pulp and paper, chemical, and oil industries) and by a collection of trade associations and even by numerous state health departments. The bill was, moreover, received coolly by the Kennedy Administration, which opposed several of its key elements and proposed weaker provisions for others. Faced with this opposition and weakened by compromise the bill was not enacted until 1965. Upon its passage the Water Quality Act of 1965 was widely hailed: it was, according to one writer, "a milestone in Federal conservation legislation." [10] Measured against the dimensions of the problem and the prolonged record of congressional inaction, this was, to say the least, an overstated judgment. Though it declared the national interest in clean water, though it provided a system of pollution abatement, and though it provided a federal agency to establish and enforce quality water standards, less can be claimed for the bill and its sponsors than is commonly thought.

The same kind of hesitation and delay marked the approach of the Kennedy Administration toward air pollution control legislation. When Kennedy declared in 1960 that "we need an effective Federal air pollution control program now," the "now" turned out to be located somewhat in the future. There were a number of complex and difficult questions associated with the question of air pollution control: What should the role of the federal government be? Should the responsibility for air pollution control be located in the Public Health Service, an administrative agency that was viewed as being in some sense "con-

[10] "Water Quality: A Question of Standards," in Cooley and Wandesforde-Smith, op. cit., p. 141.

servative," or should it be transferred to a new agency? Should the
federal government be given enforcement powers? These questions
involved a number of administrative and economic interests and were
consequently quite political in nature. For example, the Public Health
Service, supported by the Bureau of the Budget, opposed vesting enforcement authority in the federal government, while high-ranking
officials in HEW supported the establishment of strong federal enforcement powers. Conservationists, many mayors, and the American
Medical Association supported the strong legislation, while the Manufacturing Chemists Association, the American Iron and Steel Institute,
the petroleum industry, and the National Association of Manufacturers opposed the establishment of federal enforcement powers modeled
on the pattern of water pollution abatement procedures. Though the
legislation that the Administration was ultimately willing to support
was regarded as strong, conservationists were rightly uneasy. They
regarded with skepticism legislation that made federal action dependent on state initiative and that employed the same cumbersome abatement procedures that had been contained in the Water Pollution
Control Act. Nonetheless the Clean Air Act of 1963 marked a start
toward the assertion of federal responsibility for controlling air pollution. Despite the fact that the bill did not cover pollution from automobiles, President Johnson stated "under this legislation we can halt
the trend towards great contamination of our atmosphere" as he signed
the Clean Air Act into law.[11] Within three years, he was calling for
new legislation.

In other areas, the situation was not substantially different. Consequently, retrospective judgments are inevitably mixed. On the one
hand, new legislation was passed—e.g., the Wilderness Act of 1964,
and the Land and Water Conservation Fund—that represented a measure of forward movement after years of neglect. On the other hand,
the newly revived attention to matters of conservation or outdoor recreation—"environmental" was still a concept somewhat in the future
—was not strong enough to overcome the stubborn resistance of economic interests and their congressional allies. Consequently, the results fell far short of what environmentalists worked for and far short
of the expectations that the rhetoric from the White House created.
The Wilderness Act of 1964 provides an example of the situation. The
act grew out of legislation that had been initiated in the mid-1950s in
the aftermath of the Echo Park Dam struggle. Even before that conflict,
however, such groups as the Wilderness Society and the Sierra Club
had begun to press for the creation of a permanent wilderness system.

---

11 Quoted in Sundquist, op. cit., p. 355.

It was, they felt, the only way to hold back timber, mineral, tourist, and other interests who were casting a covetous eye on the remaining wilderness areas. Such a system would also limit the power of the Forest Service and the National Park Service, two agencies whose missions did not encompass the preservation of wilderness areas. Following the introduction of legislation, the "preservationists" toiled for seven arduous years in the fields of Congress to create a national wilderness system. Despite White House support, despite much-needed compromise with the Park and Forest Services, and despite growing public response, the resistance could not be fully turned back. In the end a wilderness system was created, but, as two historians of the Wilderness Act put it, "economic interests gained rather more than they were forced to give up." [12] It might, therefore, be best to say that the period of the early 1960s is significant as the beginning of the start of what came to be called the new conservation. This was an approach that began to turn away from the old-style wise-use conservation to a concern with the quality of life. In the area of legislation and policy, Kennedy's contribution lay in his symbolic commitment and in his appointment of Udall as Secretary of the Interior rather than in any set of presidentially defined policies or any fully articulated vision. At the time, any Democratic president would have done as much. Nonetheless, the commitment from the White House, however limited, was an important contribution to the more significant efforts of those who were already drawing attention to the imbalance between man and his environment.

The response of the political system, at least at the presidential and congressional levels, rose to a new level during the Johnson Administration. Much of the indifference of the Eisenhower and even the Kennedy years was replaced by a rapidly expanding recognition of questions of an environmental nature. This is not to say that the new conservation swept away before it the complex of political and economic interests that underwrote—and still underwrites—the ecological crisis. But in comparison with the past this "new conservation" movement of the 1960s became a modest political reality despite its somewhat narrow political base. The causes for the change were several: the increasing severity of the problem; the growing awareness and deep agitation in segments of the scientific community; the commitment to some form of environmental legislation by such congressional figures as Dingell, Muskie, Jackson, Blatnik, Udall; the growing volume of environmental writing by publicists; and the role played

---

[12] Delbert V. Mercure, Jr., and William M. Ross, "The Wilderness Act: A Product of Congressional Compromise," in Cooley and Wandesforde-Smith, op. cit., p. 60.

by a variety of private foundations and conservation groups in funding research, conferences, and so forth. Although the political motives and connections of the new conservation movement were mixed, the consequences of the movement were significant. At the same time the new conservation broke with the earlier emphasis on the wise and efficient use of scarce resources and displayed a greater regard for environmental quality and ecological integrity. The changing approach was captured, for example, in the titles of the Department of Interior Conservation Yearbooks: *The Quest for Quality; Man—An Endangered Species; The Third Wave—America's New Conservation*. By the end of Johnson's Administration there had been a pronounced development in environmental policy away from conservation to an ecological perspective. Nor should Johnson's own role be underestimated. Whatever the exact nature of his commitment, Johnson's public stance lent an important political weight to the new conservation. Even as the war in Vietnam, the widespread existence of poverty at home, and the persistent strength of racism mocked many of Johnson's words, and even as his desire for an all-encompassing political consensus constrained his aspirations, Johnson's rhetorical commitments and institutional support were important for the environmentalists. In his Great Society statement of May 1964 he spoke of a "place where the city of man serves not only the needs of the body and the demands of commerce but the desire for beauty and the hunger for community." Whatever the qualifications, the presidential legitimatizing of the goal of "beauty" was not without political weight. In his White House Message on Natural Beauty of February 1965, he said, "our conservation must not be just the classic conservation of protection and development, but a creative conservation of restoration and innovation. Its concern is not with nature alone, but with the total relation between man and the world around him."

Between 1964 and 1968 congressional legislation for the environment increased substantially. The legislation, which cannot be said to be uniformly proenvironmental, included the Clean Water Restoration Act, the Air Quality Act, the Land and Water Conservation Fund Act, the Wilderness Act; the Open Space and Green Span programs; the Solid Waste Disposal Act; the establishment of the Public Land Review Commission; the Highway Beautification Act; and others. Between 1961 and 1968 five additional national seashore areas were added to the one existing prior to 1961. Six national recreation areas were acquired. In this period numerous measures were taken toward creating or strengthening the national system of parks, trails, refuges, recreational areas, and lake shores. It should not be thought from this casual catalogue that the new conservationism was unmarred by all but the usual quota of compromise. Far from it. The Air Quality Act of 1967—since amended by the 1970 Clean Air Act Amendments— serves as an example of the kind of compromise that satisfied the White House, Congress, and industry while misleading the public into believing that tough, effective legislation had been passed. Early in 1967 Johnson sent to Congress a proposed air quality bill that contained two strong elements: first, national emission standards that would ensure that each major industry—e.g., paper, steel, oil, and chemicals—would have a federally established emission limit that would apply regardless of location (this latter feature would prevent industry from escaping strong legislation in one state by moving to another); second, federal regional control commissions that would cut through the complex jurisdictional difficulties of controlling air pollution across interstate lines. Because these proposals threatened not only the preeminence of state and local control and the freedom enjoyed by industry but also the very conception of pollution control that Muskie had designed, the Johnson proposals met with opposition, including that of Muskie, before they were made public. In the face of the political resistance and because the Johnson Administration was not strongly committed to even its own proposals, the Johnson bill was quietly scrapped even before public Senate hearings were held. The final situation has been succinctly described by the detailed Nader report on air pollution control as follows:

> The suggestion has been made that the White House bill was gutted by the Muskie Subcommittee as a result of enormous pressure leveled against it by American industry, and that Muskie had folded against unequal odds. While the effect was the same as if this had occurred, nothing so dramatic ever took place. What happened was that, except for the coal lobby, industry was never called upon to wield its influence. This was because relevant government views coincided with American industry's. There was a silent, unspoken unanimity in the view that nothing would be gained by supporting bold legislation to control pollution.[13]

The result of the process was a bill that gave away more than it saved for the attack on mounting levels of air pollution.

Regrettably, there is too much in the record of the Johnson years to permit even a modest discussion of the politics surrounding it— assuming the information were fully available. Any final judgment by careful historians will, however, be confronted with a severe dilemma.

[13] John C. Esposito, *Vanishing Air* (New York: Grossman Publishers, Inc., 1970), pp. 274–275.

On the one hand, a great deal was done. On the other, less was done than should have been done and less was done than the Great Society Congress of 1964–1966 might have been willing to do. Johnson's insistence, for example, early in 1965 on consulting with automobile manufacturers prior to supporting Muskie's 1965 air bill was only one example of his desire to include irreconcilable interests in an all-embracing national consensus. Whether this strategy was a viable one, given the potentially explosive nature of the environmental issue, it was one that the new conservationism of the 1960s was not ready to face.

Whatever the final balance sheet on the Johnson Administration, the change in administrations produced little optimism among observers of the environmental movement. Insofar as references to "sound conservation principles," as Nixon put it during the 1968 campaign, count for something, then the new President might have been counted as a supporter of the new conservationism. But by 1968 a concern for the environment was fast becoming a ritualistic gesture that any competent politician could painlessly make. Following the election a Nixon task force reported that federal performance in environmental policy had been "disappointingly low," but its proposals reflected little of the sense of urgency that its criticisms might suggest existed. The task force emphasis on "making existing programs work" and its call for closing the gap between authorizations and appropriations were altogether necessary but not sufficient. A similar note was struck by Nixon's Secretary of Interior, Walter Hickel, who spoke of the need for "the consolidation of the gains that have been made and . . . a reassessment of our long-range objectives." [14]

Whatever the intentions of the Nixon Administration, the pressure of events and of the new conservationism were such that the question could not be dropped from the national agenda. If proof were required, it was provided one week after Nixon took office by the disastrous Santa Barbara oil spill. Although it would be too much to claim, as some have, that it "radicalized" the American public, the spill raised the visibility of the environmental issue. By the end of the year *The New York Times* concluded that the "environment may eclipse Vietnam as a college issue." [15] In December Senator Henry Jackson felt

14 Hickel's remarks were made in his confirmation hearings. U.S. Congress, Senate, Committee on Interior and Insular Affairs, *Hearings, Interior Nomination*, 91st Cong., 1st Sess., 1969, p. 7. Nixon's 1968 election campaign statement is reprinted in U.S. Senate, Committee on Interior and Insular Affairs, *Hearings, National Environmental Policy*, 91st Cong., 1st Sess., pp. 105–108. On the Nixon Task Force, see the report in *The New York Times*, November 14, 1968.

15 November 30, 1969.

confident enough to speak on the floor of the Senate about "a new kind of revolutionary movement under way in this country . . . concerned with the integrity of man's life support system." [16]

Revolution was hardly around the corner, but the crystallization of the issue was already producing concrete results. While the press was declaring the ecological crisis the "issue of the 1970s," the campus movement was organizing the Earth Day Teach-In. This deepening concern on the campuses was, however, a mixed development. On the one hand, Earth Day employed the techniques and recreated the ambience of the antiwar movement in its early days; on the other, it did not draw heavily on either the constituency or the ideology of the student protest movement. Earth Day was a form of "safe" liberal politics: this was both its strength and its weakness. It drew on the resources not simply of the conservationists—Senator Nelson was its sponsor and it was financed by conservation-minded foundations—but of the "system" itself. Far from being a grass-roots movement, as the antiwar movement or the civil rights movements of the early 1960s had been, it was well supported by a paid staff, by a national headquarters, by the resources of major publishers, and even by speakers provided by the Nixon Administration. The press hailed it as an event based on a matter around which men of goodwill could all rally. The "environmental handbook" prepared for Earth Day called for tough pressure politics, but it also stressed the apolitical quality of the issue. In a fundamental misapprehension of the issue, the *Handbook* declared that "this issue transcends the old ideological squabbles of the left and right." [17] But Earth Day was not simply co-optive: it awakened thousands of students and ordinary citizens to the critical nature of the environmental crisis. The real question then was whether the environmental movement could go beyond the liberalism of Earth Day to develop a more effective form of political action.

For its part, the Nixon Administration dragged its feet during its first year in office. One major step taken by the Administration was the creation of a Cabinet-level advisory body, the Environmental Quality Council. Suffering from the same weaknesses that all Cabinet-level, interdepartmental, advisory bodies have, the President's Council met only three times during 1969. When viewed in the context of other actions or nonactions of the Administration—e.g., the authorization in June for the resumption of drilling in the Santa Barbara channel—

[16] U.S. *Congressional Record*, 91st Cong., 1st Sess., December 20, 1969, p. S17452.

[17] Marion Edey, "Eco-Politics and the League of Conservation Voters," in Garrett De Bell, ed., *The Environmental Handbook* (New York: Ballantine/Friends of the Earth, 1970), p. 314.

the Administration did little to encourage the environmental move-ment. As one observer wrote, "During its first year in office, the Nixon Administration was as unable as its predecessors to make its perform-ance match its environmental quality promises." [18]

This posture could not, however, be maintained for long. Long before Earth Day and its attendant publicity, it was apparent that Con-gress was worried about the state of the environment. The Ninety-first Congress amended the Clean Air Act, extended the Great Plains Conservation program, added new forest areas to the National Wil-derness Preservation system, and enacted an Endangered Species Act; in general, Congress addressed itself to environmental matters no less (but also no more) energetically than it had under Johnson. Nearly a hundred pieces of legislation were introduced, including a proposed constitutional amendment that would have provided every American with the inalienable right to a decent environment. No doubt much of this was for show. As one conservationist Senator was quoted as say-ing, "Everyone in Congress realizes that it's a good issue to talk about back home because everyone there is for it. And nobody here wants to destroy the myth that Congress is militant on this issue: it would ruin a good thing for the Congressman and his colleagues." [19] But it would be going too far to conclude that the congressional concern was simply for show: the rhetoric of public men is an important indication of the values and priorities within the system. Thus the passage of the Water Quality Improvement Act and the Clean Air Act Amend-ments in 1970, whatever their shortcomings, indicated a congressional willingness to address itself to an attack on important sources of water and air pollution, i.e., oil spills and automobile emissions. The defeat of the National Forest Timber Conservation and Management Act, a measure that would have permitted stepped-up commercial exploita-tion of timber in the national forests, signified that congressional sen-sitivity to environmental considerations could not be dismissed out of hand. Late in 1969, under intense conservationist pressure Congress appropriated $800 million for construction grants for water treatment plants, a sum which was $586 million more than the $214 requested by the Nixon Administration but less than the $1 billion authorized by law. The most dramatic demonstration of conservationist support in Congress came a year later, when the Senate—but not the House—defeated a request for funds for the SST.

The most significant act, however, was the enactment of the National

[18] Harvey Lieber, "Public Administration and Environmental Quality," Pub-lic Administration Review, Vol. 30 (May/June, 1970), p. 281.

[19] Douglas Ross and Harold Wolman, "Congress and Pollution: The Gentle-man's Agreement," Washington Monthly, Vol. 2, No. 7 (September 1970), p. 13.

Environmental Policy Act of 1969. Signed into law on January 1, 1970, its primary significance lay, first, in declaring a national policy for the environment, and, secondly, in establishing a basic structure for environmental policy-making. In both respects the National Environmental Policy Act was a substantial if long overdue measure. The declaration of a national policy for the environment was altogether new. Despite the long history of the conservation movement, the federal government had never been committed to a national policy of enhancing the quality of the environment in the way it has assumed responsibility toward the economy in the Full Employment Act of 1946. Enacted despite the muted opposition of the Nixon Administration, the Act thus represented a fairly fundamental departure in the approach of the federal government to the environment.

The stated purposes of the Act were "to declare a national policy which will encourage productive and enjoyable harmony between man and his environment; to promote efforts which will prevent or eliminate damage to the environment and biosphere and stimulate the health and welfare of man; to enrich the understanding of the ecological systems and natural resources important to the Nation. . . ." The Act continued by stating, "It is the continuing policy of the Federal Government in cooperation with State and local governments, and other concerned public and private organizations, to use all practicable means and measures . . . to create and maintain conditions under which man and nature can exist in productive harmony, and fulfill the social, economic, and other requirements of present and future generations of Americans." The precise goals of the policy were then specified as follows:

1. fulfill the responsibilities of each generation as trustee of the environment for succeeding generations;

2. assure for all Americans safe, healthful, productive, and aesthetically and culturally pleasing surroundings;

3. attain the widest range of beneficial uses of the environment without degradation, risk to health or safety, or other undesirable and unintended consequences;

4. preserve important historic, cultural, and natural aspects of our national heritage, and maintain, wherever possible, an environment which supports diversity and variety of individual choice;

5. achieve a balance between population and resource use which will permit high standards of living and a wide sharing of life's amenities; and

6. enhance the quality of renewable resources and approach the maximum attainable recycling of depletable resources.

The Act also stated that "Congress recognizes that each person should enjoy a healthful environment and that each person has a responsibility to contribute to the preservation and enhancement of the environment."

In addition to this necessarily broad statement of environmental policy, the Act also sought to overcome the chronic fragmentation of environmental agencies by creating a new top-level body, the Council on Environmental Quality. Patterned after the Council of Economic Advisers and located in the Executive Office of the President, the Council was given a wide-ranging mandate to study the condition of the environment through research; to monitor existing environmental programs and develop new programs and policies; to coordinate the tangled complex of federal environmental programs and agencies; to ensure that federal agencies take environmental considerations into account in their activities; and to assist the President in preparing an annual Environmental Quality Report. While it is too early to determine how effective the Council can be in the long run, its presence does mean that a body exists that is potentially in a position to carry out policy-oriented research, to coordinate existing government policy, to analyze the impact of private activities and technology, and to develop new policies.

Another feature of the Act should be mentioned. Section 102 requires all federal agencies to interpret, administer, and plan their policies in a manner consistent with the National Environmental Policy Act. Each agency is required to make a detailed statement to the President, the Council, and the public on the probable environmental impact of any proposed action or policy. Section 102 strikes at a very real problem, namely, the significant adverse effect of the government itself on the environment. The oil discharged from naval vessels, the thermal pollution from AEC-licensed nuclear power plants, the environmental effects of the SST, the threatened disruption of the ecological balance of the Florida Everglades by the U.S. Army Corps of Engineers, the purchase of gasoline for government cars, the use of high-sulfur fuels at federal installations, the Trans-Alaska pipeline, the location of atomic power plants—these are only a few examples of the activities that make the government itself a major polluter and a threat to the environment. Section 102 was designed as an "action-forcing" provision to ensure, as Senator Jackson put it, "that the policies and goals defined in this act are infused into the ongoing programs and actions of the Federal government." [20] Section 102 was designed, in short, to create an environmental conscience on the part of the govern-

20 *Congressional Record*, December 20, 1969, p. S17451.

ment by making governmental agencies take the environmental impact of their activities into account. Because government activities affect the private sector very extensively the "environmental impact" procedure established by the NEPA was also bound to affect many activities of private businesses (e.g., those doing business with the government or seeking government loans, subsidies, or permits) and municipalities. In this way the obligation to be sensitive to environmental impacts would create a form of federal leadership in the area of environmental management. Ultimately, therefore, the significance of the National Environmental Policy Act is found in its purpose of compelling the government to assume a stewardship role vis-a-vis the environment and to exercise this stewardship according to an ecologically defined environmental ethic. In this respect, it represents a significant advance over the more utilitarian, technological, and managerial biases of the original conservation movement. The Act could have gone further. The version of the bill passed by the Senate contained the following: "Each person has a fundamental and inalienable right to a healthful environment." In Conference this was changed to the final wording: "Each person should enjoy a healthful environment."

The rising concern over environmental quality and the passage of the NEPA seem to have pushed the Administration into taking a livelier stand on the environmental question. After a year of indifference, the Administration began to give the appearance that it was now heading in a new direction. The new line of march was revealed in the 1970 State of the Union message when Mr. Nixon pledged to submit to Congress the "most comprehensive and costly program . . . in the nation's history." Shortly thereafter, he submitted an ambitious and wide-ranging environmental program containing a "37-point action program" and accompanied by a fresh rhetorical commitment to environmental quality. The new look notwithstanding, the proposals themselves were less than what was needed. The proposed funding of waste treatment plants still fell on the short side of the estimated amounts needed, and other elements in the program reflected little more than received opinion. Undoubtdly the presentation of a full-scale presidential environmental program was an impressive and precedent-setting innovation. But the program itself, as *The New York Times* put it, lacked the commitment "to the kind of heroic effort, the ready outpouring of the national treasure, that is evoked by war— even the most unpopular war." [21]

[21] (February 11, 1970). For a relatively complete examination of the situation in a number of policy areas in 1969–1970, see Congressional Quarterly, *Man's Control of the Environment* (Washington, D.C.: Congressional Quarterly, 1970).

Insofar as the environmental issue may be conceived as having fundamental implications for an advanced industrial society, the actions of the Administration during 1970 might best be regarded as modest reform wrapped in bold pronouncements about "ecological disaster," seeking "nothing less than a basic reform," and a "war on pollution." As welcome as many of the policies were one cannot escape feeling that the modesty of the measures mocked the meaning of the rhetoric. One need not dismiss the cancellation of the Cross-Florida Canal, the terminations of the Everglades jetport, the support for New York's Gateway National Recreation Area, the Executive Order directing pollution abatement by federal agencies, the belated revival after months of bureaucratic infighting of the permit program of the 1899 Refuse Act, or the creation of the Environmental Protection Agency. Nor should one ignore the turnabout on the funding for the Land and Water Conservation Fund. But a great deal of this was simply a matter of doing what should have been done before and for some measures there was less there than met the eye. There is good reason then for reserving judgment about the Nixon record of 1970 despite the high marks that have been awarded to it. There were elements that count strongly enough on the negative side to outweigh the items on the plus side. Perhaps the most telling of these was the Administration's lobbying against passage of the Clean Air Act Amendments in the Senate. As its passage was one of the major environmental accomplishments of the Ninety-first Congress, the opposition of the Administration is a revealing example of the limited commitment of the Administration to an environmental program. As one commentator put it, Mr. Nixon got the message, but he had not got religion.

To some observers such contradictions were seen as examples of the political necessities facing the Administration. Given the impact on industry of, say, air and water pollution control and abatement requirements, Mr. Nixon was obliged, according to this view, to tread a zigzag path between the imperatives of the environmental situation and the advice of his environmental advisers, on the one hand, and the pressures of his constituency on the other. Certainly, the Administration took environmental matters more seriously in 1970 and early 1971. The President's 1971 environmental program, for example, demonstrated a programmatic awareness that had been lacking previously. Its more ambitious scope showed that Mr. Nixon was willing to listen to the advice coming from the Council on Environmental Quality and the newly formed Environmental Protection Agency. Many of its proposals—e.g., those on sulfur and lead taxes, on the regulation of toxic chemicals, on the regulation of strip mining, and on controls for power plants—reflected a tougher approach to cleaning up the envi-

ronment. The 1971 program can in fact be regarded as the environmental high-water mark of the Nixon Administration's first three years in office. Even so, it was the rare environmentalist who took real satisfaction from the Nixon program. However serious or intelligent some of the proposals were, they did not go far enough. Nor was there widespread faith that the Administration would back up its own program with the necessary political will.

These feelings were confirmed in 1971. Throughout the year an ugly reaction to the forward movement of environmental policies emerged with discouraging rapidity as one Administration spokesman after another came forward to denounce what they often pleased to call environmental extremism.[22] Triggered perhaps by the Administration's defeat on the SST, the backlash was a function of the mounting opposition to environmental reform from within the Administration and from elements in the business community. Even Mr. Nixon did not remain aloof from this blacklash. On the same day that he sent his 1971 legislative proposals to Congress, for example, Mr. Nixon reassured the corporate executives on the National Industrial Pollution Control Council that "this Administration is not here to beat industry over the head." It is true that EPA Administrator William D. Ruckelshaus told the same meeting that "industries and businessmen must change, they must adapt, they must accommodate to changes in public attitudes or they will surely die." But the words of a President are more weighty than those of his subordinates. By August the President

[22] The most notorious of these expressions was the address entitled "Wait A Minute" delivered by Maurice H. Stans, then Secretary of Commerce, before the National Petroleum Council, reprinted in *Not Man Alone* (January 1972), pp. 12–13. See also the addresses by Hendrik S. Houthakker, then a member of the Council of Economic Advisers, before the Cleveland Business Economists Club, April 19, 1971, and Hollis M. Dole, then Assistant Secretary for Mineral Resources, Department of the Interior, before the American Bar Association Section on Natural Resources Law, July 6, 1971.

"A child living within 100 feet of roadway . . . could get this much lead—(enough to cause classic lead poisoning)—by ingesting less than one sixth of a gram of atmospheric particulate fallout daily, an amount of fallout which could be contained in one twenty-fourth of a teaspoon. Therefore the contamination of outdoor streets . . . with lead fallout could easily be a significant hazard to a child with pica, and the hazard increases the closer his surroundings are to heavy vehicular traffic." From Hearings, Subcommittee on the Environment, Committee on Commerce, United States Senate, The Inner City Environment and the Role of the Environmental Protection Agency, *April 7, 1972.* [Photo by T. D. Fitzgerald.]

had so far abandoned his emphatic alarms about ecological disaster
that he was warning that "we must develop a realistic sense of what
it will cost to achieve our national environmental goals. . . ." Yet
given the Council's report on how little progress had been made on
the major environmental objectives, given the difficulties ahead for the
necessary remedial pollution-control measures, the President's warning that it is "simplistic to seek ecological perfection at the cost of
bankrupting" taxpaying enterprises was not a caution of prudence but
an expression of a differing set of values.[23] The greening of the Nixon
Administration was a thing of the past.

As the antienvironmental mood grew, the Environmental Protection
Agency encountered intense resistance from within the Administration and from various powerful elements in Congress. The situation
was a peculiar one because, under William D. Ruckelshaus, the EPA
had become a vigorous and respected presence on the Washington
scene. Nonetheless, it became politically and bureaucratically isolated
within the Administration. By August 1971 the *Christian Science
Monitor* reported that the EPA was meeting with "quite a contentious
atmosphere in the White House" and that between Ruckelshaus and
the President there existed a "thicket of Cabinet and staff men whose
instincts are chiefly protective of the polluter." Similarly, *The New
York Times* reported that industry had launched an offensive against
the EPA's implementation of the clean air and water laws. The *Times*
neatly summed up the situation in the following terms: "It is industry's complaint—a complaint that has had a sympathetic hearing in the
Department of Commerce (parent agency for the National Industrial
Pollution Control Council), the Federal Power Commission, the Office of Management and Budget and some sections of Congress—that
the standards and regulations issued by the environmental agency
are unnecessarily harsh and take insufficient account of 'economic
feasibility'—in short, costs." [24] This offensive consisted of more than
Scrooge-like rhetoric: it was a tough attack by industry, well-placed
executive agencies, and crucial congressional elements. This triadic
combination of private interests, legislative interests, and executive
agencies constitutes a potent, almost unbeatable political force in the
politics of Washington. Although the press was fond of talking about

[23] The comments of President Nixon and Mr. Ruckelshaus are found in the
Summary Minutes, National Industrial Pollution Control Council, February 10,
1971. Mr. Nixon's later remarks are found in Council on Environmental Quality,
*Environmental Quality. The Second Annual Report of the Council on Environ-
mental Quality*, p. xi.

[24] *Christian Science Monitor* (August 2, 1971); *The New York Times* (August
6, 1971).

a rhetorical backlash, there is sufficient evidence to demonstrate that antienvironmental deeds were speaking louder than words.

The most striking incident involved the EPA's guidelines for the crucial state plans for the implementation of the air quality standards that the EPA was charged with establishing under the 1970 Clean Air Act Amendments. In April the EPA first published a set of proposed guidelines and opened them for public comment; by June the EPA was prepared to publish a fairly strong set of guidelines for the states. Before they were published, however, they were referred by the White House to the Office of Management and Budget for "review." During the review process heavy pressure to rewrite the regulations was brought by several agencies. When the regulations were finally published they were so riddled with loopholes that some environmental lawyers were led to argue that the intent of the Clean Air Act Amendments was seriously weakened.[25] This was only one of several incidents. By late in the year the EPA's difficulties were apparently so great that in November there were persistent reports that Ruckelshaus had offered to resign. Judging from a considerable body of evidence, there can be little doubt that a strenuous effort to check the EPA and environmental reform was being orchestrated from within the executive branch and that at the least the President looked upon this effort with benign indifference.

Despite the hesitations in the approach of the Nixon Administration to environmental policies, a fairly steady reorganization of the federal structure for dealing with environmental affairs did occur. This development has been as significant as the programs, policies, and decisions that have flowed—or failed to flow—from Congress and the executive branch. Until recently, it should be remembered, the responsibility for federal environmental activities was fragmented unsystematically throughout both Congress and the executive branch. This situation was due in some measure to the absence of any agreed-upon definition of the concept of environmental management. It was also due to the unsystematic historical fashion in which conservation policy, resource policy, and environmentally related health policies had come into being. One study, for example, disclosed that federal responsibility for 19 environmental factors was distributed among 99 permanent or independent agencies, committees, boards, commissions, and quasi-

---

25 Jim Miller, "Clean Air, Dirty Politics," *Environmental Action* (October 16, 1971), pp. 3–5. Natural Resources Defense Council, *Action for Clean Air* (New York: Natural Resources Defense Council, 1971). U.S. Congress, Senate, Subcommittee on Air and Water Pollution of the Committee on Public Works, *Hearings, Implementation of the Clean Air Act Amendments of 1970 (Title I), Parts 1 and 2*, 92nd Cong., 2nd Sess., 1972.

official organizations. Another found that 150 environmental programs were being administered by 63 separate federal agencies. The situation was no better in Congress, where 19 committees (not to mention innumerable subcommittees) claimed some jurisdiction over environmental affairs. Understandably, then, the government as a whole, whatever its political will, could not effectively gather information about the environment, make policy, and administer policy.

Since 1969 both Congress and the President have taken significant steps toward the creation of a distinct governmental structure for dealing with environmental affairs. With the passage of the National Environmental Policy Act, Congress created the Council on Environmental Quality (discussed earlier). At the same time the Section 102 procedure contained in the NEPA laid upon administrative agencies the obligation to take environmental considerations into account in discharging routine administrative duties. Congress has, further, sluggishly attempted to overcome its own organizational diffusion by moving toward the creation of a nonlegislative Joint Committee on the Environment similar to the Joint Economic Committee. Although both Houses of Congress have passed resolutions approving the creation of such a committee, the proposal has been languishing in Conference Committee; as this is written (March, 1972), there is little prospect that the impasse will be rapidly resolved. As congressional committees are notoriously defensive about their respective jurisdictions, it is unlikely that Congress will depart from its traditional organization in environmental matters. Indeed, as environmental programs begin to gain in terms of money and importance it is more likely that congressional committees will jealously guard their jurisdictions or aggressively seek to expand them. Early in 1970, for example, the Environmental Protection Agency's budget was assigned to the conservative Subcommittee on Agriculture-Environmental and Consumer Protection of the Committee on Appropriations. Environmental programs became, in short, the hostage of some of the most conservative elements in Congress.

Perhaps the greatest step in the direction of a cohesive environmental structure was the creation of the Environmental Protection Agency. Established by Executive Order in mid 1970, the new agency began its operations late in the year. Within a short period of time, it became recognized as the heart of the government's efforts to enhance environmental quality. Although faced with the growing pains of any new agency, the EPA has managed in a short time to demonstrate a convincing administrative activism by such actions as its criticisms of the Department of Interior's impact statement on the Trans-Alaska pipeline, its attempt to establish effective clean air standards, its willingness to take polluting cities and firms to court, its efforts to establish strong state guidelines for the implementation of the air quality standards, and its apparent efforts to secure passage of a strong water pollution control law. The EPA has, indeed, acquired a reputation for independence that most shrewd administrators would covet. Indeed, whatever credibility President Nixon may still have had by late 1971 on the environmental front was due primarily to Ruckelshaus's performance as the administrator of the EPA. This is not to say that the EPA has won unqualified approval from the environmental community. In its first year, there were a number of incidents and decisions that marred the EPA's otherwise good record. Such contradictions have not come entirely from the public postures that Ruckelshaus was obliged to display as a loyal member of the Administration. They concerned, rather, matters falling within the EPA's own orbit. As one Washington observer summed it up, "One minute we are pleasantly surprised by them, the next minute, shocked."

Administratively, the EPA was formed by the consolidation into one agency of all major federal programs dealing with air and water pollution, solid waste disposal, pesticide regulation, environmental radiation, and ecological systems research. Unlike the Council on Environmental Quality, which is a small staff agency responsible for generating policy advice and reviewing and coordinating federal environmental activities, the EPA is a line agency responsible for administering and conducting federal pollution control programs. It is an enforcement and regulatory agency—the muscle of federal anti-pollution efforts. Although environmentalists have tended to urge the creation of a single Cabinet-level department for environmental affairs—a department that could take a comprehensive ecological view of environmental policy and resource development—the creation of the EPA brought several strengths to federal environmental affairs. First, it shifted programs from departments that were in the anomalous position of promoting the very activities they were also required to regulate. Second, the establishment of the EPA created a technique for dealing with the complex relationships inherent in environmental problems; it would thus be able to deal with pollutants or activities that affect several media (air, water, land) simultaneously or design more comprehensive management systems. As the lead environmental agency, finally, the EPA has the greatest statutory powers and administrative resources and the highest degree of political visibility. Even more than the CEQ, the EPA will probably determine whether the government will close the gap between promise and reality in the environmental stuggle.

In addition, the CEQ and the EPA, several other environmental bodies were established. The National Oceanic and Atmospheric Agency consolidated the major federal oceanic and atmospheric research and monitoring programs. In 1969, Mr. Nixon reconstituted Johnson's Committee on Recreation and Beauty as the Citizens' Advisory Committee on Environmental Quality. Charged with advising the President and the CEQ from the "public" point of view, the Citizens' Committee has thus far made virtually no impact on the environmental-ecological constituency it supposedly represents. In 1970, the President also established a top-level industrial advisory group, the National Industrial Pollution Control Council. Attached to the industry-promoting Department of Commerce, the NIPCC provided an enviable and one-sided institutional channel for industry to convey its advice and its outlook to the President and to the CEQ and the EPA.

In general, then, an institutional structure for environmental matters has been established. All the elements of what might be called an environmental policy arena are now in place: an agency for the enforcement of environmental programs and legislation and research; regular (if woefully small) environmental budgets; congressional committees and subcommittees with distinct environmental responsibilities; executive advisory committees; and a statutory presidential message on the environment. Although the definition of a federal responsibility for the environment and the creation of an environmental administrative-congressional structure is a step forward, they do not guarantee either that intelligent or effective environmental policies will be pursued, that adequate funding will be forthcoming, or that public officials will accord environmental questions an important priority. Those who are inclined to assume that federal responsibility and structure coupled with a growing body of environmental law will produce instant progress should remember such incidents as President Nixon's 1972 veto of the Water Pollution Control Act Amendments or the assignment of responsibility for environmental appropriations to the House Subcommittee on Agriculture. Nonetheless, the changes that have occurred since 1969 do ensure that environmental questions will no longer be ignored as they were for so many years and that they will be considered in a more integrated and comprehensive manner than they were earlier. The new structure provides a focus for an environmental constituency; it also provides the means for a future Administration that may seriously attempt to redress the imbalance between man and his natural environment.

Whatever the shortcomings, however, it is clear that the political system has responded to the escalating crisis. The character of that response can be summed up as follows.

First, there has been increasing awareness of the environmental crisis on the part of both the general public and the political and intellectual public. Given the indifference of the preceding twenty years, this altered consciousness is impressive. Given the continued existence of an alert public and the work of militant groups—ranging from old-line conservation groups to more militant ecological groups—there is little chance of the pressure's slackening. But the lesson of 1971 was a grim one for environmentalists. This lesson was that successes will not come easily, that the political struggle will be long and hard, and that the interests affected by even modest environmental reform will not hesitate to use their considerable political and institutional resources to fight what they already perceive as a very real threat. But public pressure alone is insufficient unless both the public consciousness and the political response are ultimately governed by an accurate analysis of the environmental condition and by a meaningful ecological strategy for creating a healthy balance between society and the ecosystem. All these questions remain unanswered.

Second, the creation of the Council on Environmental Quality and the Environmental Protection Agency and the declaration of policy contained in the National Enviromental Policy Act establish a legal sanction and an institutional framework for the development of meaningful ecological policies. These acts offer a fresh promise: they do not yet define a reality. But there is a stronger basis for change than might have been thought possible ten years earlier. These acts provide a mechanism for harmonizing the enforcement of existing laws, for monitoring environmental trends, and for developing fresh alternatives. To some extent, the environment has become a focus for public policy. To that extent the hopes of the environmentalists of the 1960s have been partially realized. The new situation signals a shift of concern from Congress to the Executive. Whatever the faults of Congress, the Vietnam war has taught liberals the lesson that conservatives have long been preaching: Congress must remain an involved and noisy participant in policy making. The leadership of Congress in environmental matters has been constructive: the shift of environmental policy-making to the executive branch is, therefore, a mixed blessing. But certainly the new structures—the EPA and the CEQ—provide channels of access and a bureaucratic base for the environmentalist movement.

Finally, there has been a significant if not complete shift in the framework in which the question is regarded. In rough terms there was first an awakening of the conservationist outlook in the form of the "new conservationism." From that perspective there was a shift to a concern with environmental quality, broadly defined, and from there, in the early 1970s, to the language of ecology. But it must be emphasized that the shift is not yet finished. The totalistic nature of the issue—that is, the connection between the ecological situation and the broader pattern of social and economic structures and the prevailing culture of progress, technology, and consumerism—has not yet been sharply defined by the formal political system. To be sure, the language of ecology is everywhere. Even President Nixon did not hesitate to call for "fundamentally new philosophies of land, air, and water use" as well as for "more regulation, expanded government, new programs, and great citizen involvement." But it is doubtful that this view can be translated into significant change without far-reaching alterations in patterns of economic activity and cultural belief, as the EPA proposal for gasoline rationing in Los Angeles suggests. The danger is that both policy and structure may become locked into a fixed and limited definition of the environmental problem. The concentration by both the Congress and the President on simply arresting pollution, mending its ravages, and preventing it from happening again is far from encouraging from an ecological point of view.

The decisive question then—and it is the one to which we can now turn—is whether the shortcomings in the emerging policy are simply mistakes or not yet fully developed understandings, or whether they can be traced to more systematic causes.

The Politics of Environmental Policy

Despite the body of environmental legislation that had been enacted throughout the 1960s, there existed a widespread feeling that much of it added up to very little. This feeling is shared not simply by ordinary men and women whose senses are daily assaulted by the effects of environmental decay. Those in a position to know also share it. Thus a 1969 *New York Times* survey of air pollution found that "activities across the nation to cope with smog appear to be lagging further and further behind actual needs."[26] During the first year of the Nixon Administration the Commissioner of the Federal Water Quality Administration concluded that "in the last ten years, the quality of the nation's water has probably degenerated." [27] A 1969 report by the General Accounting Office on the results of ten years of water pollution control efforts concluded that "as a result of the approaches followed in the past many treatment facilities have been constructed which . . . have not had an appreciable effect on reducing the pollution

26 (October 19, 1969).
27 *The New York Times* (March 17, 1970).

or improving water quality and uses of the waterways.[28] Despite twelve years of effort and the expenditure of $1.2 billion dollars of federal funds, the GAO found that the Federal Water Quality Administration had administered the sewage treatment grant problem in such an ineffective way that little increase in the effectiveness of controlling water pollution could be foreseen. Whether the efforts of both Congress and the Executive Branch between 1969 and 1972 had effectively turned the trends around or made an attack on other areas was problematic. By 1971 the President's Council on Environmental Quality could report that although "trends in a number of areas are promising" no clear answer could be given to the question whether overall environmental quality was getting better or worse. Despite some points of guarded optimism, however, the report found that the total nationwide emissions of air pollutants was rising, that the overall quality of the nation's waters had probably deteriorated, and that discharges of toxic substances such as mercury and lead into air and water were increasing.[29] The 1971 Environmental Quality Index of the National Wildlife Federation summed up its measures of trends in seven environmental quality areas (air, water, minerals, living areas, wildlife, timber, and soil) with the blunt conclusion that the "environmental quality trend is still headed down." [30] The 1972 election year Report of the CEQ found some improvement in air quality and a standstill in water quality.[31] But even such guarded optimism was rare. In the light of such news from the front line, one can readily sympathize with the New York Congressman who finally blurted out in despair,

28 U.S. Comptroller General of the United States, Report to Congress. *Examination into the Effectiveness of the Construction Grant Program for Abating, Controlling, and Preventing Water Pollution*, November 3, 1969, B-166506, p. 41. See also the several subsequent reports by the Comptroller General (General Accounting Office) to Congress and to the Chairman, Subcommittee on Air and Water Pollution, Senate Committee on Public Works: *Personnel, Staffing, and Administration of the Federal Water Pollution Control Administration, Department of the Interior*, April 11, 1969, B-166506; *Operation and Maintenance of Municipal Waste Treatment Plants*, July 3, 1969, B-166506; *Administration of the Construction Grant Program for Abating, Controlling and Preventing Water Pollution*, July 23, 1969, B-166506; and *Controlling Industrial Water Pollution— Progress and Problems*, December 2, 1970, B-166506.

29 U.S. Council on Environmental Quality, *Environmental Quality. Second Annual Report of the Council on Environmental Quality*, 1971, p. 41.

30 National Wildlife Federation, *1971 EQ Index* (Washington, D.C.: National Wildlife Federation, 1971), p. 16.

31 U.S. Council on Environmental Quality, *Environmental Quality. Third Annual Report of the Council on Environmental Quality*, 1972, pp. 5 and 11. See also, Virginia Brodine, "Running in Place," *Environment*, Vol. 14, No. 1 (January/February, 1972).

"The pollution situation is in a bad state, period. I thought this would be a new day and a new dawning, but it is not."

These were not simply casual expressions of impatience, disillusionment or fatigue from casual observers. They reflected a recognition by men of responsibility that a substantial body of environmental policy was having little impact on the continuing deterioration of the environment. Even on its own terms the environmental legislation of the past decade was seen as producing little meaningful change. The Council on Environmental Quality was moved to admit in its first report that after ten years of legislation, there was fresh evidence "of worsening environmental conditions in many parts of the country." Consequently, the average taxpayer might well be moved to ask whether the war on environmental decay was going the way of so many other wars for social reform, and whether the changes that occurred after 1970 might not also end up in a dead end. To pose the question in this way, of course, is to recognize that the reason for the situation lies not simply in the science of the situation but in the politics of environmental policy and in the general character of the political system.

At every point in the system, a politics intent on changing the values that govern man's relationship with the environment has been constrained both by the character of the political system itself and by the priorities that have guided American politics. On the latter point, one factor has been central in the development of a far-ranging and effective environmental policy has been the inadequate allocation of funds to such environmental areas as antipollution efforts.[32] Recent budgetary determinations at the federal level have, for example, been a reliable if discouraging indication of the lack of seriousness with which the environmental issues are regarded. In this respect, budgetary priorities suggest a different interpretation than do the customary verbal commitments to "new initiatives to fight pollution" (the 1972 State of the Union message). When looked at in this way, it seems clear that environmental programs come last in the budgetary bread line. In the fiscal 1973 budget the functional category of "natural resources and environment" constituted 1 per cent of the total budget outlays for fiscal 1973, the lowest of all functional categories. This was no surprise, however, because outlays for natural resources and environmental programs had not gone higher than 2 per cent of total budget

---

[32] Pollution is only one way in which men's activities contribute to the deterioration of the environment. If we concentrate on antipollution policy here, it is only because it is one of the more dramatic and visible examples of the environmental crisis. It is also the one part of the situation that has had a good deal of public attention. Finally, information about pollution control policy is most readily available.

expenditures since 1962. Although it is true that the absolute amounts requested and spent on environmental programs have increased sharply in the past several years, environmentalists viewing the 1973 budget—with its very modest increases—were inclined to conclude that they had been dealt a very poor hand.

To argue that that fiscal caution of the Nixon Administration, and of Administrations before it, is inconsistent with environmental needs is easy enough—perhaps too easy. To estimate the magnitude of those needs is another and very uncertain matter. Estimates of costs for pollution control alone tend to be based upon differing assumptions and differing approaches to the problem.[33] All agree, however, that pollution control costs are very high. In 1968, for example, the Federal Water Pollution Control Agency estimated that it would cost approximately $31–$79 billion, not including an approximate additional $6.5 billion in annual operating costs, to provide 90 per cent of urban areas with secondary sewage systems by 1973. Tertiary treatment would bring the total bill to somewhere between $90 billion and $100 billion. A survey made by the National League of Cities and the U.S. Conference of Mayors in 1970 estimated that between $33 billion and $37 billion in public expenditures would be necessary to meet water pollution control needs through 1976 and that $3–$4 billion a year in federal

[33] The discussion that follows draws on a wide variety of sources. The following were used directly. Marshall I. Goldman, "The Costs of Fighting Pollution," *Current History*, Vol. 59, No. 348 (August 1970), pp. 73–81. Council on Environmental Quality, *Environmental Quality. Second Annual Report of the Council on Environmental Quality*, 1971, pp. 99–155, and *Environmental Quality. Third Annual Report of the Council on Environmental Quality*, 1972, pp. 269–310. Conservation Foundation, *Newsletter* (February 1971). National League of Cities/U.S. conference of Mayors, Report on Nation's Water Pollution Control Needs, July 6, 1970, printed in U.S. Congress, *Congressional Record*, July 8, 1970, pp. 23330–23337. National Wildlife Federation, *Conservation Report*, No. 2 (January 28, 1972), and No. 2 (February 5, 1971). U.S. Congress, House Subcommittee on Agriculture-Environment and Consumer Protection of the Committee on Appropriations, *Hearings. Environmental Protection Agency for Fiscal 1972*, 92nd Cong., 1st Sess., April 1971, and ibid. *Hearings . . . for Fiscal 1973*, 92nd Cong., 2nd Sess., May 1972. See also the Budget of the United States and the special analyses on environmental programs for both fiscal 1972 and fiscal 1973, *The New York Times* (January 25, 1972). See also the GAO Report, *Examination into the Effectiveness of the Construction Grant Program . . .*, supra., n. 28, pp. 8–11. See also the annual reports of the Environmental Protection Agency entitled *The Economics of Clean Air, The Economics of Clean Water*, and *The Cost of Clean Water*. See also, *passim*, the hearings conducted on air and water pollution control and air and water pollution control legislation from 1970 through 1971 by the Senate Subcommittee on Air and Water Pollution of the Public Works Committee. For a general study of budgetary policy, including environmental budgets, see Charles L. Schultze et al., *Setting National Priorities—The 1973 Budget* (Washington, D.C.: The Brookings Institution, 1972).

expenditures would be needed. Estimates for air pollution are more imprecise, but they range from $300 million to nearly $4 billion a year. Although these estimates do not include the savings to be realized from clean air and water or from recycled wastes, they did lead economist Marshall Goldman to conclude that the cost for pollution control can add up to a staggering figure of between $140 billion and $200 billion by the mid 1970s. Other estimates differ but are no less staggering. In 1971, the Council on Environmental Quality estimated that the cost of pollution abatement for both public and private sources for air, water, and solid wastes would come to a minimum of $105 billion between 1970 and 1975.[34] Of this figure, public expenditures at all levels of government would be approximately $79.5 billion. These conclusions—which deal with only air and water pollution and not with other forms of pollution or environmental degradation—should not be read without an awareness of the somber qualification attached by the CEQ to its 1971 estimates: "Cost estimates for abatement are but rudimentary. In all probability, they underestimate the actual expenses to be incurred—probably substantially." How inexact the estimates can be was underscored the following year when the Council estimated that the cumulative cash expenditures between 1971 and 1980 for a wide range of public and private expenditures on pollution control would total $287.1 billion, excluding operating costs. The figure is undeniably great. It should be equally remembered, however, that the costs to society and to the ecosphere are incomparably greater. In monetary terms alone, it has been estimated that air and water pollution annually cost the American public $16 billion and $13 billion respectively. In terms of ultimate importance, the "cost" cannot be estimated.

In light of these needs, the Administration's 1973 budget came as a not unexpected blow to environmentalists. In this budget the Administration requested nearly $2.446 billion for the EPA, a sum that was only marginally larger than EPA's budget the year before. Because new programs had been added in that time and as inflationary pressures had forced all costs up, the budget represented a very meager advance, if that. Of the $2.446 billion requested, $2 billion was budgeted for construction grants—a figure substantially less than that contained in pending House and Senate water pollution control legislation—leaving only $446 million for all remaining environmental programs. Although there is undoubtedly a limit to the funds that any agency, especially a new agency like the EPA, can effectively employ in a given year, there seemed little doubt that the requests fell short of what a "total mobilization" such as the President once spoke of

[34] Due to a lack of data, these 1971 CEQ figures do not include the rough estimate of $18 billion to $51 billion for combined and collecting sewers.

would require. Coming after a year of strident criticisms of environmental policies from the President's official family, the budget confirmed that the Administration was unwilling to match its verbal claims with substantial commitments. Insofar as the federal budget is a central instrument of executive policy, it was simply a matter of too little too late.

The situation was not a new one. However much Nixon's fiscal caution and general values entered into the equation and however limited his so-called environmental conversion in 1970, the lack of resources for environmental programs has been a long-standing matter. Though Republicans and Democrats may fight over financing environmental programs—as President and Congress did over the water pollution control bill in 1971–1972—neither party has demonstrated a consistent readiness to place environmental affairs high on the budgetary agenda. Even before the Republicans took office in 1969, the financing of pollution control programs was characterized by insufficient funding. There has been, in fact, a permanent gap between legislative authorizations (i.e., the funding limits provided for in the original legislation) and the final appropriations (i.e., what Congress in fact provides for the Executive to spend). This gap is not confined to either Republican or Democratic Administrations, as the table shows.

AUTHORIZATIONS, BUDGET REQUESTS, APPROPRIATIONS
(in millions of dollars; fiscal years)

	1967	1968	1969	1970	1971	1972
A. Under the Air Quality Act (1967) and Clean Air Amendments (1970)						
Authorization	46	109	185	179	220	375
Budget Request	39	70	106	95	160*	158
Appropriation	40	64	89	108	116	153
B. Grants Funds for Waste Treatment Plant Construction						
Authorization	—	450	700	1,000	1,250	—
Budget Request	—	150	225	214	1,000	2,000
Appropriation	—	203	214	800	1,000	2,000

* Prior to passage of 1970 Clean Air Amendments.

Despite the rising concern about the environment and despite the absolute increase in environmental budgets in the past several years, too few funds are available for environmental affairs. Congress has in the past passed legislation that holds out some promise that pollution control and abatement efforts will receive very sizable resources. But the promise has yet to be realized. Each year the dense pages of the federal budget and the intricate steps of the budget minuet demonstrate that the underlying commitments of successive Administrations and Congresses lie in directions that cannot be reconciled in any fundamental way with the urgent need to restore the imbalance between man and nature. Though Presidents and Congressmen routinely call for a "new era" and pledge greater allocations of resources, the efforts to arrest the decay in the environment has consistently been compelled to yield before other priorities: a war in Vietnam, the military budget, the space program, an oil pipeline across Alaska. In this respect the fate of environmental policy is little different from other socially desirable programs such as welfare, urban reconstruction, education, manpower training, and health. When on December 7, 1970, the Senate voted to appropriate $110 million for the development of a space shuttle and space station and refused to restore $150 million for federal grants for water and sewer construction to an already reduced figure of $350 million in the Department of House and Urban Development appropriations bill—and $350 million was $200 million more than requested by Nixon—it simply reflected the priorities that had guided the policies of both Republican and Democratic Administrations.

But a shortage of funding is not the only problem and is probably not the major problem. The process of enforcing existing environmental laws—e.g., air and water pollution laws—has been and continues to be faced with so many difficulties that more funds could probably only relieve the situation. They could not correct it. The fault lies both in the framework of the legislation that governs pollution control and in the administration of that legislation. It should be noted, however, that these pages are being written at an uncertain and pivotal point in time. The structure of existing air and water pollution control legislation is in the process of undergoing extensive change. The passage of the Clean Air Act Amendments late in 1970 fundamentally changed the approach to air pollution control contained in the Clean Air Act of 1967. Throughout 1971 and 1972 Congress has worked at establishing new water pollution control legislation. As the process has been characterized by the existence of intense political disputes and maneuvering, the outcome is still in doubt. In the next few pages, therefore, I shall describe the structure of pollution control legislation as it operated from the mid 1960s onward, prior to the passage of the Clean Air Act Amendments.

Whatever else can be said about the legislation that has guided federal efforts in air and water pollution control, it should be remembered that the framework of legislation has been weakened by provisions that have undermined its effectiveness. The federal govern-

ment was, for example, powerless to move against part of the Santa
Barbara oil spill because it came from beyond the three-mile limit.
Although such provisions may simply be unfortunate, others tend
to work directly to the advantage not of stronger enforcements but of
the polluters. Thus, the 1966 Water Pollution Control Act came out
of committee with a provision requiring proof of "grossly negligent
or willful" polluting of water with oil. Aside from the common-sense
observation that no man willfully pollutes, court decisions have made
the burden of proof a difficult one. The consequence was that the
federal government could not sue to collect clean-up costs unless there
was proof that the oil spills were willfully or grossly negligent. Although the 1970 Act corrects this provision, it gave immunity from
criminal prosecution to any polluter who notifies the government of
his polluting discharge. At times, provisions in the laws start from
reasonable premises but then lead to contradictory results. Thus pollution control laws have tended to give discretionary powers to administrators who in turn have failed to exercise or have delayed in exercising
them. Other provisions have been open invitations for avoidance
of the goal of clean water or air. In the 1967 Clean Air Act, for
example, the states were directed to take into account the costs of
control in setting air quality standards: provisions such as this have
enabled polluters to cry poverty when faced with pressure to undertake control and abatement measures. Finally, it should be emphasized
that defects of this nature are to be found not only in the legislation
but in the administrative regulations implementing them. During the
Office of Management and Budget's administrative review of the
EPA's proposed guidelines for state implementation plans for air quality standards, language was added encouraging consideration of the
cost of pollution control strategies. Yet, as the Natural Resources Defense Council has pointed out, "It can be inferred from the Act and
its legislative history that Congress did not intend this kind of language to influence air pollution control efforts." The example illustrates vividly the ways in which impressive legislation such as the 1970
Clean Air Act Amendments can be incrementally undermined.

But even if we disregard the opportunities for evasions, avoidance,
or delay, the enforcement of the legislation that guided air and water
pollution control efforts until recently was far from easy and very far
from effective. Although the term *enforcement* summons up images
of a tough-minded official resolutely bringing polluters to heel, neither
the National Air Pollution Control Administration nor the Federal
Water Quality Administration—before they were consolidated in the
EPA—had direct authority for ordering the abatement of various
forms of air and water pollution. No criminal sanctions had existed

under the Water Pollution Control Act or the Clean Air Act. The laws themselves did not embody the notion that pollution is a form of antisocial conduct. It was regarded, rather, as an unfortunate and serious matter that should be controlled without disturbing more than necessary the normal social and economic routine. To resort to court processes was, as these laws envisioned it, a last step. The approach that underlay the Water Pollution Control Act and the Clean Air Act, according to J. Clarence Davies's book *The Politics of Pollution*,[35] was that the enforcement of standards against individual polluters was an ineffectual approach in terms of time, money, and results. Consequently, a somewhat different approach was used, namely, that of bargaining between public authorities and the polluters. Because pollution was so widespread and because there were so many individual polluters, it would be difficult indeed to approach the problem as a "criminal problem." Furthermore, as Davies argues, law depends in the end on widespread voluntary compliance: because the end purpose is to clean up, say, a stream polluted by many polluters, criminal action against individual polluters cannot really do the task. Thus, the law seeks to treat the pollution of a whole stream rather than send polluters to jail, fine them, or close them down. Resting on this kind of approach, both air and water pollution control laws employ procedures that rely heavily on cooperation and informal negotiation between federal agencies, state and local agencies, and polluters. But as Congress itself has since found, this approach led only to business as usual, that is, pollution as usual.

To describe the structure of pollution control and abatement established by the Clean Air Act and the Water Pollution Control Act [36] is to suggest some of the reasons why federal pollution efforts have succeeded so little in the past. Roughly speaking the primary procedure employed to control and abate pollution by individual polluters consisted of three stages. First, an abatement conference was to be called between the FWQA (Federal Water Quality Administration) or the NAPCA (National Air Pollution Control Administration), the appropriate state pollution control agency, and the offender. Recommendations would then be made for taking remedial action. If, after a six-month wait, nothing had been done, a hearing—the second stage— would be called. The hearing board would then issue recommendations for securing compliance. If, after another six months, these were not complied with, the federal agency could then request the Attorney

35 (New York: Pegasus, 1970).

36 It should be emphasized that the procedures described here reflected the situation prior to the passage of the Clean Air Act Amendments of 1970 and the Water Pollution Control Act Amendments of 1972.

General to bring a court suit against the polluter; this was the third stage. Much of the process was discretionary so that informal relations tended to characterize it. The process, as even this brief description suggests, was long, complex, cumbersome, time-consuming, and rich in opportunities for delay and resistance. The burden of proof rested, moreover, on the government rather than on the polluter. Whatever the virtues in principle of this procedure, its success in the real world of bureaucratic practices and industrial interest was slight. Between 1963 and 1970 only ten enforcement conferences for air pollution abatement were held. Only once has a suit been brought and in that case—against a small chicken-rendering plant—it was more than four years before a court finally ordered the plant to cease operation. The water pollution control record is slightly better. Forty-five enforcement conferences were held by 1970, but only four had gone to the hearing stage. Only one case went to court and then it took ten years for the federal government to get a court judgment against the city of St. Joseph, Missouri. In all, more than four years elapsed between the initial conference and the consent decree. The same is true in areas other than pollution control. In November 1969, the Nixon Administration announced a ban on DDT for house, garden, and various other uses. But within a month DDT manufacturers had set an appeal process in motion that, eight months later, had reached only the second of eight stages. A final ban did not come until 1972. The examples could be multiplied at depressing length.

The fact is that the rationale underlying the legislation—that compliance should flow from persuasion and voluntary action by industries and municipalities—does not work when an industry chooses not to make it work. Union Carbide has become notorious for its ability to defy the efforts of the public and the government to compel it to abate its pollution in several West Virginia communities. But the fault should not be directed solely at self-interested industries. The Nader report on air pollution [37] revealed that by 1970 the National Air Pollution Control Administration had talked seriously with only one major polluter—the air transport industry—with no appreciable success. Because it had failed to take a strong regulatory posture toward the airlines, the government had no way to oblige a major industry to act against what it perceived to be its direct economic interests. The situation with respect to both air and water pollution control enforcement efforts is well described in the conclusion reached by the Senate Public Works Committee in its 1971 consideration of amendments to the Water Pollution Control Act. "The record shows,"

[37] Esposito, op. cit.

Park Outdoor
A giant step ahead
of the law
EVINRUDE
Hear the Evinrude "Quiet" machine

the Committee stated in its report on its proposed bill, "an almost total lack of enforcement. Under this procedure, only one case has reached the courts in more than two decades." [38]

The failure of the enforcement mechanism with respect to water pollution control led in 1969–1970 to the "rediscovery" of the Refuse Act of 1899, a law that had been little known and little enforced. For those seeking a way around the cumbersome procedures of the Water Pollution Control Act, the Refuse Act appeared to be a washday miracle for dirty water. The law declared simply that it was unlawful to discharge wastes into navigable waters and that to do so was a crime. It also provided that refuse could be discharged if a permit was first secured from the federal government. Because the Act had been enlarged by the courts to apply to polluting discharges, it appeared that this permit system could be effectively used to control industrial water pollution. These conclusions notwithstanding, the Act's provisions had not been used over the years. The Department of Justice in particular was guilty of dragging its feet on the matter of using the criminal sanctions provided by the Act. Persuasion and not litigation continued to be the preferred approach; and preference was combined with a reluctance to tangle with some twenty thousand to forty thousand industrial polluters who were violating the law.

Late in 1970 the Nixon Administration established a permit program based on the Refuse Act; it was regarded as one of the Administration's chief means for controlling water pollution. But although the move was welcome, progress under the new program has been less than encouraging. The difficulties have been numerous and hard. The EPA has, for example, lacked the manpower and the funding to process fully the flood of applications due by 1971. One further difficulty is that the permit program also relies on voluntary compliance by pol-

[38] U.S. Congress, Senate, Committee on Public Works, *Federal Water Pollution Control Act Amendments of 1971*, Report 92–414 to accompany S.2770, 92nd Cong., 1st Sess., p. 5.

"*Our growing population, greater affluence and shorter work hours have combined to increase the leisure time use of recreational vehicles and powered equipment. This in turn increases the noise from such products to a noticeable degree. . . . Noise is fast becoming a psychological hazard to many people as well as a physiological problem to those subjected to high noise levels for longer than tolerable periods of time. . . . There is room for considerable improvement, particularly the newer items such as snowmobiles.*" From Leisure Time Product Noise, Leisure Sub-Council, National Industrial Pollution Control Council, 1971. [Photo by T. D. Fitzgerald.]

luters—even though noncompliance can result in court action. When the program was established, it was estimated that some 40,000 plants were discharging wastes and would be applying for permits; yet by spring 1972 only 20,000 applications had been received. The normal problems inherent in such an extensive program were compounded when, late in 1971, a court decision brought the program to a practical halt by requiring that NEPA 102 impact statements be prepared for each permit issued. Even before that, it had become apparent that the program was far from being administratively simple. Though the EPA had received 17,000 permit applicants from the Corps of Engineers (which technically issued the permits), only 3,100 were complete enough to enable the EPA to begin making evaluations. One source for the delay almost surely lay in the Administration's requirement that state certification be secured before a permit could be issued. In other words, the old idea that water pollution was a ",uniquely" local problem was introduced into the Refuse Act program—a program designed to escape limitations such as that in the Water Pollution Control Act. But even had the plan not been marred by these difficulties, other aspects of the program induced skepticism. The program did not, for example, extend to waters within states and did not contain provisions for the establishment of effluent limits. By October 1972, only twenty permits had been issued. One possible way out of the morass of the 1970 program was offered by a redesigned permit system contained in the new Water Pollution Control Act. Whether this new program can satisfy the hopes held out for it is, of course, an open question. What is clear is that the mere enactment of the program does not guarantee success: that will depend on its administration and on the compliance by polluters themselves.[39]

Even had the federal government used a different strategy, the Water Pollution Control Act and the Clean Air Act tied its hands in another way. Both acts declared that the prevention and control of

[39] There is a voluminous literature on the Refuse Act. The information in this paragraph draws in part on the following. Letter from William Ruckelshaus, Administrator of the Environmental Protection Agency, to the Office of Management and Budget, October 11, 1972, Recommending Presidential Approval of S. 2770, the Federal Water Pollution Control Act Amendments of 1972, reprinted in U.S. Congress, *Congressional Record*, October 17, 1972, p.S18454. U.S. Congress, House Subcommittee of the Committee on Appropriations, *Hearings. Agriculture-Environmental and Consumer Protection Appropriations for 1973*, Part 5, 92nd Cong., 2nd Sess., 1972, p. 456 and *passim*. U.S. Congress, Senate Subcommittee on the Environment of the Committee on Commerce. *Hearings. Refuse Act Permit Program*, 92nd Cong., 1st Sess., 1971, p. 167 and *passim*. See also, U.S. Congress, House Committee on Government Operations, *Enforcement of the Refuse Act of 1899*, Report 92-1333, 92nd Cong., 2nd Sess., 1972. Executive Order No. 11574, 3 C.F.R.188 (1970).

pollution at its source was the primary responsibility of state and local governments. Davies argues, in fact, that "the primary purpose of Federal enforcement has been to prod the states and local control agencies into taking action." [40] Although this example of "creative Federalism" may have been a tribute to the Constitution, it has been a poor way of improving the quality of air and water. A report on the proposed amendments to the Water Pollution Control Act concluded that "after five years, many States do not have approved standards. . . . Time schedules for abatement are slipping away because of failure to enforce, lack of effluent controls, and disputes over Federal-State Standards." [41] The reasons for state inaction are numerous: states have even scarcer resources than the federal government; state politics are far more subject to the influence of economic interests whose prosperity is crucial to the economic health of the state's citizenry; state administration is muddled; penalties for violations are weak. Above all, there seems to be little inclination, in most cases, to do very much about the environment: In Washington, D.C., no polluter had been brought to court (by late 1970) under a two-year "model" air pollution ordinance despite sixteen hundred citizen complaints; the federal government was obliged finally to impose water pollution standards on Iowa after more than three years of resistance by that state; thirty-two states violated federal law in meeting abatement deadlines; commonly, city, county, and state agencies spend more time arguing over jurisdiction that in cooperating to enforce pollution control laws in an aggressive manner. Where state or local penalties are imposed, they are often without effect: one large utility company, for example, has found that it pays to pay a fine rather than modernize its plant. With respect to the fight against pollution—easily the most visible and publicized aspect of the attempts to restore the environment—the states of the union have generally proved themselves an unreliable instrument of government.

To demonstrate that enforcement of pollution control laws was relatively ineffective was, however, to beg part of the question. To a considerable extent, enforcement depended upon the establishment of air and water quality standards. The Water Pollution Control Act and the Clean Air Act provided for the establishment of air and water standards. But the process of setting standards for clean air and water has been characterized by delay, uncertainty, and political entanglements. Even under the best of circumstances the drawing up of standards for air and water would be arduous. There are different kinds of standards and the relationship is neither as scientific nor as simple as

[40] Op. cit., p. 186.
[41] *Federal Water Pollution Control Act Amendments of 1971*, Report, p. 8.

it may seem. There are, first, community goals that are qualitative and nonscientific (water shall be suitable for swimming); then, there are water quality or ambient air standards that theoretically represent the translation of goals into specific numerical levels of quality to be applied to a stream of water or the air in a community [42]; finally, there are emission or effluent standards that prescribe how much of what kind of pollutant is permitted to be discharged from what source (e.g., so much sulfur oxide from factories). The establishment of goals and standards is basically a political question, although it may be masked in the somewhat sterile form of cost-benefit analysis (e.g., are the benefits of smog-free air and water clean enough for swimming and fishing great enough to offset the costs to the town of a possible loss in jobs should a given industry leave to escape pollution control measures?). The political task might be somewhat eased if the scientific part of the job could be done in a reliable manner. The fact is that despite the scientific overtones to the nature of criteria, the knowledge of the effects of pollutants is far from complete, and a common tactic of industry has been to plead for time for more study and for the further development of a technology to help control emissions. As Davies points out with respect to air pollution from stationary sources, the knowledge "is so incomplete that the distinction between goals and quality standards tends to become lost." The consequence is that "in some cases quality standards have been like Latin American constitutions, an expression of aspirations rather than intent." [43] The situation is aggravated by the need to translate quality standards and criteria into emission standards. But this process, in turn, involves a process that is far from automatic. Assume, for example, that many factories and private homes contribute to dirty air and unclean water in a given community: the problem is to calculate what sources contribute what amount of what kind of pollution—assuming also that it is possible to know where and how to measure it—and to decide which particular factories are to be required to end what kind of pollution. In other words, how is the violator to be found when the levels of pollution in a city exceed a certain level? Beyond these tricky questions, it should not be forgotten that the scheme of the pollution control laws permits some levels of pollution and that fundamentally these are subject to politically defined purposes.

The process for setting standards under the leglislation of 1965 and

[42] An added piece of confusion is that the term *criteria* is used in water pollution control to mean water quality standards; for air pollution *criteria* refers to descriptions (e.g., so much sulfur oxide is unhealthy), whereas *standards* means standards.

[43] Op. cit., pp. 154–155.

1967 was as cumbersome and subject to inaction as the enforcement process. With respect to stationary sources of air pollution, the process consisted of several stages. The NAPCA first designated air quality regions; then it issued "air quality criteria" and "control technique documents" that are simply descriptions of the effects of air pollution on humans—but not on animals or vegetation!—if the air level of a specified pollutant reaches a specified figure (e.g., so many parts per million). Next, states were required to establish ambient air standards based on the federal criteria: the standards have the force of law, whereas the federal criteria do not. Finally, the states were required to develop plans for implementing their standards. The process involved, thus, a long and complex interaction between the states and the federal government.

The process was, moreover, to be followed for each of the more than thirty different pollutants that were identified by the NAPCA. It is not surprising that between 1967 and 1970 criteria reports for only five pollutants were issued. At that rate it would have taken until 1975 to issue criteria for another twenty-nine pollutants. And this was just the first stage. In any event, the system did not work. By Spring 1970 not one state had developed a complete set of standards and plans for implementation. With respect to air standards, the full process would probably not have been completed until the 1980s. With respect to water quality standards, the prospects were equally dim. More than four years after the deadline for the submissions of standards, almost half the states did not have fully approved standards.

The ordinary citizen might have found solace on behalf of his children's children if the federal government had been seen to be exercising the kind of leadership and assistance the law envisioned. But this was far from the case. The NAPCA was tardy in designating regions as well as criteria. The reasons are numerous: lack of funds, lack of manpower, lack of experience on the part of the states with the air quality standards approach; lack of knowledge regarding air pollution; and so forth. But politics plays a role as well, as the case of the sulfur oxide criteria illustrates. These were first issued, after nearly four years of work and delay, in March 1967. Although consultations had taken place in that time between both the NAPCA and the Bureau of the Budget and the oil and coal industries, the criteria for sulfur oxides were extremely tough. If state standards were eventually to be based on them, these standards would have serious ramifications for the production and market of high-sulfur and low-sulfur fuels and for both domestic and foreign fuel producers—facts that the Department of State, the Department of the Interior, and the Federal Power Commission did not hesitate to make known. Under pressure from the coal industry, the Muskie subcommittee, then about to consider the 1967 Air Quality Act, added a provision to the bill requiring the NAPCA to reevaluate and, if necessary, modify the criteria before reissuing them. As a consequence, the new SO_x criteria were not released until February 1969, nearly six years after the 1963 Clean Air Act had been passed. In light of this and similar situations, there can be little quarrel with the conclusion of the Nader Task Force that "procrastination with respect to issuance of criteria documents contributes substantially to the decline in air quality throughout the nation." [44]

Under these circumstances, it is not surprising that pressure grew to change both the Water Pollution Control Act and the Clean Air Act Amendments of 1967 in rather fundamental ways. With the passage of the Clean Air Act Amendments of 1970 the body of federal air pollution control legislation was fundamentally restructured and immeasurably strengthened. The most dramatic provisions of the Act repair the most appalling weakness of the 1967 bill, namely, its failure to deal in any thorough way with air pollution resulting from moving sources and especially from automobiles. The new law sought to remedy this weakness by requiring that model year 1975 cars must emit 90 per cent less carbon monoxide and hydrocarbons than did model year 1970 cars; similar reductions in nitrogen oxides are required by 1976, although the deadline can be extended. The Act also requires the EPA to conduct tests on new vehicles or engines or new pollution abatement devices. Although these provisions received the most public attention, the requirements dealing with stationary sources are equally if not more far-reaching. The Act attempts to shift away from the idea that a government agency is responsible for determining what the ambient air quality in a region is and then setting controls on pollution sources to bring air quality into conformity with state-federal standards. Such a system, in effect, required the government to control the level of pollution.

In moving away from this approach, the 1970 Act strengthens, changes, and broadens the government's powers to deal with air pollution. To begin with, it enables the responsible federal agency, the EPA, to go directly to the polluting source. It does this in a number of ways. First, in retaining the concept of air quality control regions, the Act provides that areas of states not already designated as air quality control regions will be designated as air quality control regions by March 1, 1971. Second, the Act shifts the standards-setting power away from

44 Esposito, op. cit., pp. 163 and 180ff. See also, Davies, op. cit., pp. 160 and 163ff. U.S. Congress, Senate Subcommittee on Air and Water Pollution of the Committee on Public Works, *Hearings. Air Pollution—1970*, Part 1, 91st Cong., 2nd Sess., 1970, pp. 345–346 and 380–387.

the state to the federal government. It requires the EPA to set uniform primary national ambient air quality standards to protect public health and secondary national quality standards to protect public welfare (i.e., all nonhealth values such as plant and animal life, visibility, and so on) by April 30, 1970, for each pollutant for which criteria had previously been published. The EPA is required thereafter to add new pollutants to the existing list if they are found to be dangerous to public health or public welfare. These federal standards represent a maximum level of permissible pollution. States can thus set stricter standards if they wish; all areas of the country must, however, ultimately meet the national standards. Third, the Act requires the states to develop and adopt plans to implement the national standards. The plans must be adopted by January 31, 1972, and must then be approved by the EPA by April 30, 1972. If the EPA does not approve a state's plan, it can exercise a powerful hand in shaping state plans, in vetoing them if necessary, and in substituting an implementation plan for those states that fail to do their job properly. The requirements for the implementation plans are as significant. They require that the implementation plans include a description of the steps that will be taken. They require not simply that emissions be controlled but also that steps be taken to control transportation and land-use patterns as well. If vigorously enforced, it appears, the Clean Air Act Amendments can thus become an important vehicle for changing the patterns of transportation, land use, urban planning, and industrial growth. Fourth, the Act requires the EPA to establish new performance standards for various categories of stationary air pollution, such as power plants, steel mills, and cement plants. It also requires the EPA to set emission standards for pollutants that are hazardous to health. Fifth, the Act provides for stronger and more direct enforcement powers; the federal government is empowered to move directly against polluters and to enforce a state plan should the state itself fail to implement its plan. Beyond these provisions, the Act enlarges the role of the public by allowing any citizen to bring a civil suit against any polluter, including a government agency, that fails to comply with emissions limits or against the EPA itself for failing to carry out "nondiscretionary" duties under the Act. In summary, then, the Act is wide-ranging, even radical, in its dimensions and its possibilities. Whatever its limitations might be it is directed by the thought expressed in the Senate report: "The health of people is more important than the question of whether the early achievement of ambient air quality standards protective of health is technically feasible." [45] In subordi-

45 U.S. Senate, Committee on Public Works, *National Air Quality Standards Act of 1970*, Report 91-1196 to accompany S.4358, 1970, p. 2.

nating technological practicability to a secondary priority, the Act represents a major step toward a reordered approach to the environmental crisis.

The Water Pollution Control Act Amendments of 1972, passed in the closing hours of the Ninety-second Congress over President Nixon's veto, seek in similar ways to revise the structure of federal water pollution control policies. The law establishes new goals, new enforcement procedures, new strategies for pollution abatement, and a sizable amount of funding. It represents a serious and long-term attempt at cleaning up the nation's waterways. The bill establishes as a national goal the elimination of pollutant discharges into American waters by 1985 and establishes as an interim goal to be achieved by 1983 a level of water quality safe for fish, shellfish, wildlife, and recreation. The final bill as passed into law after considerable debate represented to some extent a weakening of an earlier version passed in November 1971 by the Senate. The Senate version established as a policy what the final bill established only as a goal. Even with this modification, however, the new law represents an impressive attempt to restructure federal water pollution control strategies while strengthening federal enforcement powers. Instead of relying exclusively on water standards, as the older body of legislation did, the new law requires the achievement of effluent limits for privately owned point sources of pollution. The law does not depend on the assimilative capacity of waterways but attempts rather to eliminate private (most particularly, industrial) discharges and to improve the level of treatment of municipal discharges. The law establishes a two-phase program for the application of effluent limitations. By 1977 effluent limitations must be achieved utilizing the "best practicable" control technology; by 1983 all privately owned point sources are required to utilize the "best available" technology. In the first stage the EPA will define "best practicable" by taking into account a variety of factors, including economic factors. In the second stage the economic factors are less strictly applied and the technology employed must result in reasonable progress toward the national goal of eliminating the discharge of all pollutants. For municipal sources—e.g., municipal sewage treatment systems—secondary treatment must be achieved by 1977, and by 1983 the best practicable treatment technology must be utilized. At the same time existing water quality standards for interstate waters are preserved and are extended to intrastate waters. Wherever those standards result in a higher degree of water quality than is possible through effluent limits achieved by the best practicable or best available technology, additional controls must be employed to meet the water quality standards. Consequently, the new law creates a minimum degree of water quality for all American waterways.

With respect to enforcement procedures, the EPA is granted new authority to issue abatement orders, to take violaters of the law to court, and to assess heavy fines. At the same time, a new national permit system to be regulated by the EPA is established. States are now authorized to establish their own permit programs provided that the programs are approved by the EPA. In general, then, the new law attempts to create a streamlined administrative and legal approach whereby discharges must meet effluent limitations and permit requirements and whereby speedy and effective administrative and judicial enforcement is possible.

The new law also authorized an $18.2 billion three-year program for the construction of waste treatment facilities at the local level. For hard-pressed municipalities, the law provides a flat 5 per cent federal share. And like the Clean Air Act, the bill provides for citizens' suits against the EPA, should the EPA fail to carry out its nondiscretionary duties, and against individual polluters. Citizens are thus given firm legal weapons both to attack polluters and to compel the government to discharge its obligations.

These brief paragraphs have described only some of the central provisions of what is an ambitious, complex, and far-reaching piece of legislation. Loopholes do exist and portions of the law are weaker than comparable elements in the original Senate bill. Nonetheless, it is fair to say that the new law reflects a welcome congressional intention to overcome the uncounted failures of the past.

Whether either the Clean Air Act Amendments or the new water pollution control bill can accomplish the environmental purposes that the older legislation could not is, of course, very much open to question. No doubt the change in the legislative framework will make the administration of policies and programs much easier. Nonetheless, its success will depend not merely on the political force behind it but upon the long-run capability of the EPA and upon the administrative and political capabilities of local, county, and state governments. On this score, one cannot be altogether confident that either state or federal bureaucracies will be able to administer environmental policy and programs in an ecologically sensitive manner. This judgment has less to do with the personal character or talents of the men involved than with the structural imperatives of bureaucracy and the political environments in which they operate. On the record of the past, the best efforts of talented, sophisticated, and dedicated civil servants are frequently frustrated and defeated by forces they cannot master.

Often, for example, administrative agencies have little choice in what they do. In the situation already discussed, the EPA found itself hemmed in by a cluster of other agencies during late 1971. The situation of the Forest Service in 1970 is another case in point. In February 1970, the House refused to consider the National Forest Timber Conservation and Management Act, a bill that would have directed the Forest Service to develop "optimum timber productivity" on the 97 million acres of commercial timber land in the 183 acres of national forest.[46] Four months later an Executive Order directed the Secretaries of Agriculture and Interior to prepare plans for increased timber production in the national forests. The Forest Service was thus ordered to do by Executive Order what Congress had meant for it not to do. In such cases, agencies find their activities and their resources defined by President and Congress, a pressure that cannot be resisted whatever the agencies' basic mission. In July 1971, the House-Senate Conference Report on the EPA's budget contained the "belief" that in the review and appraisal of federal programs and activities agencies should take into account not merely "environmental" impact but "the significant economic impact on the public and the affected areas and industries."[47] Such casual suggestions acquire the force virtually of an authoritative command when made by committees as powerful as the Appropriations Committee of the House and the Senate. Similarly, shifting or contradictory laws, developing technology, overlapping jurisdictions, and interagency politics can all defeat the best intentions of a pollution control agency.

At the same time, however, the close connection between most agencies and the industries that form their clientele group has resulted in a too-ready responsiveness to the needs and demands of industry. The Nader Task Force's description of the watering down of the sulfur oxides criteria leaves little doubt that the unrelenting efforts of industry contributed substantially to that process. How can it be otherwise when agency officials are subjected to what Dr. Herbert Ley, former Food and Drug Administration Commissioner, has termed "constant, tremendous, sometimes unmerciful pressure" from industry.[48] The views of industry need to be heard, but the exclusion of public representatives from the activities of many agencies produces an environment that is naturally disposed to respond to industrial outlooks. But even where agencies have not been captives of the interests they are obliged to regulate, they have often been unnecessarily cau-

[46] *The New York Times* (November 19, 1970). Congressional Quarterly, *Man's Control of the Environment* (Washington, D.C.: Congressional Quarterly, 1970), p. 37.

[47] U.S. Congress, House, *Agriculture-Environmental and Consumer Protection Programs, Fiscal Year 1972,* Report 92–376, Conference Report to accompany H.R. 9270, 92nd Cong., 1st Sess., 1971, p. 7.

[48] Quoted in James S. Turner, *The Chemical Feast* (New York: Grossman Publishers, Inc., 1970), p. 236.

tious in pursuing their task. From this perspective, the presence of the EPA poses a potent possibility. Undoubtedly it is off to a good start and should accomplish much that the FWQA or the NAPCA did not. Despite the favorable judgment on the EPA thus far, therefore, the history of public regulation has taught us not to be too quick in assuming that all is well.

The reasons for this skepticism are worth pursuing. In general, the continued division of environmental policy-making and administration among several agencies and congressional committees, the access that industry enjoys in the administrative process, and the severe inter-agency politics that routinely take place all make coherent policy-making and policy execution difficult if not illusory. Yet despite the growing importance of an environmental crisis, it is not easy—it is vir-tually impossible—for the ordinary citizen to understand the labyrin-thine bureaucratic politics that characterizes the Washington scene. The inner motifs of agency decision-making are obscure and go un-reported. It is impossible, for example, to discover whether the ma-neuvering between the Department of Justice, the U.S. Army Corps of Engineers, and the Federal Water Quality Administration over the enforcement of the Refuse Act of 1899 flowed from a simple expres-sion of the bureaucratic territorial imperative or whether it flowed from a desire to minimize tough enforcement pressure on industry. It is equally difficult to determine what happened during the period of time when the EPA's draft guidelines for state plans for implementa-tion of the air quality standards were under review by the Office of Management and Budget. Whatever the answers to these questions, there is little doubt that interagency cooperation cannot be taken for granted. With respect to the enforcement of water pollution control statutes, a former U.S. Attorney General, Jack Schmetterer, has given the following account of the relations between the Department of Jus-tice and the FWQA:

> we have received excellent cooperation from the Coast Guard which detects pollution discharges and takes samples and other evidence, from the Corps of Engineers which aids in evaluation of the evi-dence produced by the Coast Guard, and from the Metropolitan Sanitary District which has aided us greatly with technical assist-ance. . . . The one Federal agency that has sophisticated technical staff and information sufficient to help us move forward against major water problems in the Northern District of Illinois has re-fused to give us that aid. . . . Any concept of professional Govern-ment service means interagency cooperation to attain important public goals, and we usually have that cooperation in the Federal

Government. But the absolute refusal of the Interior Department to permit the Federal Water Pollution Control Administration (FWPCA) office to supply us *any* information or technical advice defies understanding. Our request for specific information on specified companies has gone unanswered. Our request for general advice and judgment as to which companies pose the most critical problems has gone unanswered. Our final request for just such information as would be made available to any member of the public upon request has not been complied with. Apart from a few published reports and transcripts, we have received nothing. The technical information and advice held by Interior Department and made available to the states is not available to the United States Attorney. It has proved difficult even to get the FWPCA laboratory to analyze samples picked up by Coast Guard, and we have asked the Guard to return to its former procedure of delivering samples to the Corps of Engineers for a time-consuming analysis by a private laboratory.

Agency cooperation is absolutely necessary to an effective prosecution program by our office. We are chronically understaffed, spread thin with criminal and civil responsibilities in every conceivable field of federal law, and face an uncredible trial and appeal case load. Many assistants average up to 70-hour work weeks already. We therefore lack time and facilities to do basic research in technical subjects and search nation-wide for our own experts, as we now must. Therefore, lack of Interior Department assistance has made much more difficult our effort to analyze pollution by major offenders through the Grand Jury process.

Facing this lack of cooperation we tried to persuade the agency to change its views. We have tried for several months to work quietly to bring about that change in attitude. Perhaps that attitude is due to the view of an Interior Department official who called me from Washington to ask why I wanted to prosecute "those nice people." Perhaps it is due to other reasons.[49]

The reasons sought by Schmetterer are to be found in part in the breakdown of the structural system by which the federal government has sought to regulate corporate power in the twentieth century. Whether conducted through independent regulatory commissions or through agencies located in Cabinet departments, this system has in practice betrayed the aspirations of a generation of idealist Progres-

[49] Address by Jack B. Schmetterer, First Assistant United States Attorney. "Federal Enforcement of Pollution Law," Chicago, Illinois, April 1970. Used by permission of Jack B. Schmetterer.

POLITICS [161

sives and New Dealers. An aggregate of social and organizational as well as economic power, the modern corporation has shown a remarkable ability to accommodate itself to the countervailing power of social reform movements and organized labor and to adjust to the regulatory character of the modern state. It has been able to convert control into a system of regulatory partnership that works to the long-run advantage of industry. The prevailing situation has been described cogently by Grant McConnell in *Private Power and American Democracy* in the following terms: "More important and more characteristic of American government is the conquest of segments of formal state power by private groups and associations. Although it would be impossible to state with any precision what portion of the power of American government has been taken possession of in this way, it is certain that the portion is substantial and that the control involved is considerable." The pattern by which this condition has developed historically varies from issue area to issue area as do the precise arrangements through which the relationship is expressed. But the result is the same: "The function of policy-making is often turned over to the private groups in what amounts to delegation." The distinction between public power and public interest and private power and private interest is thus eliminated and what is private interest becomes fused with public policy. "The pattern," McConnell argues, "is very pervasive . . . what is visible here is the rise of a scheme of representation alternative to the machinery of Congress, legislatures, President, and governors." [50] If we view environmental policy not as a unique policy area populated by ecologically minded administrators starved of resources and burdened with weak statutes, but as another forum for the normal government-business relationship, then the persistent failures of agencies administering environmental policy can be explained. The earlier failures of such agencies as the FWQA or the NAPCA or the FDA and the obstacles now facing the EPA and the CEQ are just the latest chapter in the continuing story of the decline of a scheme of government checks on corporate power and the development of private government through public authority.

It has become common to describe the ways in which outside influence is brought to bear on the independent agency and on the slow transformation of the agency from the regulator to the promoter and ally of the regulated industry. It is equally important, however, to understand not simply the "outside" influence of industry but its strategic "inside" position and the significant influence it exercises in the process of making policy. In the United States—as in most West-

50 (New York: Alfred A. Knopf, Inc., 1967), pp. 162–164.

162]   OUR ECOLOGICAL CRISIS

ern political systems—private interests have been accorded a regular, institutional, and legitimate role in the formal structure of decision making. The old image of the industrialist wining, dining, and browbeating a vulnerable administrator must be replaced by the image of the sterile committee room where representatives of industry and government regularly and habitually consult in a spirit of mutual understanding and cooperation. Although a diversity of interests—e.g., labor—are often included when appropriate, it would be misleading to underestimate the position accorded industry in the process of environmental policy-making. One institutional mechanism by which industry participation is assured is the advisory committee; another, the appointment of men of industry to appointive government bodies.

Several examples illustrate the nature of this system with respect to environmental policy. In all but a handful of states, important responsibilities for administering air and water pollution control statutes rests in the hands of appointed state boards: insofar as responsibility for controlling pollution under the 1965 Federal Water Pollution Control Act and partial responsibility for implementing the Clean Air Act Amendments falls to the states, these boards are the decisive links between the federal government and the states in the national system of pollution control. Yet a *New York Times* investigation in 1970 revealed that the membership of pollution control boards in thirty-five of the forty-two states that had such boards was heavily weighted with representatives of manufacturing, mining, agricultural, and municipal and county governments. Under the impact of public and group pressure for stronger antipollution efforts, the situation began to change. But a year later a similar *Times* survey showed that the number of states with air or water boards reflecting pollution interests went down by only three (from thirty-five to thirty-two) whereas the number of states without part-time citizen boards rose by only one (from eight to nine). By 1972 there were still thirty-one state boards of air or water pollution control or both that contained implicit conflicts of interest. Only ten states had shifted in the three years to pollution regulation by full-time agencies, and only ten state boards of pollution control were free of perceptible conflict-of-interest situations. Despite the change in public opinion and despite subtle pressure from the EPA, therefore, more than half the states still had state boards that had representatives of polluters sitting on pollution control boards.[51] (See the figure.)

[51] The three surveys were published in the *Times* on December 7, 1970, December 19, 1971, and December 13, 1972. See also follow-up dispatches in the *Times* on December 8, 1970, and December 15, 1970. The quotations in the paragraphs that follow are from the several 1970 and 1971 *Times* reports.

● Means state pollution board with regulatory authority contains members associated with basic pollution sources (industry, agriculture, county and city governments)

◐ Means state board is free of such representation

"No Boards" means air and water pollution regulation statewide is handled by a full-time state agency

	Air Board	Water Board	Combination Air-Water Board		Air Board	Water Board	Combination Air-Water Board
Alabama	◐	◐		Montana			◐
Alaska	No Boards			Nebraska			●
Arizona	●	*		Nevada			●
Arkansas			●	New Hampshire	●	●	
California	◐	●		New Jersey	No Boards		
Colorado	●	●		New Mexico	◐	●	
Connecticut	No Boards			New York	No Boards		
Delaware			●	North Carolina	●	●	
Florida			◐	North Dakota	●	●	
Georgia			◐	Ohio	No Boards		
Hawaii			◐	Oklahoma	*	●	
Idaho			◐	Oregon			●
Illinois	No Boards			Pennsylvania			●
Indiana	●	●		Rhode Island	No Boards		
Iowa			●	South Carolina			●
Kansas			◐	South Dakota	●	●	
Kentucky	No Boards			Tennessee	●	●	
Louisiana	●	●		Texas	●	●	
Maine			●	Utah	●	●	
Maryland	No Boards			Vermont	●	◐	
Massachusetts			◐	Virginia			◐
Michigan	●	●		Washington	No Boards		
Minnesota			●	West Virginia	●	●	
Mississippi			●	Wisconsin			●
Missouri	●	●		Wyoming	●	●	

*Air or water pollution regulation is handled by a full-time state agency

Composition of state pollution boards. (This figure is not a classi-fication of states' air and water pollution conditions.) [From New York Times, December 13, 1972. © 1973 by The New York Times Company. Reprinted by permission.]

As the *Times* noted, these board members are men whose activities and organizations "are in many cases in the forefront of pollution." The Times study revealed that

the roster of big corporations with employees on such boards reads like an abbreviated blue book of American industry, particularly the most pollution-troubled segments of industry. The state boards

—statutory part-time citizen panels of gubernatorial appointees and state officials—are in most states the entities that set policies and standards for pollution abatement and that then oversee enforcement. They are the agencies that the Federal Government usually has to deal with. . . . Federal officials . . . say privately that the composition of such boards is perhaps a major reason why abatement has not progressed faster.

Although industry representatives undoubtedly bring a special competence to bear, the simple need for expertise or for keeping in touch with the person affected by antipollution policies in no way justifies industries' acting as policemen and judges in their own cases. Thus one Colorado state hearing on water pollution by a brewery was presided over by the pollution control director of the brewery. In Indiana the governor was obliged to dismiss a board member when both he and his company were indicted as water polluters. Although it is not possible to make a precise measure of the outcomes influenced by industry representatives, there is, according to the *Times*, "abundant circumstantial evidence that they do not expedite pollution abatement." As a Republican member of the Michigan state legislature said, "While the individuals can be of a very high caliber, they basically represent polluters on the board. They represent a constituency and the constituency includes the people in organizations the commission is set up to regulate."

The presence of state officials on such boards is, moreover, no guarantee that the boards will be unaffected by industry perspectives. All too often members of such boards from state departments of, say, industrial development or agriculture may well have close connections with industry or agriculture. The real objection to such membership is not the possibility of a direct conflict of interest but rather the persistence of an outlook that is inconsistent with an uncompromising concern with environmental policy. Although some states, e.g., Virginia, have made special efforts to guard against conflicts of interest, elsewhere the influence of crucial industries is pervasive on the boards. "The chief problem," one Midwestern state official is quoted as saying, "was a general atmosphere of timidity (on the board) due to a hostile, lobby-ridden legislature and an apathetic Governor. We had money troubles constantly. . . . Some members would knuckle under if industry seemed to be getting to the Governor (who) had some ties with the power industry, which restrained us from adopting tough emission restrictions." The presence of representatives of the regulated interest on the regulating boards and the fairly systematic exclusion of representatives of the public are then one important way in which governments are institutionally fused with the prevailing structure of economic activity.[52]

A second way in which industry is institutionally made part of the structure of governmental decision-making is through regular membership on advisory bodies attached to administrative agencies. The rationale for this arrangement is that government should have available the special knowledge of industry representatives and that such committees provide decision makers with a familiarity with the special problems and conditions in different policy areas. In reality, however, these committees provide an institutionalized channel of access for private interests. Even when disinterested "public" representatives or unattached professional experts are included, administrators and decision makers are often inclined to defer to the claims of industry that, say, technology is not ready to control emissions or that thousands of jobs may be affected or that more scientific study is needed or that industry will be forced to move or that trade secrets must be guarded or that the government must prove the danger to health or that compromises in air-water standards can be found to suit everybody or that some pollution is the price of progress. The role of the system of advisory groups, and especially of advisory groups composed exclusively of industry representatives, should be carefully noted. For some time, they have formed what one Congressman termed "the fifth branch of government." Created to provide a means of communication, cooperation, and consultation for administrator and private interest alike, advisory committees have developed as a little-known mechanism that provides industrial interests with access to the administrative process.

[52] Although a continuing fact of life, industry-dominated boards are in tension with a political culture that seeks to serve the public interest. Following the publication of the *Times* report, W. D. Ruckelshaus, the head of the EPA, wrote the fifty governors telling them that "it is imperative that the men and women who sit on those boards . . . be influenced only by the general public interest and not by any vested interests." "It's not an ideal situation," he told the press. A year later, Ruckelshaus said, "I think it's very encouraging that the states are moving in this direction. Governors seem to be responding to this problem very well, and should be encouraged by their constituents." In part, his comments reflect the significant tendency of numerous states to strengthen antipollution or environmental quality laws. At least one state, Oregon, has been so zealous that the predictable environmental backlash has begun to set in. The body of legislation enacted in Oregon may not be as exemplary as it should be: a *Times* dispatch in August 1971 reported that hundreds of environmental bills introduced in state legislatures "for the third year in a row . . . ran into more determined opposition, mainly from industry lobbyists." There was opposition, the report continues, to bills intended to reorganize diverse state agencies into one environmental office "on the ground that environmentalists were exerting too much power."

Whatever the rationale for a system of advisory committees, pollution control efforts have suffered materially as a consequence. The Nader Task Force on air pollution control demonstrates, for example, the role of the National Advisory Committee on Air Quality Criteria in providing industry with a forum for influencing the preparation of the all-important criteria report on which the air standards were based. Another case in point is the Business Advisory Council on Federal Reports attached to the Office of Management and Budget (until 1970 the Bureau of the Budget). Formed during World War II to assist the government in compiling information relating to industry, the BACFR has now secured for itself a decisive role in controlling the flow of information to the government. Beginning in 1964, for example, officials of the government sought to conduct a federal inventory of water-contaminating industrial waste disposal. Required by law to collect this information in order to develop and enforce water pollution abatement programs, the federal officials turned to the advisory committees for assistance. When industry representatives on the committee—all of whom came from such industrial giants or trade associations as U.S. Steel, the American Petroleum Institute, the National Association of Manufacturers, American Paper and Pulp—objected, the Bureau of the Budget quietly shelved the proposed inventory. Federal pollution control officials tried again in 1965 and 1966, and again the Bureau of the Budget, whose approval is necessary for the collection of such information, blocked the inventory. Now desperate for accurate data on industrial water pollution, FWPCA officials made another attempt in 1968; again, no success. Despite the obvious need for an inventory of industrial wastes, an intense struggle had developed within the FWQA itself over the question of conducting a survey. The final resolution of the dispute was a half loaf: In late 1970 the FWQA announced that it would conduct a voluntary survey of industry, and at the same time the Nixon Administration rejected proposals for making the pollution inventory mandatory. The ineffectualness of a voluntary survey is hardly in doubt: in 1963 the Bureau of the Budget had told industry that with respect to corporate disclosures, "When you are in doubt, resolve the doubt to your own advantage." The NAPCA, on the other hand, had secured approval for an emission survey but had done so only by yielding to industry objections and preparing an innocuous questionnaire. Even then the Chattanooga Manufacturers Association urged its members to withhold information sought through the emissions survey. To these facts might be added the fact that neither have the meetings of the Bureau of the Budget's committees been open to the public until recently nor is the information gathered made public.

As Vic Reinemer has concluded from his investigation [53] into the advisory panels, the advisory committee system "gives large industries and their trade associations exceptional advantages. The process of disclosing or withholding information goes to the heart of Government decision-making and law enforcement. Members of the committee have a vantage point deep within an extraordinarily powerful agency. They can anticipate and affect government policy. They can better protect their own interests and adversely affect the interests of others. And they do—especially with regard to pollution."

That involvement of industry in government decision-making with respect to environmental policy would continue at the highest levels was confirmed with the establishment in spring 1970 of the President's National Industrial Pollution Control Council.[54] The significance of the NIPCC cannot be underestimated for it may well have an impact on environmental policy equal to that of any other governmental agency. That the Council was not intended to have merely a passive, advice-giving role was indicated at the start in President Nixon's statement in creating it. Acknowledging that "our productive economy and our advancing technology" have created many environmental problems, Nixon called on industry to employ the "same energy and skills" in improving the environment. More precisely—his words are worth quoting at length:

> The effort to restore and renew our environment cannot be successful unless the public and the private sector are both intensively involved in this work—with their efforts closely coordinated. The new Industrial Council will provide an important mechanism for achieving this coordination. It will provide a means by which the business community can help chart the route which our cooperative ventures will follow. The new Council will allow businessmen to communicate regularly with the President, the Council on Environ-

[53] "Budget Bureau: Do Advisory Panels Have an Industry Bias?" *Science* (July 3, 1970), pp. 36–39. A reply by Robert P. Mayo, then Director of the Bureau of the Budget, is found at p. 35. The preceding paragraphs have drawn on Reinemer's article. See also the Reuss Hearings on the subject: U.S. Congress, House Subcommittee on Conservation and National Resources of the Committee on Government Operations, *Hearings. The Establishment of a National Industrial Wastes Inventory*, 91st Cong., 2nd Sess., 1970; and Committee on Government Operations, *The Establishment of a National Industrial Wastes Inventory*, H.Report 91-1717, 91st Cong., 2nd Sess., 1970.

[54] See my paper, "Power and the Policy Process: Advisory Committees in the Federal Government," delivered at the 1972 Annual Meeting of the American Political Science Association, Washington, D.C., September 1972.

mental Quality and other government officials and private organizations which are working to improve the quality of the environment. It will also provide a direct opportunity for business and
industry to actively and visibly support the drive to abate pollution
from industrial sources.

Although the Council was charged with a number of functional
tasks—surveying industrial plans and actions and investigating the
effects of industrial practices on the environment—the function most
consequential for the power relationships governing environmental
policy was this: "Advise on plans and actions of Federal, State, and
local agencies involving environmental quality policies affecting industry which are referred to it by the Secretary [of Commerce], or by
the Chairman of the Council on Environmental Quality through the
Secretary." It need hardly be said that the control of the information,
advice, and support given to policy makers and the granting or withholding of cooperation to policy makers and the granting or withholding of cooperation to policy enforcing agencies constitute a kind of influence that a public official can ill afford to ignore and that determines
the success of the policy itself.[55]
Nor can there be any doubt that the NIPCC seeks to secure for industry a privileged position in the process of environmental policy-
making. As its first report stated, "The Council seeks to inform itself
in advance concerning those areas of priority attention on which its
advice may be sought by the President and the Council on Environmental Quality." [56] Nor, further, can there be doubt that the NIPCC
seeks to secure for industry a confidential position. The Department
of Commerce refused to permit representatives of ten environmental
and consumer groups to be present at the October 1970 meeting of the
NIPCC and refused to make transcripts of the meeting public. As
Bert S. Cross, Chairman of the Council and Chairman of the Board of
the 3M Company, put it, "Our new Government-industry partnership
can and will do the job if we remember the basic facts."
Whereas Cross' disclaimer that the NIPCC will "in any manner . . .
pre-empt, supplant or duplicate any real or assumed prerogatives of
any other public or private institution" can be taken as a genuine
expression of intent, the realities of organizational relationships may
produce a somewhat different situation. It would be hard for it to be

[55] The White House, "Statement by the President on Establishing the National
Industrial Pollution Control Council," April 9, 1970. Executive Order 11523, 3
C.F.R. 915 (1966–1970 Comp.), April 9, 1970.
[56] National Industrial Pollution Control Council, First Progress Report, July 14,
1970.

otherwise when the NIPCC seeks for itself the prerogative of being, to quote Cross again, "the central source of industry information and planning concerning (pollution) control problems," the "communication mechanism between plans and programs of the government and the activities . . . programs of the industries most closely involved," and *"the principal consulting organization* as to economic problems of proposed standards and/or criteria and schedules being considered by National, State or local governmental bodies" (emphasis added). In addition to providing a transmission belt between industry and government, the Council is apparently designed to provide an important element of self-regulation for industry in matters of environmental policy. Thus one of its main responsibilities is to "provide liaison among members of the business and industrial community" on environmental matters.[57]

Although the cooperation and competence of industry is undoubtedly necessary to any serious attempt to redress the ecological imbalance, the mandate and structure of the NIPCC suggests that the Council is not simply an advice- and information-giving body in a narrow technical or organizational sense. The membership, for example, consists of top executives, e.g., presidents and chairmen of the board, of most major American industries. All the members of the Council are from major corporations. None are drawn from newer environmental groups, older conservation groups, universities, law firms, labor unions, consumer groups, nonindustrial laboratories, state or local governments, or the public—all of whom can be regarded as having a direct interest in the control of industrial pollution. Although the Council itself consists of 62 members, 136 additional members have been added to serve on 30 subcouncils embracing all areas of industrial activity. The energy that the Council has brought to its work suggests that membership on the Council and its subcouncils is not simply honorary. The Council has been a serious, hard-working body. Since its establishment it has been preoccupied with such related questions as the impact of environmental regulation on the operations of industry, the economic impact of environmental regulations, the allocation of costs of pollution control, and the overall consequences of environmental policy for the economic system. With respect to the question of economic impacts, for example, the Council has concluded that "the extent of impact was both more severe and more disruptive and that the benefits of pollution expenditures in the near term are unlikely to occur in such a way as to offset the specifics of unemployment and

[57] The remarks by Mr. Cross are from his statement on Organization of the Industrial Council and Sub-Councils and before the First Meeting of the NIPCC, April 14, 1970.

other disruptions in prospect." [58] It goes almost without saying that such views do not reflect a strong willingness by industrial policy-makers to assign an urgent priority to environmental restoration. Although the Council has been involved from time to time in high-level lobbying, it chiefly influences the shaping of the broad outline of evolving Administration environmental policy. One result of the Council's work, for example, was the flood of "environmental backlash" speeches that flowed steadily from high Administration officials during 1971—climaxed by President Nixon's call for "greater realism" in the approach to clean up the environment. For many environmentalists, the President's message added up to one thing: go slow where costs are involved!

In one of its early reports, the NIPCC spoke of the need for the determination of "national priorities compatible with our economy and society." The point is rather crucial. To take but one example of the kind of priority-setting decisions that must be made, the all-important question of costs is one that the industrial community has been forced to confront rather directly. Here the advice of industrial advisory groups like the NIPCC is liable to carry a good deal of weight as it will—and apparently has—on other tough, practical, complex matters. This is not to suggest that the business community will uncritically resist attempts at pollution control. Over 80 per cent of businessmen surveyed by Fortune felt that environmental protection should be taken into account even if it means inhibiting the introduction of new products, forgoing an increase in production, and reducing profits. At the same time, the question of the government's role is a foremost one. Business looks to the government for help, and at the present time government includes support (e.g., through research grants, special amortization allowances, tax credits, and so on) for the development of pollution control strategies and technology.[59] In these cases of emission control devices on automobiles, each individual consumer will also contribute. No doubt the American public, as the cliche goes, is willing to pay to improve the environment. But it does matter whether

[58] NIPCC Discussion Paper, "Economic Impact and Transitional Compliance Assistance," October 14, 1971.

[59] It did not go unnoticed by Russell Train, Chairman of the CEQ, in his remarks to the NIPCC that "pollution is itself creating a whole growth industry with important opportunities for new investment." Moralists and others can ponder at their leisure the paradox (or dialectics) involved. An August 1972 report by the Steel Sub-Council of the NIPCC recommended to President Nixon that more liberal tax treatment be provided for pollution control facilities and that $3 billion in low-interest loans be provided. See The Economic Impact of Pollution Control, a study prepared for the Council on Environmental Quality, Department of Commerce, and the Environmental Protection Agency, March 1972.

and to what extent each individual person will bear the cost, either as a taxpayer or as a consumer.

The decisions as to who pays how much and who gets what is, of course, a political decision. It is political because—to return to the NIPCC reference to priorities—it reflects the determination of priorities and the values guiding those determinations. These decisions will not, of course, be made at one time nor will the priorities be unambiguously enunciated. Given the slow, bargaining style of much of our politics, decisions will be made in gradual, incremental steps. Only in retrospect—and perhaps not even then—will it be clear what the priorities were, who had access to the decision makers, who made the decisions, and who bore the cost of the decisions. But because of a peak role in the authoritative decision-making process, such high-level advisory bodies as the NIPCC must be regarded as having an influential if not decisive voice. Certainly environmentalists looking back on the role of the NIPCC in the decision-making process could not have been encouraged to find Secretary of Commerce Maurice Stans telling the Council:

This Council is an effective new institutional communication and leadership link for industry and government. Virtually no major move is made in environmental policy without drawing on your advice and criticism. The rough spots in administration of environmental laws, standards, and implementation actions have been easier to spot and smooth out because you are always available to give help.[60]

In light of this statement, environmental and public-interest groups might well envy the institutional advantages afforded industrialists for mobilizing their persuasive forces in the making of environmental policy.[61]

What we have so briefly surveyed here gives little comfort. A decade of environmental legislation has yet to produce significant change in man's relationship with his natural environment. The new legislation of the past three years and the several victories by environ-

[60] Remarks by Secretary Stans, Minutes, Meetings of the National Industrial Pollution Control Council, October 14, 1971.

[61] It should be noted that the situation now holds out some interesting possibilities for citizens and citizen groups. In September 1972 Congress enacted the Federal Advisory Committee Act (P.L.92-463), which goes a long way toward opening advisory committees up to the public in terms of their operations and records. In June 1972 the Administration had issued an Executive Order (E.O. 11671, 37 F.R. 11307, June 7, 1972) that sought to realize many of the same objectives.

mentalists in courts offer some hope that some improvement may be probable. But the long-term prospects are far from cheerful. Despite the changes there is still a lack of money, a lack of manpower, a lack of strong legislative authority in all areas, a lack of political will to back up strong unified agencies, and, above all, a lack of an ecological ethic. It all adds up. Even though advances are made in some environmental fronts—e.g., the passage of the 1970 Clean Air Act or the 1972 Water Pollution Control Act Amendments—there is still a limited sense of the need for land-use policies, for a comprehensive approach to energy use and conservation, for an environmentally sensitive transportation policy, for a radical reassessment of the use of chemicals in producing food: the list is a long one. In viewing the situation, then, one is led to conclude that thus far the commitment of most of our political leadership lies in directions that cannot be reconciled in any fundamental way with a meaningful commitment to restore the imbalance between man and nature. For even the casual observer, the records of the past several administrations appear motivated by a common desire to pursue those environmental goals that do not seriously infringe on those values that are given a higher priority. These include economic growth, national economic and technical strength, technological development, national prestige, corporate preeminence in the economic system, and a desire to limit government expenditure on domestic social reform. Whatever has occurred since the mid 1960s has not, in other words, demonstrated that the political system is inspired by anything like an environmental ethic.

ENVIRONMENTAL POLICY AND THE AMERICAN POLITICAL SYSTEM

What we have surveyed here is not altogether unique to the area of environmental policy. Environmental policy is only one policy area, and the defects to be found in this area reflect more general characteristics of the political system. The task of describing these characteristics accurately has exercised a generation of social theorists. For some, the system remains true to the pluralistic prescriptions that James Madison so accurately set forth in Federalist Paper #10. For those holding to the pluralist model of power, the system remains characterized by a substantial diversity of organized groups, each pursuing its own discrete interest. Robert Dahl has summarized a rich and intricate pluralist model in the following terms:

The fundamental axiom in the theory and practise of American pluralism is . . . this: Instead of a single center of sovereign power there must be multiple centers of power, none of which is or can be wholly sovereign. . . . The existence of multiple centers of power, none of which is wholly sovereign, will help . . . to tame power. . . .[62]

Dahl describes the politics of pluralism as follows:

There exist many different sets of leaders; each set has somewhat different objectives from the others, each has access to its own political resources, each is relatively independent of the others. There does not exist a single set of all-powerful leaders who are wholly agreed on their major goals and who have enough power to achieve their major goals. Ordinarily, the making of government policies requires a coalition of different sets of leaders who have diverging goals. . . . It makes for a politics that depends more upon bargaining than upon hierarchy; that resolves conflicts more by negotiation and compromise than by unilateral decision; that brings about reform more through mutual adjustment and a gradual accumulation of incremental changes than through sweeping programs of comprehensive and coordinated reconstruction. . . . The system rarely yields unchecked power to leaders and rarely leaves any group of citizens powerless. To this extent, the accent of the system is not so much on power as on consent.[63]

For Dahl and other pluralists, power is dispersed unequally among groups but the inequalities are not cumulative: coalitions of groups change according to the issue area involved. Because the system is open and because there is a multiplicity of access points, organized groups can enter the system and participate in the making of decisions. Although actual participation may be confined to a political stratum composed of leaders of diverse groups, ordinary citizens exercise indirect influence by such means as voting. Because the system is characterized by balancing and counterbalancing among competing groups and because bargaining and compromise are the characteristic political mode, ultimate policy is in the public interest. Accordingly, environmental policy will develop bit by bit, and as problems arise, over the course of time as a result of compromise between competing groups.

For other theorists, the structure of power is described in different terms. For them the system is characterized by the concentration of power in the hands of a relatively unified elite of power that can realize

---

[62] *Pluralist Democracy in the United States: Conflict and Consent* (Chicago: Rand McNally & Co., 1967), p. 24.

[63] Ibid., pp. 188–190.

its will on key issues despite the contrary will of the majority and despite the countervailing efforts of parties, groups, and ordinary politicians. For C. Wright Mills, who gave this theory its most cogent and extended formulation,

> The power elite is composed of men whose positions enable them to transcend the ordinary environments of ordinary men and women; they are in positions to make decisions having major consequences. Whether they do or do not make such decisions is less important than the fact that they do occupy such pivotal positions: their failure to act, their failure to make decisions, is itself an act that is often of greater consequence than the decisions they do make. For they are in command of the major hierarchies and organizations of modern society. They rule the big corporations. They run the machinery of the state and claim its prerogatives. They direct the military establishment. They occupy the strategic command posts of the social structure, in which are now centered the effective means of the power and the wealth and the celebrity which they enjoy.

As for voters, parties, and politicians,

> The top of the American system of power is much more unified and much more powerful, the bottom is much more fragmented, and in truth, impotent, than is generally supposed by those who are distracted by the middling units of power which neither express such will as exists at the bottom nor determine the decisions at the top.[64]

According to this conception, environmental policy would develop in a meaningful way if and only if the elite of power decided it should and then on the terms set by the elite structure of power.

Neither model is wholly adequate for understanding the system of power as it affects environmental matters. Both, however, provide necessary and analytically valuable perspectives. The political system can be best described as showing two faces of power.[65] Let us put it

[64] *The Power Elite* (New York: Oxford University Press, Inc., A Galaxy Book, 1956), pp. 3–4 and p. 29.

[65] The phrase is taken from the exceedingly important article by Peter Bachrach and Morton S. Baratz, "Two Faces of Power," *American Political Science Review*, Vol. 56 (1962), pp. 947–952. Indebted though I am to the article, Messrs. Bachrach and Baratz must be wholly absolved of responsibility for my argument. See the invaluable book by the same authors, *Power and Poverty* (New York: Oxford University Press, Inc., 1970). See also my testimony on the National Industrial Pollution Control Council, Hearings, U.S. Senate Subcommittee on Intergovernmental Relations, Committee on Government Operations, *Advisory Committees*, June 17, 1971.

this way: for some groups and some issues, the system appears benign, open, and pluralistic; for other groups with other issues, the system appears hostile, exclusionary, and monolithic. Consider the image of an administrative conference at which earnest administrators gather around a table to hammer out a compromise decision while "in the audience" spectators sit quietly. As the men around the table argue over, say, the amount of thermal waste a power plant will be permitted to discharge, the spectators believe no discharges whatsoever should be permitted. While the administrators debate, the spectators remain silent and are not heard. For the men around the table, the process is open and fair: all sides of the issue are heard—should one degree above the lake's temperature be permitted or should there be a heat quota of 2 billion BTUs per hour?—and all agenda items are covered. For all spectators the process is closed and unfair—they cannot say they want all thermal discharges banned—and their alternative is not considered by the men of power at the table.[66] In sum, the structure of the situation is different for different participants and nonpartici-pants; to each the process of decision making shows a different face.

Taking this image as a schematic model of the political system, we can use it to make several observations about the pattern of power in America. To begin with, the system is not neutral and therefore im-personally open and responsive to any group seeking any outcome. The system is biased in favor of some things and against other things because it is in the nature of political organization to contain bias. E. E. Schattschneider has expressed this point with great force in *The Semisovereign People:* "All forms of political organization have a bias in favor of the exploitation of some kinds of conflict and the suppres-sion of others because *organization is the mobilization of bias.* Some issues are organized into politics while others are organized out"[67] (emphasis in original). The American system, according to Schatt-schneider, has an upper-class bias. That need not concern us here; simply let it be said that the bias of the system upholds the dominant values of society, economy, and culture. This is not to say that there is a monolithic ruling class or an all-powerful power elite. It is to say some groups, some issues, and some techniques of political action are defined as unacceptable if not illegitimate. As Schattschneider puts it, *"the definition of the alternatives is the supreme instrument of power;*

[66] The image is not farfetched. Representatives of conservation and environ-mental groups were physically barred from the October 1970 meeting of the NIPCC; representatives of public groups claim that industry dominated the air quality standards public hearings in Cincinnati in December 1969 and that citizen groups were denied adequate consideration. The chairman of the Ohio Air Pollu-tion Control Board denied the allegation.

[67] (New York: Holt, Rinehart & Winston, Inc., 1960), p. 71.

the antagonists can rarely agree on what the issues are because power is involved in the definition. He who determines what politics is about runs the country, because the definition of the alternatives is the choice of (political) conflicts, and the choice of conflicts allocates power." [68]

To return to the image of the conference room: though the men around the table may differ deeply among themselves, collectively they occupy a differential position vis-à-vis the spectators. They are at the table, the spectators are not. They have authority to be at the table; the spectators do not. They determine the rules of the meeting according to which the spectators are excluded; they draw up the agenda and so decide what shall be talked about and what shall not be talked about; they define what the disagreements over the issue shall be. If the spectators demand to be heard, those at the table decide whether they shall be heard or whether the spectators shall be evicted. If they permit the spectators to speak, the men at the table may listen but they may not hear. Finally, the administrators at the table decide, leave, and execute the decision.

The bias of the political system thus consists of the cumulative totality of a multiplicity of differential relationships among those who are "in" and those who are "out." Those whose interests are favored exercise a hegemony over those whose interests are not, and this relationship is expressed through the network of values, groups, resources, and authoritative positions that make up the system. Drawing on Schattschneider's concept that the definition of alternatives is the supreme instrument of power, Bachrach and Baratz describe the hegemonic relationship in terms of "nondecision-making." As they put it,

A nondecision . . . is a decision that results in suppression or thwarting of a latent or manifest challenge to the values of interests of the decision-maker. . . . Nondecision-making is a means by which demands for change in the existing allocation of benefits and privileges in the community can be suffocated before they are even voiced; or kept covert; or killed before they gain access to the relevant decision-making arena; or, failing all these things, maimed or destroyed in the decision-implementing stage of the policy process.[69]

Although the system is exclusionary, it is not closed. Some values, for example, work toward opening the system, whereas others tend to narrow the scope of conflict or restrict the participants. Changing circumstances can, further, force the channels to become unblocked. Those who benefit from the system may accommodate themselves

68 Ibid., p. 68.
69 Op. cit., p. 44.

to rising social forces or new issues by sharing, in fact or form, participation in the decision-making system. Because new groups or new issues may be resolutely, even repressively, resisted, excluded groups may frequently need to resort to extrasystem, but democratic, techniques of action to break through the barriers imposed by cultural and ideological values, by established procedures, by strong opposition, or by imperfect administration of policy. Whether, in this respect, the ecological movement will ultimately need to imitate the more militant (but nonviolent) tactics of civil rights, antiwar, and student movements is very much an open question.

For those outside, the system is monolithic; for those inside, it is pluralistic. The pluralism that exists within the system is, however, a special kind. It does not fit the classical pluralistic model that assumed a multiplicity of free-floating groups balancing and checking one another's power, forming and reforming winning coalitions on principles, as Madison put it, "of justice and the general good." The pluralistic system of special-interest groups that does prevail is described well by Dahl (writing in another context) as a pattern of "independent sovereignties that managed to avoid severe conflict by tacit agreement on spheres of influence." [70] The pluralism of the American system is, then, a system of quasi-autonomous sovereignties in which groups representing similar if not identical interests and sharing views about policy have acquired an inordinate influence over particular areas of public policy. These groups have maximized their advantage by securing institutionalized participation in the defining of issues, the making of policy, and the administration of policy. As McConnell observes in *Private Power and American Democracy*, this pattern is "in many ways at odds with the formal plan embodied in the Constitution. . . . The large extent of autonomy accorded to various fragments of government has gone far to isolate important matters of public policy from supposedly coutervailing influences. Moreover, the picture of government as mediator among different interests is falsified to the extent that government itself is fragmented and the various fragments are beholden to particular interests." [71]

The same pattern has prevailed and to a large extent still prevails with respect to environmental policy. Until recently it was true that industrial-governmental or agricultural-governmental links on environmental policy were dispersed according to the particular area, e.g., air pollution, water pollution, pesticides, food, atomic energy, and so on. But the creation of the Council on Environmental Quality, the Environmental Protection Agency, and, above all, the National Industrial

[70] *Who Governs?* (New Haven: Yale University Press, 1961), p. 190.
[71] Op. cit., p. 164.

Pollution Control Council signifies the growing consolidation of environmental policy-making into a very few central areas. (We can indeed expect soon the creation of a Department of National Resources.) Although this development is undoubtedly welcome for many reasons, it also gives industry a legitimate and institutionalized access to the arenas of power that is not shared by conservation and environmental groups. The power that industry has, it should be noted, consists to an important extent of the ability to control the flow of information and advice, to help define the alternatives open to policy makers, and to cooperate in the enforcement of policy.

These developments represent an important change in the system of environmental policy-making. Just as we now speak of a military-industrial complex or a medical-industrial complex—however lacking in analytical rigor those terms may be—we can also speak of an emerging environmental-industrial complex. By this we refer simply to the stable relationship between those organized segments of industry interested in and those governmental units (congressional committees and bureaucratic agencies) responsible for environmental policy. Brought into existence by the growing role of government (through statute, administrative regulation, and expenditures) in environmental matters and based on much older traditional links between government and industry, the environmental-industrial complex is characterized chiefly by the inclusion of representatives of individual corporations and trade associations in the process of environmental policy-making and execution. We can also expect an increasing similarity of outlook to develop between industrial advisers and public officials on questions of environmental policy. This outlook will accept the need for arresting pollution, for employing technology to do so, for planning production to take environmental considerations into account, and for a high degree of industrial-governmental cooperation. Although the environmental-industrial complex may not monopolize the issue area of environmental policy—it must contend with old-line conservation groups who have played pressure groups politics for years, with increasingly militant groups using a range of tactics, and with tough-talking liberal politicians—its preeminence is assured.

Conservation and environmental groups are not, to be sure, closed out entirely; they have strong allies in Congress and throughout the bureaucracy. Nor can industry always be assured of seeing its interests translated into law: the emission-reduction requirements for automobiles contained in the Clean Air Act Amendments of 1970 are a dramatic example of that. But overall it seems reasonable to say that industry is well placed to realize its will and that, on the evidence thus far available, it is doing just that, whatever its several setbacks.

Environmental groups are, further, at a severe disadvantage in their attempts to break into the system and gain for themselves the power to define issues and values. To the extent that they uphold an alternate set of values, their access to the system will be limited and their ability to influence the outcomes slight. They do not enjoy the hard political advantages of well-organized economic groups. The latter, especially if they are small, can usually lay their hands on the kinds of resources—money, committed members, social status, invocation of dominant cultural and ideological values, and effective organization—that result in success in the game of pressure politics. By contrast, large "cause" groups are at a disadvantage if they seek to bring about fairly substantial change. They are disadvantaged by the exclusionary nature of the system, now expressed in the fusion of governmental-corporate roles in environmental policy-making. They are disadvantaged by the need to work within the institutional pluralism of the system: Congress with its decentralized conservative structure of decision making; the President with the innumerable constraints on his ability to move as freely as he and the public might wish; the fragmented localistic party system; the slow-moving courts; and the pluralistic nature of the federal bureaucracy. They are also disadvantaged by the nature of large, mass cause groups. Where such groups pursue goals that are not direct, immediate, and personal—as economic rewards are—and where individual commitment is expressed in terms of time, energy, and devotion, there is a tendency for these resources to dry up as time passes and the bright tomorrows seem increasingly composed of dusty yesterdays. Finally, the environmental groups may be disadvantaged insofar as the American public—committed to progress and consumption and disinclined to respond to forms of ideological politics—may fail to distinguish between the technocratic environmentalism that the government suggests and the alternate vision of society that the ecological view creates. Although it is true that the crisis nature of the environmental situation will continue to produce government action and although the American public will doubtlessly become increasingly alarmed, the possibilities for a meaningful ecological politics hardly seem to exist.

SUGGESTED READINGS

A short bibliography can convey only a partial glimpse of the profuse literature on environmental policy and politics. The bibliographical task is made more difficult by the current outpouring of popular writings. Readers interested in a fuller bibliography would do well to consult the following: Nedjelko D. Suljak, *Public Policymaking and Environmental Quality* (University of California at Davis, Institute of Governmental Affairs, 1971); and

Daniel H. Henning, "A Selected Bibliography on Public Environmental Policy and Administration," *Natural Resources Journal*, 11:1 (January 1971).

GOVERNMENT PUBLICATIONS

The best starting point for an introduction to recent federal policy is the annual reports of the Council on Environmental Quality for 1970, 1971, 1972, all published under the title *Environmental Quality*. Both the Council on Environmental Quality and the Environmental Protection Agency publish materials of interest; environmentally minded citizens should contact these agencies directly. There is also a vast congressional literature on virtually all aspects of environmental policy. The committees in both the House and the Senate that have been continuously involved are the Interior and Insular Affairs Committees; the Public Works Committees, especially the Air and Water Pollution Subcommittee of the Senate Public Works Committee; the Commerce Committees; the Committees on Government Operations; the Agricultural and Environmental Subcommittees of the Appropriations Committees; and the House Merchant Marine and Fisheries Committee. On the public lands, see the Public Land Law Review Commission Report, *One Third of the Nation's Land* (1970).

CONSERVATIONIST, NATURALIST, AND ECOLOGICAL

HAYS, SAMUEL P. *Conservation and the Gospel of Efficiency.* Cambridge, Mass.: Harvard University Press, 1959.

LEOPOLD, ALDO, *A Sand County Almanac.* New York: Ballantine Books, Inc., 1966 (1949).

MARSH, GEORGE PERKINS. *Man and Nature.* Cambridge, Mass.: Harvard University Press, 1965 (1864).

NASH, RODERICK. *Wilderness and the American Mind.* New Haven: Yale University Press, 1967.

SIERRA CLUB WILDERNESS CONFERENCES. *Wilderness in a Changing World* (1966).

SMITH, FRANK E. *The Politics of Conservation.* New York: Colophon Books, Harper and Row, Publishers, 1966.

WHITE, LYNN, JR. "The Historical Roots of Our Ecologic Crisis." *Science,* **155** (March 1967).

ENVIRONMENTAL LAW

BALDWIN, MALCOLM, and JAMES K. PAGE, JR., eds. *Law and the Environment.* New York: Walker & Company, 1970.

LANDAU, NORMAN J., and PAUL D. RHEINGOLD. *The Environmental Law Handbook.* New York: Ballantine Books, Inc., 1971.

SAX, JOSEPH L. *Defending the Environment.* New York: Alfred A. Knopf, Inc., 1970.

ENVIRONMENTAL POLICY, POLITICS, AND ADMINISTRATION

CALDWELL, LYNTON K. *Environment: A Challenge for Modern Society.* New York: Natural History Press, 1970.

COOLEY, RICHARD, and GEOFFREY WANDESFORDE-SMITH, eds. *Congress and the Environment*. Seattle: University of Washington Press, 1970.

CRENSON, MATTHEW A. *The Un-Politics of Air Pollution*. Baltimore: Johns Hopkins University Press, 1971.

DAVIES, J. CLARENCE, III. *The Politics of Pollution*. New York: Pegasus, 1970.

DITTON, ROBERT B., and THOMAS I. GOODALE, eds. *Environmental Impact Analysis: Philosophy and Methods*. University of Wisconsin Sea Grant Program, University of Wisconsin, Green Bay, 1972.

ESPOSITO, JOHN C. *Vanishing Air*. New York: Grossman Publishers, Inc., 1970.

GOLDMAN, MARSHALL I. *The Spoils of Progress: Environmental Pollution in the Soviet Union*. Cambridge, Mass.: MIT Press, 1972.

GRAHAM, FRANK, JR. *Since Silent Spring*. Boston: Houghton Mifflin Company, 1970.

HOLDREN, JOHN, and PHILIP HERRERA. *Energy*. San Francisco: Sierra Club, 1971.

LOVE, SAM, and DAVID OBST, eds. *Ecotage*. New York: Simon & Schuster, Inc., Environmental Action, Pocket Books, 1972.

MITCHELL, JOHN G. and CONSTANCE L. STALLINGS. *Ecotactics: The Sierra Club Handbook for Environmental Activists*. New York: Simon & Schuster, Inc., Pocket Books, 1970.

RATHLESBERGER, JAMES, ed. *Nixon and the Environment: The Politics of Devastation*. New York: Village Voice Book, 1972.

RIDGEWAY, JAMES. *The Politics of Ecology*. New York: E. P. Dutton & Co., Inc., 1971.

ROOS, LESLIE L., JR., ed. *The Politics of Ecosuicide*. New York: Holt, Rinehart & Winston, Inc., 1971.

STECK, HENRY. "Power and the Policy Process: Advisory Committees in the Federal Government." Paper delivered to American Political Science Association annual meeting, 1972.

THOMPSON, DENNIS L., ed. *Politics, Policy and Natural Resources*. New York: The Free Press, 1972.

ZWICK, DAVID. *Water Wasteland*. New York: Bantam Books, Inc., 1972.

EPILOGUE

The perspectives contained in this volume were first formulated in a tentative manner in 1970; they have been completed in the closing days of the 1972 election campaign. In that time concern for what is loosely called the environmental issue has assumed many forms and has taken diverse directions. The horror stories that filled the press in 1970 are now either routine or subjected to more careful judgment. The excitement and missionary zeal of Earth Day 1970 has faded for some and become a matter of tough, serious work for others. Although it is now common to find writers denouncing "environmental extremists" or cynics declaring that the ecological movement was "just another fad," the environmental question does remain firmly on the agenda of public men. For the international community, the Stockholm Conference has been a sharp reminder that the environmental situation is neither an exclusively national problem nor a product of a particular socioeconomic system. For Americans, environmental questions have been ever present in the 1972 campaign: in Colorado one Congressman, one Senator, and the 1976 Winter Olympics went down to defeat at the hands of an environmentally sensitive electorate; the struggle over the Water Pollution Control Act cut across the party lines as Congress passed it over a President's veto; in New York a $1 billion environmental bond issue was passed; in many states and communities governmental structures were changed to deal with environmental policies; the National Environmental Policy Act has given rise to a growing body of environmental law. Similarly, the economy of the country is affected, albeit in small ways thus far, by the impact of environmental policy; land and commercial developers are forced to take environmental impacts into account in their planning; industries are obliged to adopt costly pollution-control and abatement technology; farmers must adapt to new pesticides legislation; the energy industry finds itself faced by social and political forces and by environmental considerations it never dreamed of ten years ago; ordinary consumers find their "free choice" constrained by a host of environmental factors. The environmental question is not, after all, another fad that will fade away. It is, rather, an issue of great moment. Although the headlines and noise of 1970 may have disappeared, the central question is still there: Can modern societies—characterized

[183]

by population increase, by advanced technologies, and by a growth-oriented, man-centered culture—adapt to the constraints of the environment in such a way as to ensure not simply survival but a decent life for future generations?

THE QUESTION RECONSIDERED

By posing the question in this way, we mean to insist upon a broad view of the subject. To many observers the environment problem is seen primarily as a problem in pollution. In economic terms, they view pollution as the disagreeable externalities, that is, side effects, of otherwise socially beneficial productive activity. Thus, the paper mill may ruin the river for swimming and fishing, but it nonetheless provides jobs for the town. As production grows, the noxious side effects also increase and eventually must be controlled. When put in this way, the problem resolves itself in terms of the measurement of the rate of growth of production in relation to the increase in the unpleasant side effects. It is then only a short step to drawing up an equation that places economic benefits on one side and environmental costs on the other. Once a community decides how much pollution to allow it expresses its decision by establishing standards of environmental purity. It may even decide to stop pollution altogether, as the 1972 Water Pollution Control Act Amendments propose to ao. Once these decisions of policy have been made, the problem becomes one of effluent technology, of measurement, and of administrative action. But although technology, measurement, and effective administration are necessary to any sound environmental policy, they are not sufficient. They are not sufficient because pollution as such is only one aspect of the disharmonious relationship between man and his natural environment.

If we go beyond pollution to seek an understanding of the environmental situation, we find—as we have argued in this volume—an inner logic in man's relationship to his environment. The logic of our relationship to nature and to ourselves is not susceptible to administrative engineering. Millions of years of natural history have bequeathed to modern societies a complex, interrelated, and diverse ecosphere. At some point in his evolution, however, man has presumed that his well-being is best served by his orienting himself in an exploitive rather than in a harmonious manner toward his natural environment. Modern societies especially appear to operate on the premise, as we have argued, that nature is to be conquered and subdued. Our contemporary culture is, in fact, replete with metaphorical expressions reflecting our overriding desire to dominate our natural environment. Man cannot, of course, permit himself to be the plaything of natural forces. But managing the environment in order to secure food, clothing, shelter, and civilization need not entail, as it now does, a disregard for man's role in his ecological niche. An ecological sensibility does not require mankind to return to some primitive state. What it does require is an alternative cultural and ethical outlook on the relationship between man and nature. This alternative outlook is not novel, for it finds expression in such figures as Thoreau, Marsh, Muir, and Leopold. Indeed, Aldo Leopold's conception of a land ethic can stand as the premise of a modern ecological sensibility. "A land ethic," Leopold writes, "changes the role of *Homo sapiens* from conqueror of the land-community to plain member and citizen of it. It implies respect for his fellow-members, and also respect for the community as such." [1] This view is an alternative view precisely because we are used to seeing our basic purpose on earth as wresting control away from nature and as expanding that control so as to realize our wildest dreams.

Seemingly, we have succeeded. Modern development-oriented societies have been the leading wedges of domination and have successfully generated incredible growth. Our material standard of life has progressed remarkably for many and promises to continue to do so for all mankind in the future. But, we have argued, this success is short-lived. Just as miners use the canary in the mines to detect the odorless poison gases that bring quiet death, so we should use the signs of ecological decay to warn of impending disaster. That disaster, we should add, need not be defined in terms of survival: ecosystems may adapt, survive, and so continue to support life. Disaster need be defined only in terms of a greatly diminished quality of life for us to raise the flag of distress.

ARE THERE ANY SOLUTIONS?

With this volume we have sought to examine the meaning of the environmental crisis. We believe that the crisis is inevitably cultural, economic, and political in its various dimensions. We have thus examined the operation of the market culture and the assumptions upon which its rests. In examining the economics, politics, and culture of the environmental crisis, we have been inescapably drawn to several conclusions. First, we have seen that both "free enterprise" and "socialist" systems are characterized by concentrated industrial structures that are committed to economic growth, national economic and technological development, national prestige, and corporate preeminence. Second, we have seen that the network of interests and the structure

[1] *A Sand County Almanac* (New York: A Sierra Club/Ballantine Book, 1970 [first pub. 1949, 1953]), p. 240.

of power that characterize the political system cannot be reconciled with a meaningful commitment to restore the imbalance between man and nature. Although great strides have been made in the development of a federal policy, that policy is not yet underwritten by a commitment to an environmental ethic. Underlying the political and economic structures, therefore, the essential premises of our culture are still at work. From an ecological perspective, growth, expansion, and domination remain the central sociocultural objectives of most advanced societies and comprise the aspirations of the developing societies.

To focus on growth as a central factor in the environmental crisis is not, however, to define the problem but merely to suggest an approach to understanding it. It is now common for writers on the environmental situation to focus on one or another form of growth as the primary cause of the inability of human societies to achieve a stable ecological balance. Thus, some argue that unchecked population growth will ultimately lead to an exhaustion of resources and to an intensification of a variety of environmental assaults; others focus on man's tendency to consume ever greater quantities of the finite resources of the spaceship Earth; still others have concentrated less on population growth or the exhaustion of resources than on the growth of an environmentally unsound technology. All point, however, to man's increasingly unstable relationship to the environment, which grows out of his unchecked tendency to take from the common good without regard to the future. When more than ever before take from the commons, when they take without regard to the technique of taking, and when they take without regard to the ecological condition of the commons, then prosperity for all leads to tragedy for all.

The argument that unchecked growth produces the environmental crisis has received its most dramatic expression in the recently published report of the Club of Rome, *Limits to Growth*.[2] Based on a model of long-term interactions among five basic factors—food availability, population, capital investment and depreciation, population, and resource availability—the study argues that future developments will be characterized by the exponential growth of pollution, population, and industrialization and by the linear growth of food and resource supplies. The study argues that mankind faces a very bleak future if current growth rates continue unchecked along their exponential trajectory. Although the Club of Rome argument against growth does have a compelling quality, it does raise as many questions as it seeks to answer. It assumes, for example, that no changes will occur that

[2] Donella H. Meadows et al., *The Limits to Growth. A Report for the Club of Rome's Project on the Predicament of Mankind* (New York: Universe Books, 1972).

might naturally check the exponential growth trends before the constraints of complete starvation, environmental decay, or resource exhaustion are reached. It can be argued that changes in technology or responses in the price system will slow down the growth rates far short of disaster.

But if the growth that gives rise to environmental disruption can be checked short of disaster, there still remains the question of establishing a strategy for "no growth" that is consistent with a decent quality of human life and is guided by a sound strategy for environmental management. The alternatives to unchecked growth that meet these criteria are often couched in terms of a steady-state economy. Basically, a steady-state economy has been characterized by some of its proponents, such as the economist Herman E. Daly, as the maintenance of a constant stock of energy, natural wealth, and people, each of which is held at some well-defined low rate of births, energy utilization, resource consumption, and even technological innovation.[3] If the rates are held down, then societies can begin to move toward a more desirable equilibrium with the environment.

Like the argument contained in *Limits to Growth*, the argument for a steady-state economy is not without its difficulties. How does society achieve constant stocks of capital, births, consumption, energy, and resource use? What institutional rearrangements would they necessitate? Even though it is recognized by proponents of the steady-state economy that a major problem of such a society would be redivision of the fixed pie, how can such a redivision be effected? How equal would the shares be? Would an elite take it upon itself to decide that the interests of society would be best served by a stationary state and then dictate policy consistent with its views? Who would do the menial, mind-dulling labor of the assembly line, the trash collection? How would power be wrested from those now making decisions?

Clearly, the transition from a growth-state to a steady-state economy can occur only through fundamental structural change and through the development of a new consciousness about economic purpose and policy. As Herman Daly himself observes, "Environmental conservatism is economic radicalism."[4] However, a very real problem remains that cannot be easily dismissed. How is this radicalism to be expressed? Is it to be brought about by a revolution in values and consciousness? Is it to be a function of the enlightened self-interest of cor-

---

[3] "Toward a Stationary-State Economy," in John Harte and Robert H. Socolow, eds., *Patient Earth* (New York: Holt, Rinehart & Winston, Inc., 1971), pp. 226–244.

[4] "Debunking Madison Avenue," *Environmental Action*, Vol. 4, No. 22 (October 14, 1972), p. 9.

porate leaders and political elites? Where would one start in moving toward a stationary state or would no movement at all be necessary in any self-conscious fashion? It might be possible to argue, for example, that the current energy crisis—with the accompanying concern for energy conservation, reduced energy consumption, more energy efficient technologies—represents one state in an advance toward steady-state economic policy. Despite these questions and despite the objections to a no-growth economy, one could still maintain that the steady-state economy is inevitable even if it does not represent an optimal situation in terms of human values. Beyond this consideration, however, it should be noted that some people do not see growth as the heavy in the piece. From this point of view, it is not growth per se that has created disharmony with nature. Rather it is the manner in which we have developed technology and the type of technology we have developed that bear close scrutiny. Such a point of view might welcome some greater degree of steadiness in the economy, but it would also emphasize the need to redesign technology, both industrial and agricultural, in order to make it more compatible with ecological principles.

Whether socialist or capitalist, technology is massive and centralized rather than diffuse and adaptive to nature. Such large-scale industrial processes have required an efficiency orientation, loss of individuality, and compartmentalization, as well as increased interference with natural processes. There is nothing wrong with a better standard of life dependent upon material advancement; rather the problems reside in the types of energy sources and techniques that man's ingenuity has fashioned. Additional problems arise from the manner in which these sources and techniques are put to use. The environmental problem is exacerbated if the necessary decisions are made by a small band of powerful vested interests, but it does not go away when such arrangements are changed. Why haven't we developed energy sources consistent with the natural processes such as tides and winds? Why is it necessary to have urbanized, centralized, mass, assembly-line production? Why do we need the automobile? Why couldn't man live a good life (materially) in small, semi-self-sufficient communities where emphasis would be placed upon intense interpersonal relations, philosophy, and the arts? [5]

OUR VIEW

This brief concluding discussion on the role of growth and of technology in producing the environmental crisis serves to reaffirm our

[5] See Murray Bookchin's essay "Toward a Liberatory Technology" in his *Post-Scarcity Anarchism* (Berkeley: Ramparts Press, 1971), pp. 83–140.

The dialectics of recycling. [Photo by T. D. Fitzgerald.]

conviction that the long-term relationship between man and his environment is produced by forces that are not immediately governed by piecemeal administrative action. As we have argued throughout this volume, the environmental question touches on fundamental issues in our culture, our economy, and our policies. Indeed, it is not too extravagant to say that our contemporary culture in its success has drawn battle lines with the complex ecosphere that is nature's success. Although we may reduce the telltale signs of this battle with timely and effective administrative measures, more fundamental adjustments are necessary in the long run.

Viewed in this way, the environmental question is necessarily a political question, touching as it does on the overall allocation of values and resources. But to raise the question in a political context and to urge on our public and our policy makers the acquisition of an environmental ethic is also to reveal a multitude of painful dilemmas. Thus we are forced to rely upon careful and rational calculations of costs and benefits and upon contingent scientific predictions; at the same time the wisdom of Thoreau and Muir reminds us that there is no technical solution for the current environmental problems that confront us. Although some environmentalists are inclined to call for a halt to economic expansion and material progress, we are reminded daily that most of the world's population has yet to enjoy the well-being that is commonplace for most of the industrialized world. The arguments for achieving stable population growth are compelling, but we are also apprehensive in the face of the political implications of the neo-Malthusian position. Although we would welcome the redirection of our technological development, we are also fearful of the socially and economically disruptive effects of a too rapid change in the rules of the game. At the same time we are persuaded that the rules of the game need changing. These are not easy dilemmas for our politics—so beset with other woes—or our culture. In thinking of the tasks facing an ecological consciousness, therefore, we are repeatedly reminded of Leopold's comment that "on the back forty we still slip two steps backward for each forward stride."

The struggle to liberate nature from men's action and so liberate man requires the creation of an ecologically sensitive politics that transcends the conventional distinctions of party and ideology. Man's relation to the environment is not a matter entirely of public and economic policy. Cleaning up pollution, preserving some wilderess, planning the rational use of resources and land, developing a coherent energy policy are necessary but not sufficient. The unavoidable need is for a consciousness that achieving a balance between man and his environment depends on ecological principles and that these principles must lead to a fundamental reordering of our social patterns. This is not to say that man will not survive in the absence of an ecological movement. Perhaps the technocratic planners will ensure that man survives. But an ecological ethic involves not simply survival but the terms on which man and nature and man and man relate to one another. In reflecting on the meaning of an environmental ethic, therefore, we are also reminded that the confrontation with modern society began with the romantics. The ecological movement will offer little and come to nothing if it cannot infuse its politics and consciousness with the aesthetics and morality of the romantic tradition. In his essay "Walking," Thoreau defines well the ecological sensibility:

> What is it that makes it so hard sometimes to determine whither we will walk? I believe that there is a subtle magnetism in Nature, which, if we unconsciously yield to it, will direct us aright. It is not indifferent to us which way we walk. There is a right way; but we are very liable from heedlessness and stupidity to take the wrong one. We would fain take that walk, never yet taken by us through this actual world, which is perfectly symbolic of the path which we love to travel in the interior and ideal world; and sometimes, no doubt, we find it difficult to choose our direction, because it does not yet exist distinctly in our idea.[6]

SUGGESTED READINGS

The issues discussed briefly in the Epilogue are taken up at greater length in the following:

"Blueprint for Survival." *The Ecologist* (London), **2**:1 (January 1972).

BOOKCHIN, MURRAY. *Post-Scarcity Anarchism.* Berkeley: Ramparts Press, 1971.

Commission on Population and the American Future, *Report: Population and the American Future.* Washington, D.C.: Commission on Population and the American Future, 1972.

COMMONER, BARRY. *The Closing Circle.* New York: Alfred A. Knopf, Inc., 1971.

DALY, HERMAN E. "Toward a Stationary-State Economy" in John Harte and Robert H. Socolow, eds. *Patient Earth.* New York: Holt, Rinehart & Winston, Inc., 1971.

——"Debunking Madison Avenue." *Environmental Action*, **4**:11 (October 14, 1972).

EHRLICH, PAUL R. and ANNE H. *Population, Resources, Environment.* San Francisco: W. H. Freeman & Co., Publishers, 1970.

[6] In Carl Bode, ed., op. cit.. pp. 602–603.

HARDIN, GARRETT. "The Tragedy of the Commons." *Science,* **162** (December 1968).

LEOPOLD, ALDO. *A Sand County Almanac.* New York: Ballantine Books, Inc., 1966 [1949].

MADDOX, JOHN. *The Doomsday Syndrome.* New York: McGraw-Hill Book Company, 1972.

MEADOWS, DONELLA, et al. *Limits to Growth.* New York: Universe Books, 1972.

Report of the Study of Critical Environmental Problems (SCEP). *Man's Impact on the Global Environment.* Cambridge, Mass.: MIT Press, 1970.

WEISBERG, BARRY. *Beyond Repair.* Boston: Beacon Press, 1971.

INDEX